# PORTABLE SHELL PROGRAMMING:
## An Extensive Collection
## of Bourne Shell
## Examples

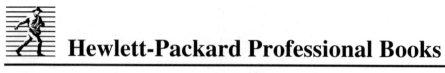

# Hewlett-Packard Professional Books

| | |
|---|---|
| **Blinn** | Portable Shell Programming: An Extensive Collection of Bourne Shell Examples |
| **Costa** | Planning and Designing High Speed Networks Using 100VG-AnyLAN, Second Edition |
| **Fristrup** | USENET: Netnews for Everyone |
| **Fristrup** | The Essential Web Surfer Survival Guide |
| **Grady** | Practical Software Metrics for Project Management and Process Improvement |
| **Grosvenor, Ichiro, O'Brien** | Mainframe Downsizing to Upsize Your Business: IT-Preneuring |
| **Gunn** | A Guide to NetWare® for UNIX® |
| **Helsel** | Graphical Programming: A Tutorial for HP VEE |
| **Lewis** | The Art & Science of SmallTalk |
| **Madell, Parsons, Abegg** | Developing and Localizing International Software |
| **McMinds/Whitty** | Writing Your Own OSF/Motif Widgets |
| **Phaal** | LAN Traffic Management |
| **Poniatowski** | The HP-UX System Administrator's "How To" Book |
| **Poniatowski** | HP-UX 10.x System Administrator's "How To" Book |
| **Thomas** | Cable Television Proof-of-Performance: A Practical Guide to Cable TV Compliance Measurements Using a Spectrum Analyzer |
| **Witte** | Electronic Test Instruments |
| **Witte** | Spectrum & Network Measurements |

# PORTABLE SHELL PROGRAMMING:
## An Extensive Collection of Bourne Shell Examples

**Bruce Blinn**

*Hewlett-Packard Company*

*For book and bookstore information*

**http://www.prenhall.com**

Prentice Hall PTR
Upper Saddle River, New Jersey 07458

**Library of Congress Cataloging–in–Publication Data**

Blinn, Bruce, 1950-
　　Portable shell programming : an extensive collection of bourne
shell examples / Bruce Blinn.
　　　　p. cm.
　　Includes index.
　　ISBN 0-13-451494-7
　　1. UNIX (Computer file)　2. UNIX Shells　3. Microcomputers–
–Programming　I. Title.
QA76.76.063B593　1996　　　　　　　　　　　　95-39657
005.13'3—dc20　　　　　　　　　　　　　　　　　CIP

Editorial/production supervision: *Rainbow Graphics, Inc.*
Cover design director: *Jerry Votta*
Cover design: *Amy Rosen*
Manufacturing buyer: *Alexis R. Heydt*
Acquisitions editor: *Karen Gettman*

© 1996 by Hewlett-Packard Company
Published by Prentice Hall PTR
Prentice-Hall, Inc.
A Simon & Schuster Company
Upper Saddle River, New Jersey 07458

The publisher offers discounts on this book when ordered
in bulk quantities. For more information, contact:

　　　　Corporate Sales Department
　　　　Prentice Hall PTR
　　　　One Lake Street
　　　　Upper Saddle River, NJ 07458
　　　　Phone: 800-382-3419
　　　　Fax: 201-236-7141
　　　　E-mail: corpsales@prenhall.com

10　9　8　7　6　5

ISBN　　0-13-451494-7

Prentice-Hall International (UK) Limited, *London*
Prentice-Hall of Australia Pty. Limited, *Sydney*
Prentice-Hall Canada Inc., *Toronto*
Prentice-Hall Hispanoamericana, S.A., *Mexico*
Prentice-Hall of India Private Limited, *New Delhi*
Prentice-Hall of Japan, Inc., *Tokyo*
Simon & Schuster Asia Pte. Ltd., *Singapore*
Editora Prentice-Hall do Brasil, Ltda., *Rio de Janeiro*

# Contents

## 12   Portability ........................................... **208**

# Introduction

The most frequently asked question in shell programming is:

*Where can I find examples of shell scripts?*

Most engineers find that the easiest way to learn shell programming is to learn from the examples of others. Similarly, the easiest way to write a shell script is to use an existing shell script as a template. This stems from the fact that there are innumerable commands and techniques that can be used to solve any particular problem. Seeing an example helps you sift through the chaff to get to a solution quickly. Oftentimes shell programming is used to solve a short-term problem, and, therefore, it is important to get something working quickly; the task might not be worth doing if it requires a significant amount of learning or trial and error to come up with a solution.

Seeing examples also helps you to remember the peculiarities of the shell syntax and the idiosyncrasies of the UNIX commands. Since writing shell scripts is not an everyday task for most engineers, it is easy to forget those infrequently used details. It is usually easier to modify a shell script that contains many of the ideas that you need than it is to develop a new shell script from scratch.

Shell programming is too useful to avoid simply because you find the syntax difficult to remember or the number of UNIX commands overwhelming. Besides executing simple commands such as `echo`, `date`, `cp`, and so forth, the shell defines a command language that allows you to combine commands into complex shell scripts. The shell supports variables, control flow statements (such as `if`, `while`, and `for`), functions, parameter passing, and even interrupt handling. Coupling the capabilities of the shell with the wide variety of commands available on UNIX, very powerful shell scripts can be written in just a few lines. In addition, since the shell is an interpretive language, there is no compiling or linking to worry about. You can create simple and powerful shell scripts in just a few minutes.

When I first began to write shell scripts, I found it difficult to find useful examples of shell scripts, and when I did find them, they were often difficult to understand. To this end, I believe it is useful to have a reference of relevant, well-documented examples, which is what I have tried to provide in this book. I have also tried to provide enough variety in the examples and their explanations that you will become familiar with many of the common practices used in writing shell scripts, and, therefore, it will be easier for you to understand the code in other shell scripts that you find.

This is not a book on how to use UNIX, as most books on shell programming are. This book is intended for people who are already familiar with UNIX and, for one reason or another, have decided to write a shell script. This book is intended for people who already know what an `if` statement is, but they do not know or cannot remember how an `if` statement is implemented in the shell. If they could just see an example, they would be off and programming. The examples in this book cover everything from simple shell statements to complex shell scripts, and unlike most books on shell programming, this book contains examples that you are likely to use.

This book is intended to be useful as a reference book. The style of presentation is straightforward. Each topic is self-contained, which allows you to skip directly to the information that you are interested in. This book provides an extensive collection of examples that are organized and indexed so that you have a ready reference to a wide variety of shell programming tasks. If you choose to read the book from cover to cover, you will be exposed to a variety of techniques and practices that would normally take you years to discover.

All of the examples in the book are written using the standard Bourne shell[1] (`sh` or `/bin/sh`), which allows these examples to be used on any UNIX system. While there are several shells to choose from on most UNIX systems, and many of them are more suitable than the Bourne shell for interactive work, the standard Bourne shell is available on all modern UNIX systems, and therefore, is the most common choice for writing shell scripts. In addition, the Korn shell and the POSIX shell contain all of the syntactic constructs of the Bourne shell, which makes the examples in this book compatible with those shells as well.

Some of the examples in this book have dependencies on the flavor of UNIX (e.g., System V or BSD) and some of the examples are dependent upon the particular implementation of a command by the vendor, but these dependencies are explained in the text, and in each case a portable solution is shown. This makes the examples in this book especially useful to those who write shell scripts that must execute on more than one type of UNIX system.

---

[1] The Bourne shell was developed and named after Stephen R. Bourne, formerly with Bell Laboratories. Any references in this book to the "shell" refer to the Bourne shell unless otherwise noted. Similarly, the Korn shell was developed and named after David Korn, also at Bell Laboratories.

When reading this book, it is important to remember that there are many ways to perform most tasks on UNIX systems. I have chosen implementations for the examples in this book that are easy to understand, but not necessarily the most efficient solution, or in some other way, the most desirable solution. I will sometimes comment on alternatives, but for the most part, I leave it up to you to determine when an example from this book should be altered for your particular situation.

There is no warranty of any kind on the examples in this book. I have tested each example on several different UNIX systems, but because of the wide variety of UNIX systems and configurations available, it is possible that some examples will not work exactly as I have indicated. I welcome any comments that you might have about the content of this book, including problems with examples and suggestions for improvements.

## HOW THIS BOOK IS ORGANIZED

The first four chapters in this book describe the syntax of the Bourne shell. Chapter 1, "Shell Syntax," begins by introducing you to the basic syntax of the Bourne shell. This chapter describes simple commands, quotes and quoting, file name expansion, and control flow statements.

Chapter 2, "Shell Variables," continues the presentation of shell syntax. It describes how to assign values to variables, how to retrieve those values, variable initialization techniques, and variables that are built into the shell.

Chapter 3, "Shell Functions and Built-in Commands," presents the syntax for shell functions and discusses techniques for using them. This chapter also lists the commands that are built into the shell and gives a brief description of each one.

Chapter 4, "Using Files," presents the shell syntax for input-output redirection. It shows a variety of examples that use the shell's redirection syntax to redirect the standard input and the standard output of commands, and it also discusses how to use the shell's redirection syntax to read and write other files.

Chapter 5, "The Environment," describes the process environment and how it affects shell scripts. This chapter discusses how parent and child processes can affect each other, how signals can be used in shell scripts, and it presents a variety of examples on how to execute commands on remote systems.

Chapter 6, "Parsing Command Line Parameters," explains the conventions used to pass parameters to shell scripts and presents examples of common techniques that are used to parse the command line parameters.

Chapter 7, "Using Filters," explains what a filter is, how to write one, and how they are used. This chapter contains many examples of filters that can be used to process text files.

Chapter 8, "Shell Utilities," has examples of how to perform many common tasks that are frequently used in larger shell scripts. This chapter covers such things as doing arithmetic, manipulating strings, manipulating files and directories, asking questions, presenting output, and much more.

Chapter 9, "Examples of Shell Functions," has examples of complete shell functions. These functions demonstrate a variety of reasons to use shell functions, and each function in this chapter contains a line-by-line explanation describing exactly how the function works.

Chapter 10, "Examples of Shell Scripts," has examples of complete shell scripts. Each example is complete with comments and demonstrates good shell programming practices. Each shell script in this chapter contains a line-by-line explanation describing exactly how the shell script works

Chapter 11, "Debugging," describes the debugging options in the shell and other techniques that are useful for debugging shell scripts. This chapter also describes a variety of common problems and unusual coding styles that can lead to errors.

Chapter 12, "Portability," explains the most common issues surrounding the portability of shell scripts and how to avoid portability problems. This chapter also discusses some of the portability issues that arise with specific UNIX commands.

Chapter 13, "Common Questions and Problems," is structured as a question and answer discussion. It explains many of the problems that inexperienced users are likely to encounter, and it answers many of the questions they are likely to ask.

Appendix A, "Comparison of UNIX Shells," provides a brief description of each of the major shells available on UNIX systems

Appendix B, "Syntax Summary," is a complete but brief summary of the syntax of the Bourne shell.


## CONVENTIONS USED IN THIS BOOK

To differentiate the text of the explanations in this book from the examples of shell code, `typewriter font` is used to represent the examples of shell code. `Typewriter font` is also used to indicate command names, file names, or anything else that must be entered literally as it is shown in the text.

```
echo "Hello world."
```

Text in *italics* is used to indicate text that should be replaced with an appropriate value rather than entering the text literally as it is shown.

```
rm file
```

When expressing command syntax, square brackets ( [ ] ) indicate an optional entry, a vertical bar ( | ) separates multiple selections, and ellipses ( . . .) indicate that the previous entry may be repeated.

```
cp file1 [file2 ...] target
```

Nonprinting characters are represented by the name of the character in italics and surrounded by angle brackets. This notation is only used where the additional clarity is necessary.

```
<tab> <space>
```

Even though this book does not cover using the shell interactively, it is frequently useful to use the shell interactively to test new ideas. Some of the examples in this book are presented this way. These examples will use the dollar sign ($) as the shell prompt and the greater than sign (>) as the prompt for continuation lines.

```
$ if command
>   ...
> fi
$
```

## SOFTWARE INCLUDED WITH THIS BOOK

Many of the examples in this book are complete, ready-to-use shell scripts. These examples (which include all of the examples in Chapter 9, "Examples of Shell Functions," and Chapter 10, "Examples of Shell Scripts") are contained on the floppy diskette attached to this book and they are also available electronically from the Prentice Hall FTP server.

The files on the floppy diskette are stored as a `tar` archive. To extract the files from the floppy diskette, enter the following command:

```
tar -xvf device
```

Where *device* is the name of the floppy diskette device on your system (for example, /dev/fd0). This command will create a subdirectory named shbook that contains the examples from this book.

To obtain the examples electronically from the Prentice Hall FTP server, you can use the ftp command to connect to ftp.prenhall.com. The files are contained in the compressed, tar archive file /pub/blinn/shbook.tar.Z. The following example shows a sample dialog to obtain this file from the Prentice Hall FTP server. The underlined text is the portion of the dialog that you enter, the remainder of the text is the information displayed by the ftp command.

```
$ ftp ftp.prenhall.com
Connected to ...
220 ... FTP server (...) ready.
Name (ftp.prenhall.com:username): anonymous
331 Guest login ok, send ident as password.
Password: username@xxx.xxx.xxx (Your user name and full host name; it will not echo)
230 Guest login ok, access restrictions apply.
ftp> cd /pub/blinn
250 CWD command successful.
ftp> binary
200 Type set to I.
ftp> get shbook.tar.Z
200 PORT command successful.
150 Binary data connection for shbook.tar.Z (n.n.n.n,n) (n bytes).
```

```
226 Transfer complete.
n bytes received in n.n seconds (n.n Kbytes/s)
ftp> quit
221 Goodbye
$
```

After executing this command, the file shbook.tar.Z should be in the current directory. To unpack this file, enter the following commands:

```
uncompress shbook.tar.Z
tar -xvf shbook.tar
```

This will create a subdirectory named shbook that contains the examples from this book.

## ACKNOWLEDGMENTS

I would like to thank the following people for reviewing this book during its various stages of development: Bob Campbell, Lisa Chen (watch for this name in the poetry section of your bookstore), Peggy Chen, Marshall Gaddis, Jeff Gitlin, Paul Kay, Tom McNeal, and Ellie Quigley. Your valuable suggestions and contributions have made this book a truly useful collection of examples of shell programming.

I would also like to thank my editor Karen Gettman and the people that work with her at Prentice Hall for helping me throughout the publishing process.

Finally, I would like to thank my friends at Clarity Software, Inc. If it wasn't for our work together, I probably never would have learned all this stuff in the first place. Thanks for your help and patience.

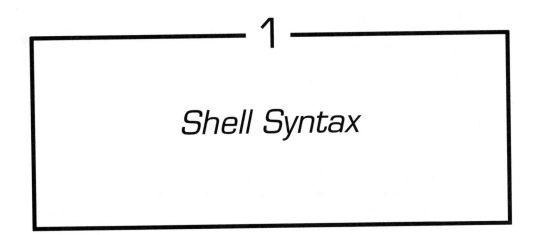

# 1

## Shell Syntax

### CREATING A SHELL SCRIPT

Shell scripts are ordinary text files that contain commands to be executed by the shell. The first line of a shell script should identify which shell will be used to execute it. This line is not always necessary, but until you know otherwise (see "Identifying Shell Scripts" in Chapter 5), the first line of all shell scripts should be:

```
#!/bin/sh
```

Following this line, you enter the commands that are to be executed. For example, a shell script to append one file to another file might look like this:

```
#!/bin/sh
case $# in
    1 ) cat >> $1 ;;
    2 ) cat $1 >> $2 ;;
    * ) echo "Usage: append [fromfile] tofile" 1>&2 ;;
esac
```

Once you have written a shell script, you need to save it in a file using a name that describes what the command does. In this example, you would probably use a file name such as append.

After you save the file, you need to give it execute permission. The owner of a file can assign execute permission to a file using the `chmod` command as follows:

```
chmod +x append
```

When changing the permission of a shell script, be sure not to remove read permission; the shell needs to read the file in order to execute it.

Now to execute the shell script, all you need to do is enter its name followed by any parameters that it needs.

```
$ append fromfile tofile
```

## COMMENTS

The hash character (#) is used to indicate the beginning of a comment. It must be the first character of a word. That is, it must be at the beginning of the line or it must be preceded by a tab or space. The comment continues to the end of the line.

Block comments are customarily formed by stacking individual comments so that the hash characters form a column.

```
#
# This is
# a typical
# block comment.
#
echo "Hello world."       # This is a trailing comment.
```

## LINE CONTINUATION

It is often desirable to break a line into more than one line to improve its readability. When the backslash character is the last character on a line, the backslash will be ignored by the shell and the following line will be treated as a continuation of the current line.

```
$ VALUE=abc\
> def
$ echo $VALUE
abcdef
$
```

In the example above, the line is continued in the middle of a string of characters. While a line can be continued anywhere, it is better practice to continue the line where there is already a break in the words. This prevents accidentally introducing whitespace where it is not wanted. In the following example, notice that the whitespace used to indent the second line is not removed. Only the backslash and the newline are removed when a line is continued.

```
$ VALUE="abc\
>       def"
$ echo "$VALUE"
abc     def
$
```

When writing shell code, it is easy to accidentally put a space after the backslash. Since the backslash would no longer be the last character on the line, it would not be interpreted as a line continuation character. If you are not getting the behavior you expect when ending the line with a backslash, look for spaces following the backslash. You may also want to make sure that you have not tried to put a comment on the end of the line. The following examples show some common mistakes that are made when trying to use line continuation.

```
echo "This will not work."    \<space>
echo "This will not work."    \    # Comment
echo "This will not work."        # Comment    \
```

You can also break lines following any command separator without changing its meaning. For example, it is common to see a pipeline separated into multiple lines following each pipeline symbol ( | ). (The command separators are discussed later in this chapter.)

```
cat file1 file2  |
     sort        |
     more
```

## FILE NAME EXPANSION

The shell supports certain file name abbreviations, called *wildcards,* that can be used to express long file names and multiple file names in just a few characters. The shell performs file name expansion on the command line before each command is executed. Each word on the command line, whether it is a file name or not, is scanned to see if it contains any wildcard characters. If it does, the word is replaced with the sorted list of file names that match the pattern.

The following wildcards can be used to specify file names:

```
*           matches any (zero or more) characters
?           matches any single character
[...]       matches any single character in the enclosed set
[!...]      matches any single character that is not in the enclosed set
```

When using the [. . .] wildcard notation, a pair of characters separated by a hyphen will match any character in the range between those characters. If you want to include the hyphen in the set of characters, the hyphen must be the first character in the set.

Here are some examples of using wildcards:

| | |
|---|---|
| `*tmp` | any file name ending in `tmp` |
| `*tmp*` | any file name containing the string `tmp` |
| `[a-z]*` | any file name starting with a lower case alphabetic character |
| `[-a-z]*` | any file name starting with a hyphen or a lower case alphabetic character |
| `[a-zA-Z]*` | any file name starting with an alphabetic character |
| `*[0-9]*` | any file name that contains a numeric digit |
| `[!0-9]*` | any file name that does not begin with a numeric digit |
| `??` | any file name that contains exactly two characters |
| `??*` | any file name that contains two or more characters |
| `*/tmp` | file named `tmp` in a subdirectory |

## Hidden Files

A *hidden file* is a file in which the first character of the file name is a period (.). This refers to the convention that the `ls` command does not usually list these files, and thus, they are considered hidden. There is an exception to the use of wildcards when trying to match hidden files. If the first character of a file name is a period, the period must be matched explicitly. That is, the first character of a pattern must be a period or it will not match a file name that begins with a period. This prevents inadvertently matching the . and . . file names.

Here are some examples of using wildcards to match hidden files:

| | |
|---|---|
| `*` | any file name that does not begin with . |
| `.*` | any file name that begins with ., including . and . . |
| `.?` | any file name that contains two characters and the first character is . |
| `?` | any file name that is one character except . |
| `[.a]*` | any file name that begin with a, but this will not match files that begin with . because the first character of the pattern is not . |
| `\.*` | matches nothing since . is not the first character in the pattern, and only files that begin with . are to be matched (mutually exclusive conditions) |
| `directory/*` | any file name in the directory that does not begin with . |
| `directory/.*` | any file name in the directory that begins with ., including . and . . |

## USING QUOTES

The shell separates its input into individual commands to be executed. In doing so, it processes a variety of metacharacters,[1] whitespace, keywords, variable names, and so forth. It is sometimes useful to shield some text from interpretation by the shell so that it will simply be used as is.

---

[1] Characters that have special meaning to the shell are often called *metacharacters*.

The shell provides three methods of quoting to shield text from interpretation by the shell:

- the backslash character
- single quotes
- double quotes

When quoted text is processed by the shell, the quotes are removed and the text is used as is. In the following example, quotes are used to prevent the shell from interpreting the characters in a string being passed to the `echo` command.

```
$ echo "The secret word is #!%**."
The secret word is #!%**.
$
```

Most characters other than letters and numbers have special meaning to the shell and need to be quoted when that special meaning is not intended. In particular, the following characters should be quoted when they are used in strings.

```
; & ( ) | ^ < > ? * [ ] \ $ ` " ' { } newline tab space
```

## Backslash

The backslash is convenient for quoting the single character that follows it. This is often referred to as *escaping* the character, since it directs the shell to ignore any special meaning normally associated with the character. The backslash is essentially the same as using single quotes around a single character (single quotes are discussed in the next section); you will find both methods used frequently.

The backslash character can be used to quote itself. For example:

```
$ echo abc\\def
abc\def
$
```

**Note:** The backslash followed by a newline is used for line continuation. The shell treats a backslash followed by a newline as if it were not there at all. This is not the same as a quoted newline where the quotes are removed and the newline remains. If you want to quote a newline, you need to use single or double quotes.

The following example assigns the newline character to the variable NEWLINE. Be careful here; if the second single quote is not the first character on the following line, both the newline character and the leading whitespace on the second line will be assigned to the variable.

```
NEWLINE='
'
```

## Single Quotes

Single quotes are the most restrictive form of quoting provided by the shell. Any text enclosed in single quotes (' . . . ') is ignored by the shell. The only character that cannot be quoted by single quotes is another single quote.

Be sure not to confuse the single quote (') with the back quote (`), sometimes called the grave quote. These characters look similar, but they have very different meanings to the shell. An easy way to remember this is that the single quote and the double quote are on the same key on the keyboard.

## Double Quotes

Text that is enclosed in double quotes (" . . . ") instructs the shell to ignore *most* of the special characters within the quoted text. The shell continues to interpret $, `, and \. However, the \ is only interpreted if it precedes a $, `, \, or ". If the backslash precedes any other character, it will be ignored and passed on as part of the text.

Simply stated, double quotes allow variable and command substitution within the quoted string.

Here are some examples of using quotes:

```
$ FOO=foo
$ echo "$FOO"      # The value of FOO is printed
foo
$ echo "\$FOO"     # \ causes the shell to ignore the $
$FOO
$ echo "F\OO"      # \ not before $, `, \, or " is left as is
F\OO
$ echo '$FOO'      # $ is left as is in single quotes
$FOO
$ echo '\$FOO'     # \ and $ are left as is in single quotes
\$FOO
$
```

## When Should You Use Quotes?

Quotes are used when you do not want the shell to interpret parts of the command line; for example, when a parameter contains whitespace or metacharacters. However, if a parameter is stored in a variable, you may not know whether or not the parameter contains characters that need to be quoted. Thus, there is no answer that is always right, but in general, it is better to use quotes unless you know that quotes are not necessary.

The following examples demonstrate some of the problems that can occur when quotes are needed, but not used. These examples use the test command to compare two strings. The `test` command is discussed in "The `test` Command" in Chapter 3, but for now, it is enough to know that the `test` command in these examples expects three parameters: a string, the equal sign (=), and another string. Since each of these is a separate parameter, they must be separated from each other by whitespace as shown here.

```
test string1 = string2
```

In the first example, neither string contains characters that need to be quoted; therefore, quotes can be used, but they are not necessary.

```
test John = John            # Right
test "John" = "John"        # Right
```

On the other hand, if one of the strings contains whitespace, that string needs to be quoted. In the next example, the first string is not quoted, but it contains whitespace. This will cause the shell to interpret that string as two separate parameters. Since the second parameter will be `Doe` instead of the equal sign, the `test` command will print an error message indicating that it is an invalid operator.

```
test John Doe = John        # Wrong
```

To prevent this error, the quotes are required around the first string to prevent the shell from interpreting the whitespace as a separation between two parameters.

```
test "John Doe" = "John"    # Right
```

A similar problem occurs when one of the strings is empty. You can probably guess that the following example will produce an error because the first parameter to the `test` command is missing.

```
test = John                 # Wrong
```

On the other hand, the following example is correct. It passes an empty string as the first parameter. There is a significant difference between not passing a parameter and passing an empty parameter.

```
test "" = "John"            # Right
```

This problem is more subtle when a variable is used to pass the string to the `test` command as in the next example. Even though it looks like the first parameter is being passed to the `test` command, after the shell replaces the variable with its value, which is empty, the parameter will disappear.

```
STRING=
test $STRING = John         # Wrong
```

As before, this problem is solved by putting quotes around the parameter as shown below.

```
test "$STRING" = "John"      # Right
```

These examples stress the use of quotes, whether they are needed or not. While this is usually true, it is not always true. Remember that quotes are used to prevent the shell from interpreting the text inside the quotes. Sometimes you want the shell to interpret the text. In the following example, an asterisk is passed as a parameter to the `echo` command. If you want the shell to interpret the asterisk as a wildcard character, it cannot be quoted.

```
echo *
```

## Which Type of Quotes Should You Use?

If you want to use quotes but allow variable and command substitution in the quoted string, you should use double quotes. This is the most common type of quoting. The following examples show variable and command substitution into quoted strings.

```
$ FILE=foobar
$ echo "Cannot remove $FILE"
Cannot remove foobar
$

$ echo "Today is `date`"
Today is Tue Jan  1 00:00:01 PDT 1991
$
```

Single quotes are used when you do not want the shell to interpret anything in the quoted string. This usually occurs when the string contains dollar signs, back quotes, or double quotes. Single quotes are frequently used to quote command sequences that are passed to `sed` and `awk`, since these strings usually contain many of these characters.

The backslash is usually reserved for special situations in which you want to quote a single character; for example, a dollar sign inside a double quoted string.

## Examples of Quoting

Single quotes can be used to quote double quotes and vice versa.

```
$ echo '"abc"'
"abc"
$

$ echo "'abc'"
'abc'
$
```

Single quotes can be used to quote the backslash.

```
$ echo '\'
\
$
```

The backslash can be used to quote itself.

```
$ echo \\
\
$
```

In more complicated situations, you can use a mixture of quoted and unquoted text, and you can use a mixture of single quoted and double quoted text as long as they do not overlap. You cannot nest quotes, except when using the backslash inside double quotes to escape the $, `, \, or ".

When trying to decipher the use of quotes in a command line, scan the command line from left to right. The first instance of a quote character begins the quote, and the second instance of the quote character ends the quote (except that a double quote can occur in a double quoted string if it is preceded with a backslash). If there is another quote character, it begins another quoted section, and so forth. For example, the following string consists of three parts: a single quoted part (Part1), an unquoted part (Part2), and a double quoted part (Part3).

```
'Part1'Part2"Part3"
```

If you want to substitute a variable into a single quoted string, you can simply end the quote before the variable and start the quote again after the variable. Since the variable might contain whitespace or other metacharacters, it is usually best to use double quotes around the variable. For example:

```
'Part1'"$VARIABLE"'$Part2'
```

This is a common technique for passing the value of a variable to an awk script. Since awk scripts are loaded with spaces and dollar signs, they are usually enclosed in single quotes. The following example uses this technique to pass the value of the variable USER to an awk script. This example prints the names of the terminals you are logged into.

```
who | awk '/^'"$USER"'/ {print $2}'
```

## COMMAND SUBSTITUTION WITH BACK QUOTES

The back quote is used to delimit a command that is to be replaced by its standard output. That is, the command is executed and the output from the command is substituted in its place in the command line.

Be sure not to confuse the back quote (`` ` ``) with the single quote ( ' ). These characters look very similar, but they have different meanings to the shell.

The following example shows the output of the date command substituted into a string that is then passed to the echo command.

```
$ echo "Today is `date`"
Today is Tue Jan 1 00:00:01 PDT 1991
$
```

Command substitution can be nested, but quotes are necessary to prevent the shell from pairing from the back quotes from left to right. That is, the quotes prevent the shell from pairing the first two back quotes together and then pairing the next two back quotes together, and so forth. The following example shows how to use quotes to nest command substitution.

```
$ STRING=`echo "abc \`echo def\` ghi"`
$ echo $STRING
abc def ghi
$
```

This same example can be rewritten using a temporary variable instead of nesting the command substitution as shown here:

```
$ TMPSTR=`echo def`
$ STRING=`echo "abc $TMPSTR ghi"`
$ echo $STRING
abc def ghi
$
```

## COMMAND EXIT STATUS

In the Bourne shell, logical operations are based on the exit status of the last command executed to determine whether a condition is true or false. By convention, commands return a value of zero to indicate successful execution and a value of nonzero to indicate an error. For example, in the if statement below, the test command will return a value of zero if the file exists; otherwise it will return a value other than zero.

```
if test -f file
then
    echo "file exists"
fi
```

A command is successful (true) if its exit status is zero; any other value implies the command was not successful (false).

| 0 | Success | True |
| Not 0 | Unsuccessful | False |

This may seem backwards when compared with other languages. For example, when the C shell evaluates an expression, if the result is zero it represents false, and any other value represents true. The difference is that the Bourne shell is not evaluating an expression, it is simply testing the exit status of the last command that was executed.

The command exit status is used in the conditional test of the `if`, `elif`, `while`, `||`, and `&&` statements. These statements are all discussed in the remaining sections of this chapter.

The exit status of the last command that was executed is saved in the variable `$?`.

When commands are grouped, the exit status of the group is the exit status of the last command that was executed in the group.

## COMMAND SEPARATORS

A command is usually terminated by the end of the line. However, each of the following shell operators is also a command separator.

| | |
|---|---|
| newline | command separator |
| ; | command separator |
| \| | connect stdout of command to stdin of following command |
| & | execute command in the background |
| \|\| | conditional OR |
| && | conditional AND |

### Semicolon

The semicolon (`;`) separates commands for sequential execution. The command following the semicolon will not begin execution until the command preceding the semicolon has completed. The semicolon is equivalent to a newline, but it allows more than one command to be on the same line. For example, the following two examples are equivalent.

```
cd /tmp; ls

cd /tmp
ls
```

### Pipe

The vertical bar (`|`) causes the standard output of the command before the vertical bar to be connected, or *piped,* to the standard input of the command following the vertical bar. For example:

```
cat file1 file2 | sort | more
```

This sequence of commands is called a *pipeline*. Each command in the pipeline is executed as a separate process, and the commands are all executed at the same time.

The exit status of the pipeline is the exit status of the last command in the pipeline. A pipeline such as:

> *command1* | *command2*

is equivalent to the following commands except that, when using a pipeline, temporary files are not necessary and the commands are executed in parallel.

> *command1* >*tmpfile*; *command2* <*tmpfile*

## Background Execution

The ampersand (&) causes the command that it follows to be executed in the background. That is, the process created to execute the command executes independently of the current process, and the current process does not wait for it to complete.

The ampersand is not usually used as a command separator; instead, it is used to execute a command in the background while other commands are executed from the terminal. For example:

```
make &
```

When a command is run in the background, its standard input is connected to /dev/null. This prevents the current process and the background process from trying to read the same standard input.

## ORed Execution

The double vertical bar ( | | ) causes the command following it to be executed only if the previous command fails. The following two statements are equivalent:

> *command1* | | *command2*

```
if command1
then
     :   # This is the null command; it does nothing.
else
     command2
fi
```

In the following example, if the rm command fails, the echo command is used to print the name of the file that could not be removed. If the rm command succeeds, the echo command is not executed.

```
rm file || echo "ERROR - Cannot remove file" 1>&2
```

This separator can be used to write conditional statements that resemble the C programming language such as shown in the next example.

```
if command1 || command2
then
    . . .
fi
```

This example will only execute the commands between the `then` and the fi if either *command1* or *command2* is successful. If *command1* is successful, *command2* will not be executed. In practice, using this separator in this way is almost never done; perhaps because when the commands are followed by their parameter list, the resemblance to C diminishes.

## ANDed Execution

The double ampersand (`&&`) causes the command following it to be executed only if the previous command executes successfully. The following two statements are equivalent:

```
command1 && command2

if command1
then
    command2
fi
```

In the following example, the `mkdir` command creates a new directory. If `mkdir` is successful, a file is copied to the directory, otherwise the file is not copied.

```
mkdir directory && cp file directory
```

Like the double vertical bar, this separator can be used to write conditional statements that resemble the C programming language such as shown in the next example.

```
if command1 && command2
then
    . . .
fi
```

This example will only execute the commands between the `then` and the fi if both *command1* and *command2* are successful.

## COMMAND GROUPING

### Grouping with Parentheses

When commands are grouped between an opening parenthesis ( ( ) and a closing parenthesis ( ) ), the commands will be executed in a separate shell process, or subshell. The shell creates a *subshell* and passes the commands inside the parentheses to it. The current shell waits for the subshell to complete before it continues.

Since a subshell is executed in a separate process, it will inherit the environment of the current shell, but it will not be able to alter the environment of the current (parent) shell (see "Changing the Parent Environment" in Chapter 5). Thus, when commands are executed in a subshell, changes to the environment, such as changing the current working directory and changing the value of a variable, are lost when the subshell finishes (that is, they revert to their previous values). This can be either good or bad, depending upon what you are trying to accomplish.

Parentheses are usually used to prevent a section of code from altering the environment of the current shell. In the following example, the parentheses are used to temporarily change the directory while the `make` command is executed. Since the directory is changed while in a subshell, the directory in the current shell is not changed.

```
(cd $HOME; make)
```

An ampersand can be used following the right parenthesis to execute the subshell in the background.

Parentheses can be nested, which in turn, will cause more than one subshell to be created.

### Grouping with Braces

When commands are grouped between an opening brace ( { ) and a closing brace ( } ), their treatment is similar to commands grouped with parentheses. The primary difference is that commands grouped with braces are executed in the current shell and commands that are grouped with parentheses are executed in a subshell.

For example:

```
{ command1; command2; ...; }
```

Notice that the last command inside the braces must be followed by a semicolon and the braces must have whitespace around them. Braces are commonly used on a line by themselves with the commands appearing between them. When the braces and commands are separated by newlines, the semicolons are not necessary.

```
{
    command1
```

```
        command2
        . . .
  }
```

Braces are usually used to redirect the combined standard input or standard output of the commands within the braces as shown in the following examples. However, when the standard input or standard output of commands grouped with braces is redirected, the shell will execute the commands in a subshell.[2] Thus, when braces are used in this way, they are equivalent to using parentheses.

```
{ date; make; } > make.list
```

```
{ ...; } < file
```

```
command | { ...; }
```

When braces are used to group commands, the group is treated as a single command. This can be used with the `||` and `&&` command separators to execute, or not execute, the group of commands following the separator. This is demonstrated in "Another `if` Statement" in Chapter 11.

Braces can be nested, and they can be followed by an ampersand to cause the commands within the braces to be executed in a subshell in the background.

## CONTROL FLOW STATEMENTS

The control flow statements are defined by a set of keywords. Each keyword is usually the first word on a line, but it may follow any command separator. The following is a list of the control flow keywords:

```
if          then        elif        else        fi

case        in          esac

for         while       do          done
```

### The `if` Statement

```
if command-list
then
        command
        . . .
[else
```

---

[2] The Korn shell and the POSIX shell do not create a subshell in this instance.

```
        command
        ...]
fi
```

The `if` statement enables you to execute commands conditionally depending upon the result of a conditional test. The conditional test of an `if` statement is based on the exit status of the last command executed in the command list. If the exit status is successful, the commands following the `then` are executed.

An `if` statement can contain an optional `else` section that will be executed if the conditional test of the `if` statement is not successful.

An `if` statement is always terminated by an `fi` statement.

The command list is usually, but not necessarily, a single command. The command list must be terminated by the keyword `then`. The `then` key word is frequently on the same line as the command list, but when it is, a semicolon is needed to separate the command list and the `then` keyword as shown in the following example.

```
if test -f file; then
      echo "The file exists."
else
      echo "The file does not exist."
fi
```

## The `elif` Statement

```
elif command-list
then
      command
      ...
```

One or more `elif` statements can be used in an `if` statement to test for additional conditions. Each `elif` statement contains a separate command list. If the command list of the `if` statement is not successful, the command list of each `elif` statement will be executed, one at a time, until one of them is successful.

The last `elif` statement can be followed by an `else` statement. The commands following the `else` statement will be executed if none of the `elif` statements were successful.

The following example shows an `if` statement that tests for three separate conditions. The last `elif` statement is followed by an `else` statement.

```
if condition1
then
      ...
elif condition2
then
      ...
```

```
elif condition3
then
      . . .
else
      . . .
fi
```

## The for **Statement**

```
for variable [in word-list]
do
      command
      . . .
done
```

The `for` statement enables you to execute a set of commands repeatedly, once for each value in the word list. Each time the loop is executed, the next value in the word list is assigned to the variable and the commands between `do` and `done` are executed.

The word list is a string that is parsed into words using the characters in the IFS (internal field separators) variable as delimiters. Initially, the IFS variable is set to space, tab, and newline; therefore, the word list is parsed by whitespace.

If the word list is omitted, the `for` loop is executed once for each positional parameter that is set. That is, it is equivalent to the following example. (The positional parameters are discussed in Chapter 2.)

```
for parm in "$@"
do
      . . .
done
```

The `break` command can be used to exit the loop early, and the `continue` command can be used to go to the next iteration of the loop. (These commands are discussed in Chapter 3.)

## The while **Statement**

```
while command-list
do
      command
      . . .
done
```

The `while` statement enables you to execute a set of commands repeatedly as long as some condition is true. The condition is based on the exit status of the last command executed in the command list.

The command list following the `while` is executed repeatedly. Each time the command list is successful, the commands between `do` and `done` are executed. The loop terminates when the command list is not successful. If the command list is not successful the first time it is executed, the commands between `do` and `done` are never executed.

The `break` command can be used to exit the loop early, and the `continue` command can be used to go to the next iteration of the loop. (These commands are discussed in Chapter 3.)

The following example shows a `while` statement where the condition of the `while` statement is always true; that is, it will loop forever. The body of the `while` statement must detect the condition needed to terminate the loop and execute the `break`, `exit`, or `return` command to stop it.

```
while :
do
      if ...
      then
            break
      fi
done
```

The null command (`:`), used for the conditional test in this example, is a special command that does nothing but always returns a successful exit status. This command is discussed in more detail in "The : (null) Command" in Chapter 3.

## The `case` Statement

```
case string in
      pattern [| pattern] ...) command-list ;;
         ...
esac
```

The `case` statement enables you to execute one of several lists of commands. The value of the string is compared to the patterns that precede each command list to determine which command list to execute.

If the string matches more than one pattern, only the commands associated with the first matching pattern will be executed. If no pattern matches the string, then no commands will be executed.

The same command list can be matched by more than one pattern by separating the patterns with a vertical bar (`|`). The last pattern must be followed by the right parenthesis to mark the end of the patterns and the beginning of the command list.

Following the right parenthesis is a list of commands terminated by a double semicolon (`;;`). The list of commands may be empty, or it may contain one or more commands.

The following example shows a simple `case` statement.

```
case string in
      pattern1) command-list ;;
      pattern2) command-list ;;
```

```
        pattern3)   command-list  ;;
         . . .
        *)          command-list  ;;        # Default case
esac
```

When a command list is short, it is common to put the pattern, the command list, and the double semicolon all on the same line as shown in the example above. If the double semicolon is on the same line as the last command in the command list, it must be separated from that command by whitespace.

A pattern may contain the same wildcard characters that are used for file name expansion.

| | |
|---|---|
| * | matches any (zero or more) characters |
| ? | matches any single character |
| [...] | matches any single character in the enclosed set |
| [!...] | matches any single character that is not in the enclosed set |

A single * is a pattern that matches any string and therefore is useful as the default case.

The following code shows some examples of pattern matching in a case statement. This is just sample code rather than a working example. Some of the cases cannot be reached because the string will always be matched by one of the preceding patterns, and some of the examples are not very practical, but they are shown so that they can be contrasted with similar examples.

```
case string in
    abc )           echo "It is abc"                            ;;
    def | ghi )     echo "It is def or ghi"                     ;;
    abc* )          echo "It begins with abc"                   ;;
    *abc )          echo "It ends with abc"                     ;;
    [Yy]* )         echo "It begins with Y or y"                ;;
    "[Yy]" )        echo "It is literally [Yy]"                 ;;
    "[Yy]*" )       echo "It is literally [Yy]*"                ;;
    "[Yy]"* )       echo "It begins with [Yy]"                  ;;
    [!Nn]* )        echo "It does not begin with N or n"        ;;
    [a-z]*[AB] )    echo "It begins with a lower case" \
                         "letter and ends with an A or B"       ;;
    \* )            echo "It is an asterisk"                    ;;
    "*" )           echo "It is an asterisk"                    ;;
    '*' )           echo "It is an asterisk"                    ;;
    \? )            echo "It is a question mark"                ;;
    ? )             echo "It is a single character"             ;;
    "" )            echo "It is empty"                          ;;
    '""' )          echo "It is two double quotes"              ;;
    \"\" )          echo "It is two double quotes"              ;;
    * )             echo "It is some other value"               ;;
esac
```

## The `test` Command

The `test` command is used to evaluate expressions and set its exit status to success if the expression evaluates to true; otherwise it sets its exit status to failure. This makes the `test` command useful with the shell syntaxes that support conditional execution, such as the `if` and `while` statements.

The following example shows the `test` command used in the conditional test of an `if` statement. The option supplied to the `test` command causes it to return true (success) if the file exists and is readable; otherwise it will return false.

```
if test -r file
then
    echo "The file exists and I can read it."
fi
```

The `test` command supports a wide variety of options that can be used to create complex expressions. These options are described in the section on the `test` command in Chapter 3.

To improve the readability of the `test` command, the shell provides an alternate syntax specifically for the `test` command. To use this alternate syntax, the command name, `test`, is omitted and the expression is enclosed in brackets. The following example shows the previous example of the `test` command after it has been modified to use the brackets.

```
if [ -r file ]
then
    echo "The file exists and I can read it."
fi
```

The bracket syntax may be used in place of the `test` command anywhere you would normally use the `test` command, but the most common place that it is used is in the command list of the `if` and `while` statements. The following example shows the bracket syntax used in a `while` statement.

```
while [ expression ]
do
    . . .
done
```

## STATEMENTS WITHOUT NEWLINES

A semicolon can be used to put more than one keyword on the same line. The following examples show several equivalent ways to write an `if` statement.

```
if command-list
then
      command
      . . .
fi

if command-list; then
      command
      . . .
fi

if command-list; then command; ...; fi
```

Sometimes it is necessary to write a command without newlines—for example, when the command is passed to the remote shell command (see "Remote Command Execution" in Chapter 5) or when the command is used in a makefile. When this is necessary, you can use a semicolon wherever you would normally use a newline, except you cannot put a semicolon immediately following a keyword.

The following examples show how you could write each of the control flow statements without using newlines.

```
if command-list; then command; [...;] [else command; [...;]] fi

elif command-list; then command; [...;]

for variable [in word-list]; do command; [...;] done

while command-list; do command; [...;] done

case string in [pattern [| pattern] ...) command-list ;;] ... esac
```

# 2

# *Shell Variables*

A variable name can be composed of letters, digits, and the underscore. The first character of a variable name must be a letter or the underscore.

The value of a variable is always a string of characters. Even when a variable contains a number, it is stored as a string of numeric characters. The string may be whatever length is necessary.

A value is assigned to a variable by specifying the variable name followed by the equal sign and the value. Whitespace is not permitted on either side of the equal sign. More than one assignment statement can be on the same line. Since whitespace is not allowed in an assignment statement except within quotes, whitespace is used to separate multiple assignments on the same line.

> *variable=value* [ *variable=value* ]

It is not necessary to declare a variable before it is used. The shell will create the variable the first time it is used. If a variable is used before it has been assigned a value, the value will be an empty string.

## USING VARIABLES

The value of a variable is retrieved by prefixing the name of the variable with the dollar sign ($). The variable name may be enclosed in braces.

> $*variable*
> ${*variable*}

The dollar sign and the braces are not part of the variable name; they are only used to retrieve the value of the variable. When this syntax is used, the shell replaces the variable with its value. In the following example, the first line shows the string /tmp being assigned to the variable DIR. In the second line, the value of DIR is retrieved and substituted into the command line of the cd command before it is executed.

```
$ DIR=/tmp
$ cd $DIR
$
```

When characters are appended to the value of a variable, the variable name may be enclosed in braces to remove any ambiguity of where the variable name ends and the string being appended to the value begins. The braces are not necessary if the first character following the variable name is not a legal character in a variable name, that is, it is not a letter, digit, or underscore. In the following example, the braces are necessary. Without the braces the shell would look for a variable FOOBAR.

```
$ FOO=abc
$ echo ${FOO}BAR
abcBAR
$
```

In the next example, braces would be permitted, but they are not necessary. Since the first character following the variable name is a period, which is not a valid character in a variable name, the shell has no difficulty locating the end of the variable name.

```
$ ROOT=main
$ CFILE=$ROOT.c
$ echo $CFILE
main.c
$
```

### Passing Variables to Commands

Passing the value of a variable to a command is as simple as putting the variable name, prefixed with the dollar sign, wherever it is needed on the command line. When a variable name is preceded with a dollar sign, the shell will replace the variable with its value before executing the command.

If it is necessary to use a variable within a quoted string, such as in a `sed` script, be sure to use double quotes; single quotes will prevent the shell from performing variable substitution. Also, when a variable that contains whitespace or other metacharacters is used on the command line, be sure to enclose that variable in double quotes.

In the following example, the shell will insert the values of `OLD_TEXT` and `NEW_TEXT` into the command line before it is executed. This command is used to perform text substitution in a file; it is described in more detail in "Replace Text" in Chapter 7.

```
OLD_TEXT=abc
NEW_TEXT=def
sed -e "s/$OLD_TEXT/$NEW_TEXT/g" <file >newfile
```

## UNDEFINED VARIABLES

In the shell, variables are defined the first time they are assigned a value. Usually, a variable is used for the first time when it is assigned a value, but that is not necessary. If the value of a variable is retrieved before it has been assigned a value, its value is an empty string.

In many shell scripts, you will see each variable assigned a value at the front of the shell script. This is a convention that is used to list the variables and provide a simple comment describing how each variable will be used. Except when a value other than an empty string is assigned to these variables, these assignments have no functional purpose; they are used to make the shell script more understandable. For examples of this practice, you can look at the shell scripts in "Examples of Shell Scripts" in Chapter 10.

Before a variable has been assigned a value for the first time, it is not known to the shell, and therefore, it is undefined. A variable may also be defined, but assigned the empty string. This is not quite the same as being undefined, which will be discussed further in the following section. The following two statements are equivalent; they both assign an empty string to the variable.

```
VARIABLE=
VARIABLE=""
```

## UNINITIALIZED VARIABLES

The shell supports four syntaxes to specify a default value or action when an uninitialized variable is used. These syntaxes can differentiate between a variable that is undefined (has never been assigned a value) and one that has been assigned an empty string. The colon in each form of the initialization syntax is optional.[1] If the colon is present, both

---

[1] Some older versions of the shell, such as `/bin/sh` on ULTRIX, do not support the colon in these syntaxes.

undefined variables and empty variables will be treated as uninitialized variables. If the colon is omitted, only undefined variables will be treated as uninitialized variables.

${*variable*:=*value*}
${*variable*=*value*}

This statement is used to specify a default value for an uninitialized variable. If the variable is initialized, this statement simply returns its value. If it is not initialized, *value* is assigned to the variable and then *value* is returned. Since this form of initialization can result in the variable being assigned a value, it cannot be used with read-only variables, such as the positional parameters. (The positional parameters are discussed later in this chapter.)

In the following example, the value of the variable DIRECTORY will be substituted into the string passed to the echo command. If the variable DIRECTORY is undefined or empty, /tmp will be assigned to DIRECTORY before its value is passed to the echo command.

```
echo "The directory ${DIRECTORY:=/tmp} will be used."
```

${*variable*:-*value*}
${*variable*-*value*}

This statement is similar to the previous statement, except that the value is not assigned to the variable when the variable is not initialized. If the variable is initialized, this statement simply returns its value as before. If the variable is not initialized, *value* is returned and the variable remains uninitialized. Since this statement does not assign a value to the variable, it can be used with read-only variables.

The following example is similar to the previous example, except that the positional parameter $1 (which is discussed later in this chapter) is used in place of the variable DIRECTORY. The value of the variable $1 will be substituted into the string passed to the echo command unless it is undefined or empty. If it is undefined or empty, /tmp will be substituted into the string before it is passed to the echo command, and $1 will not be changed.

```
echo "The directory ${1:-/tmp} will be used."
```

${*variable*:?*message*}
${*variable*?*message*}

This statement is used to ensure that a variable is initialized. When this statement is evaluated, if the variable is not initialized, the message is printed and the shell script is terminated. The message may be omitted, in which case "parameter null or not set" is printed. If the message contains whitespace, you need to enclose the message in quotes.

The first example below shows the statement without a message, and the second statement shows the message in quotes.

> $ { *variable* : ? }
> $ { *variable* : ? *"message"* }

In the following example, because the variable is within a quoted string, additional quotes around the message are not needed.

```
echo "The directory ${DIRECTORY:?missing parameter} will be used."
```

When the message is printed, it will be prefixed with the name of the variable. The message from the previous statement will look like this:

```
DIRECTORY: missing parameter
```

${*variable*:+*value*}
${*variable*+*value*}

This statement returns *value* if the variable is initialized; otherwise it returns an empty string. This statement does not change the variable.

## Testing Uninitialized Variables

The initialization syntaxes are only used to retrieve the value of a variable. If you want the initialization behavior, but not the variable substitution, you can precede it with a colon (:). The colon is the null command, that is, a command that does nothing (see "The : (null) Command" in Chapter 3). When used in this way, the variable is being passed as a parameter to the null command. The result is that the shell will perform the variable initialization that you want and execute a command that does nothing.

> :  $ { *variable* :=*value* }

To test whether a variable has a value other than an empty string, you can simply compare it with an empty string as shown in the next example. Be sure to use quotes around the variable, otherwise you will not get a syntax error when the variable is empty.

```
if [ "$VAR" = "" ]; then
    echo "VAR is not set."
fi
```

Some people prefer to write this statement as shown here:

```
if [ ! "$VAR" ]; then
    echo "VAR is not set."
fi
```

## POSITIONAL PARAMETERS

Before a shell command is executed, the command line is processed (metacharacters are processed, quotes removed, etc.) and separated into parameters. The parameters are put into the positional parameters $0, $1, $2, ..., $n. Positional parameter $0 contains the command name as it was entered on the command line, $1 contains the first parameter, $2 contains the second parameter, and so forth.

Positional parameters are available for the first nine parameters only (i.e., $1 through $9). If more than nine parameters are present, the shift command can be used to move parameter values from $2 to $1, $3 to $2, and so forth. The remaining parameters are shifted into $9 one at a time. The shift command may be followed by a number to specify the number of positions to be shifted. If the number is omitted, the parameters will be shifted one position. The parameter $0 is not affected by the shift command.

The current number of parameters specified on the command line is contained in the variable $#. The value of this variable is the actual number of parameters specified, not counting the command name in $0; it may be greater than nine. This variable is automatically decremented each time the shift command is executed.

Either of the variables $* or $@ can be used to refer to all of the positional parameters. Using either of these variables will return a string that contains all of the positional parameters, starting with $1, with a space inserted between the value of each parameter. The variables $@ and $* are the same except when enclosed in double quotes. When $* is enclosed in double quotes, it returns all of the positional parameters as a single value, but when $@ is enclosed in double quotes, it returns each positional parameter as a separate value.

| | | |
|---|---|---|
| $* | is equivalent to: | $1 $2 ... |
| $@ | is equivalent to: | $1 $2 ... |
| "$*" | is equivalent to: | "$1 $2 ..." |
| "$@" | is equivalent to: | "$1" "$2" ... |

If $* is used to copy the parameter list, it may cause a problem if one or more of the parameters contains whitespace. For example, if $* is used to pass the parameter list to another command, any parameter that contains whitespace will be separated into individual parameters. If $* is quoted, then all the parameters would be passed as a single parameter. Neither of these options reproduces the parameter list as it was passed to the current command. To do that, you can use "$@". However, when the parameter list is empty, some implementations of the shell interpret "$@" to mean one empty parameter. Since one empty parameter is not the same as no parameters, you will sometimes see the following notation used since it more accurately reproduces the parameter list.

```
${@+"$@"}
```

The following example shows this notation used to pass the entire command line to another command:

```
command ${@+"$@"}
```

This is equivalent to the following sequence of commands:

```
if [ $# -eq 0 ]; then
    command
else
    command "$@"
fi
```

The variables $0-$9, $#, $*, and $@ are read-only variables; that is, they cannot be assigned values. However, except for $0, these variables can be altered indirectly by using the set command or the shift command. For more information on the set and shift commands, see "Built-in Commands" in Chapter 3.

## SPECIAL VARIABLES

The special variables described in this section are all read-only variables.

### $? Variable

The variable $? contains the exit status of the last command that was executed. This does not apply to commands that were executed in the background using the ampersand. By convention, a value of zero implies success and any other value implies failure. The following two commands are equivalent:

```
if command
then
      . . .
fi

command
if [ $? -eq 0 ]
then
      . . .
fi
```

### $$ Variable

The variable $$ contains the process ID of the current command. The value of $$ will not be changed if a portion of the shell script is executed in a subshell. For example, if some commands are enclosed in parentheses to force them to be executed in a separate process, the value of $$ will not change.

This value is commonly used to provide a number that uniquely identifies a particular invocation of a command. For example, you will frequently see temporary file names appended with this value to make a unique file name. This prevents two simultaneous executions of the shell script from trying to use the same file name.

```
/tmp/tmp.$$
```

## $! Variable

The variable $! contains the process ID of the last command that was executed in the background using the ampersand.

```
command &
...
wait $!        # Wait for command to complete.
```

## $- Variable

The variable $- contains the set of flags that were specified when the shell was invoked or that have been set using the set command.

# ASSIGNMENT STATEMENT ON THE COMMAND LINE

It is possible to put a variable assignment statement in front of a command. When this is done, the variable with its new value is exported to the environment of the command, but the value of the variable is not changed in the current environment. The first command below shows an example of this, and the second command shows an equivalent way to do the same thing. This topic is revisited in "Changing the Child Environment" in Chapter 5.

```
CFLAGS=-g make

(CFLAGS=-g; export CFLAGS; make)
```

When using this method of exporting a variable to a command, the variable assignment must be on the same line as the command, and it must be in front of the command name. Be sure not to put a semicolon between the variable assignment and the command since that would be the same as putting them on separate lines.

This technique of exporting a variable to the environment of a command requires a separate process to be created. Since a shell function executes in the current shell, this technique cannot be used to export a variable into the environment of a shell function. Shell functions are discussed in the next chapter.

# 3

# *Shell Functions and Built-in Commands*

## SHELL FUNCTIONS

Shell functions were added to the Bourne shell in UNIX System V Release 2; therefore, they are available in most versions of the shell that you are likely to encounter.[1]

A function defines a set of commands that are executed when the function name is invoked. A function must be defined before it is executed. The following example shows the syntax of a function where *name* is the name of the function. The parentheses are always empty, but they are required as part of the function definition.

```
name ( )
{
    command
    . . .
}
```

If the function is defined on a single line, be sure to leave a space following the left brace and use a semicolon following the last command.

```
name ( )  {  command-list ;  }
```

---

[1] The default shell on ULTRIX, /bin/sh, does not support shell functions, but you can use /bin/sh5, which does support them.

To return from a function, you can either fall through the end of the function, or you can execute the `return` command.

```
return [n]
```

The parameter passed to the `return` command is the exit status of the function. This value is the same as the exit status returned by a command. Therefore, when the function returns, its exit status is in the variable `$?`, and a function can be used in the conditional test of the shell statements such as the `if` statement or the `while` statement.

If there is no `return` statement, the exit status of the function is the exit status of the last command that is executed in the function.

## Function Execution

Functions are normally executed in the current shell without creating a subshell; however, this is not always the case. Whenever the standard input or standard output of a function is redirected, most versions of the shell will execute the function in a subshell. For example, enclosing the function in back quotes to capture its standard output in a variable will cause the function to be executed in a subshell.

There are several differences in the way a function behaves, depending upon whether it is executed in the current shell or a subshell:

- If a function is executed in the current shell and the current directory is changed in the function, it will remain changed after the function exits. If the function is executed in a subshell, the current directory will revert to the directory where it was before the function was executed.
- If a function is executed in the current shell, any changes made to variables while executing the function will remain after the function exits. If the function is executed in a subshell, the value of all variables will revert to what they were before the function was executed.
- If a function is executed in the current shell, the `exit` command will exit the entire shell script. If the function is executed in a subshell, the `exit` command will only exit the subshell and return to the current shell; thus, it behaves like the `return` command.

## Passing Parameters to Functions

To execute a function, you specify the function name followed by the parameters, just as you would to execute a command. When a function is entered, the parameters are made available to the function through the positional parameters `$1`, `$2`, . . ., etc. Positional parameter `$0` is not changed when a function is called; it still contains the name of the shell script.

On some systems, there is only one set of positional parameters for both the parameters of the shell script and the parameters of the functions executed by the shell script.

Therefore, be sure to save any of the command line parameters that are still needed before executing a shell function.

## Using Variables in Functions

There is only one set of variables in a shell script; it includes all the variables of the shell script and its functions. If a variable in a function has the same name as a variable outside the function, they are the same variable.

When local variables are needed within functions, special care must be used to ensure that the variable name does not unintentionally collide with a variable used outside the function. This is especially important when the function is included from another file (see the next section) where the caller of the function may not check to see what variable names are used inside the function.

The simplest method to avoid conflicts between variables used inside a function and variables used outside the function is to adopt a naming convention that prevents the conflict. For example, in the shell functions in this book, the name of any variable that is only used within a function begins with the underscore character.[2]

Notice that recursive function calls, while possible, are not very useful because a new set of variables is not created for each instance of the function.

## Reusing Functions

Shell functions can be defined in a file that is included by a shell script. If a shell script executes a statement such as the one below, the commands in the file will be executed in the current shell without creating a new process. If the file contains a function definition, the statement behaves the same as if the function is defined in the current shell script.

```
. file
```

The shell uses the PATH variable to locate files included by this command in the same way that it uses the PATH variable to locate commands. Thus, if shell scripts and include files are kept in the same directory, the following statement can be used to ensure that the include files will be found when the shell script is executed. This statement is explained in "The PATH Variable" in Chapter 5.

```
PATH=$PATH:`dirname $0`
```

To avoid confusion, the file name suffix .sh is sometimes used for files that contain shell code, but are not intended to be executed as commands.

---

[2] Some older versions of the shell may require variable names to begin with a letter, in which case, you will have to adapt the convention to your own needs.

## BUILT-IN COMMANDS

This section discusses the commands that are built into the shell. Each command is discussed briefly, but some of the commands are discussed in more detail in other sections of this book. In those cases, the description refers you to that discussion.

Not all shells support the same set of built-in commands. The commands listed in this section are generally available in all shells. You should check the manual page for the `sh` command on your system for information on additional commands that may be built into the shell.

Some commands are both independent command files and commands that are built into the shell, namely the `cd`, `echo`, `expr`, `pwd`, `test`, and `umask` commands. These commands are documented by their own manual pages, which contain more information about these commands than the manual page for the shell. The rest of the built-in commands are only documented in the manual page for the shell.

Some built-in commands are part of the shell because they provide an integral part of the shell's functionality while others, such as the `echo` command and the `test` command, are part of the shell to make shell scripts execute more efficiently. In general, any command that is built into the shell will execute more efficiently than that same command if it is executed in a separate process.

### The : (null) Command

`:` [*parm* . . .]

This is a special command built into the shell that does nothing but is always successful. The name of the null command is the colon character (`:`). Parameters may be passed to the null command, and the command line will be evaluated the same as any other command.

The null command always returns an exit status of zero (success). This allows the null command to be used in conditional tests to force a "true" condition. The following example shows a `while` statement in which the condition of the `while` statement is always true; that is, it will loop forever. The body of the `while` statement must detect the condition needed to terminate the loop and execute the `break`, `exit`, or `return` command to stop it.

```
while :
do
    if ...
    then
        break
    fi
done
```

The null command can also be used as a place holder in situations in which a command is required but none is needed. For example, you may want to use the `else` clause of the `if` statement, rather than to reverse the conditional test of the `if` statement, as shown in the following example.

```
if command-list
then
      :
else
      command
fi
```

The null command is also used for the side effects caused by having its parameter list evaluated. The following example shows how this can be used with one of the variable initialization syntaxes to test whether or not a variable is set. The value returned as a result of using the syntax is discarded because it is passed as a parameter to the null command.

```
: ${VAR?"VAR is not set."}
```

Another common example is to use the following command to truncate a file. When the shell evaluates the command line, it will reset the length of the file to zero if the file exists (see "Truncating a File" in Chapter 4).

```
: >file
```

## The . (dot) Command

```
. file
```

This command is usually referred to as the dot command, but the actual command name is . (that is, the period character). This command reads a file and executes the commands in the file without creating a new process. The effect is equivalent to replacing this command with the contents of the file.

The name following the dot is the name of the file containing the commands to execute. If the name of the file does not contain a slash ( / ), the `PATH` variable will be used to locate the file just as it is used to locate other commands to execute (see "The `PATH` Variable" in Chapter 5).

Files referenced by the dot command must be readable by the shell, but they do not need to be executable.

## The break Command

```
break [n]
```

The `break` command is used to immediately exit from an enclosing `for` or `while` loop. When more than one loop is executed at the same time (that is, the loops are nested), the value of *n* can be used to exit from more than one loop at the same time.

The earlier discussion about the null command shows an example that uses the break command to exit from an infinite while loop.

## The cd **Command**

cd [*directory*]

The cd command changes the current directory to the directory named on the command line. If the directory is omitted, this command changes the directory to the value specified in the variable HOME.

The variable CDPATH defines search paths that will be used to locate the directory if it is not an absolute path name (that is, it does not begin with a slash character).

## The continue **Command**

continue [*n*]

The continue command is used to skip to the next iteration of the enclosing for or while loop. When more than one loop is executed at the same time (that is, the loops are nested), the value of *n* can be used to skip to the next iteration of the *n*th enclosing for or while loop.

## The echo **Command**

echo [*parm* ...]

The echo command writes its parameters to the standard output. Each parameter is separated from the next by a single space, and the output is followed by a newline.

There are two common versions of the echo command: the System V version and the BSD version. The differences between these two versions of the echo command are a common source of problems when writing shell scripts. The section "The echo Command" in Chapter 12 discusses the differences between these two versions of the echo command.

## The eval **Command**

eval [*parm* ...]

The eval command is provided for situations in which more than one evaluation of the command line is needed. The eval command takes its parameters and makes a command line out of them. It then evaluates the command line by performing variable substitution, command substitution, wildcard expansion, and so forth. The result is then executed by the shell, which will cause the command line to be evaluated again.

The eval command is used for things like storing variable names in variables.

Two evaluations are needed since the first evaluation retrieves the name of the variable and the second evaluation retrieves the value of that variable. This is demonstrated in the following example. The name of VAR1 is stored in VAR2. When the value of VAR1 is retrieved, it is necessary to specify two dollar signs, one to retrieve the value of VAR2 during the first evaluation, and one to retrieve the value of VAR1 during the second evaluation. The dollar sign needed during the second evaluation is quoted with a backslash so that it will be ignored during the first evaluation.

```
$ VAR1=value
$ VAR2=VAR1
$ eval echo \$$VAR2
value
$
```

The eval command is also used when a command returns some commands that the caller is expected to execute. For example, the resize command returns commands that the user is expected to execute to set variables to the current window size. For example, the output of the resize command might look like this:

```
COLUMNS=104;
LINES=37;
export COLUMNS LINES;
```

Thus, by executing the following command, the COLUMNS and LINES variables are automatically set and exported.

```
eval `resize`
```

During the first evaluation of this command line, command substitution causes `resize` to be replaced with the standard output from the resize command. Then the command line is executed, which, after command substitution, consists of the statements returned by the resize command.

### The exec **Command**

```
exec [parm ...]
```

The exec command is used to execute a command in place of the current shell without creating a new process. Once the new command begins to execute, there is no way to return to the current shell.

The exec command takes its parameters and makes a command line out of them. This command line is similar to any other command line, including the use of file redirection operators.

If the command line consists of nothing but file redirection operators (that is, there is no command to execute), any file redirection operators will be applied to the current shell, and the current shell will continue to execute. This allows the `exec` command to redirect the standard input, standard output, or standard error of the current shell. This is discussed further in "Opening Files" in Chapter 4.

## The `exit` Command

    exit [*n*]

The `exit` command is used to exit from the shell. The value of *n* is the exit status of the shell. If *n* is omitted, the exit status of the shell is the exit status of the last command that was executed.

If a shell script reaches the end of the file, the shell script will exit and the exit status will be the exit status of the last command that was executed in the shell script.

If the `exit` command is executed from a subshell, it only exits the subshell, not the entire shell script.

## The `export` Command

    export [*name* ...]

The `export` command marks the variables named on the command line to be automatically exported to the environment of any commands that are executed. Normally, shell variables are not put in the environment, and they will not be seen by commands that are executed from the shell (see "Environment Variables" in Chapter 5).

## The `pwd` Command

    pwd

The `pwd` command prints the full name of the current directory. Also, the section "The `pwd` Command" in Chapter 12 discusses the value returned by the `pwd` command when, through the use of symbolic links, there is more than one path to a directory.

## The `read` Command

    read [*name* ...]

The `read` command is used to read one line from the standard input. The `read` command returns zero (success) unless the end of the file is encountered, in which case it returns nonzero.

As each line is read, it is parsed into fields using the characters in the `IFS` (internal field separators) variable as delimiters. Initially, the `IFS` variable is set to space, tab, and newline, which causes the line to be parsed by whitespace. The fields are then assigned to the variables listed on the `read` command line. If the line contains more fields than variables, the extra fields are all assigned to the last variable on the command line. When more than one field is assigned to the last variable, the fields will be separated by spaces. If there are more variables than fields, the unused variables are assigned the empty string.

For example:

```
while read field1 field2 field3 remainder
do
    ...
done
```

The `read` command is discussed further in "Reading Files" in Chapter 4 and "Parsing Data" in Chapter 8.

### The `readonly` Command

```
readonly [name ...]
```

The `readonly` command is used to prevent the variables named on the command line from being changed by a subsequent assignment.

This command is almost never used in shell scripts; it may be more useful when the shell is used interactively.

### The `return` Command

```
return [n]
```

The `return` command is used to return from a shell function. The value of *n* is the exit status of the function. If *n* is omitted, the exit status of the function is the exit status of the last command that was executed in the function.

### The `set` Command

```
set [-ekntuvx] [parm ...]
```

This command is used to turn shell options on and off, and it is used to load new parameters into the positional parameters. In addition, if the `set` command is used without any options or parameters, it will list the name and value of the currently defined variables.

These different functions of the `set` command are discussed under a variety of topics throughout this book. In particular, see "Positional Parameters" in Chapter 2, "Environment Variables" in Chapter 5, "Parsing Data" in Chapter 8, and "Debugging Options" in Chapter 11.

## The `shift` Command

```
shift [n]
```

The `shift` command is used to shift the positional parameters so that $2 moves to $1, $3 moves to $2, and so on. The value that was in $1 is lost. The value of *n* indicates the number of positions to shift. If *n* is omitted, the positional parameters are shifted one position.

In older versions of the shell, the `shift` command did not allow a value to indicate the number of positions to shift. To shift multiple positions, the `shift` command was executed more than once, which is a technique that is still frequently used to perform multiple shifts.

## The `test` Command

```
test [expression]
[ [expression] ]
```

The `test` command is used to evaluate an expression and set its exit status to indicate whether the expression is true (success) or false (failure). This makes the `test` command useful with the shell syntaxes that support conditional execution, such as the `if` and `while` statements.

As shown above, there are two syntaxes for the `test` command; this was discussed in the section on the `test` command in Chapter 1.

The expression to be evaluated by the `test` command is specified by using one or more of the options to the `test` command. The `test` command supports a wide variety of options that allow you to create complex expressions. However, not all versions of the `test` command support the same set of options. The following list of options are generally available on most systems, but you should check the manual page for the `test` command on your system to determine which options are actually available.

**File Tests**

| | |
|---|---|
| -r *file* | true if *file* is readable |
| -w *file* | true if *file* is writable |
| -x *file* | true if *file* is executable[3] |
| -f *file* | true if *file* is an ordinary file |
| -d *file* | true if *file* is a directory |
| -s *file* | true if the length of *file* is greater than zero |
| -t [*filedes*] | true if the file descriptor number (default=1) is associated with a terminal |

**String Tests**

| | |
|---|---|
| -z *str* | true if the length of *str* is zero |
| -n *str* | true if the length of *str* is greater than zero |
| *str* | true if *str* is not an empty string |
| *str1* = *str2* | true if *str1* and *str2* are the same |
| *str1* != *str2* | true if *str1* and *str2* are not the same |

---

[3] This option may not be available on ULTRIX systems.

**Numeric Tests**

| | | |
|---|---|---|
| *int1* -eq *int2* | | true if *int1* is equal to *int2* |
| *int1* -ne *int2* | | true if *int1* is not equal to *int2* |
| *int1* -lt *int2* | | true if *int1* is less than *int2* |
| *int1* -le *int2* | | true if *int1* is less than or equal to *int2* |
| *int1* -gt *int2* | | true if *int1* is greater than *int2* |
| *int1* -ge *int2* | | true if *int1* is greater than or equal to *int2* |
| ! | | NOT operator, true if the next expression is false |
| -a | | AND operator, true if the previous and the next expression are true |
| -o | | OR operator, true if the previous or the next expression is true |
| ( *expr* ) | | parentheses for grouping expressions |

When using the test command, be sure to leave spaces between each of the options in the expression; they are actually parameters to the test command and need to be parsed as such. For the same reason, do not try to insert newlines to improve the readability of an expression without using a backslash to continue the line.

If you use parentheses to group expressions, both the left and right parentheses are separate options to the test command, and thus, must be surrounded by whitespace. Also, since parentheses are special characters to the shell, they need to be quoted so that the shell will pass them on to the test command without trying to interpret them itself. For example:

```
if [ ! \( -r file -a -w file \) ]
then
    echo "The file is not readable and writable."
fi
```

## The times **Command**

```
times
```

The times command prints the amount of execution time consumed by the shell and the processes executed from the shell. The execution time is broken down into the amount of system time and the amount of user time.

## The trap **Command**

```
trap [command-list] signo ...
```

This command is used to control the behavior of the shell when a signal is received. This command is discussed in "Using Signals" in Chapter 5.

## The type **Command**

```
type [name ...]
```

For each name in the parameter list, the type command will print a message indicating how the shell will interpret the name if it is used as a command. For example:

```
$ type echo date
echo is a shell builtin
date is /bin/date
$
```

## The umask Command

```
umask [nnn]
```

The umask command is used to set the file creation mask to the octal value *nnn*. This value is used to determine the access permissions for a file when it is created. The mask will be subtracted from 777 to determine the access permissions for the file. For example, a mask value of 002 will give read, write, and execute access to the owner and group members, and read and execute access to others.

If *nnn* is omitted, the umask command will print the current value of the file creation mask.

The following example shows how you can temporarily change the file creation mask for a section of code and then restore the original value.

```
OLDMASK=`umask`       # Save current value
umask 002
       .
       .
       .
umask $OLDMASK        # Restore previous value
```

## The unset Command

```
unset [name ...]
```

The unset command will remove the variable or function corresponding to each name in the parameter list. Some variables that are defined by the shell, such as PATH and IFS, cannot be unset using the unset command. You also cannot unset read-only variables.

This command may not be available in some older shells.

## The wait Command

```
wait [n]
```

The wait command will wait for the specified process to terminate and return the exit status of that process as the exit status of this command. If *n* is omitted, this command will wait for all child processes to terminate, and in this case, the wait command will return a successful exit status.

# 4

# *Using Files*

## STANDARD FILE DESCRIPTORS

There are three files that are opened for every process when the process is created, and they are always assigned the following file descriptor numbers.

| | |
|---|---|
| 0 | standard input |
| 1 | standard output |
| 2 | standard error |

These files are usually associated with the user's terminal. Thus, the standard input can be used to read what the user types, and the standard output can be used to send output to the user. The standard error is usually used for error messages so that they can be kept separate from the ordinary output.

## REDIRECTION SYNTAX

The following syntaxes are provided by the shell to redirect the input and output of commands. Each of these syntaxes will be discussed in one of the sections that follow.

| | |
|---|---|
| >*file* | write standard output to *file* |
| >>*file* | append standard output to *file* |
| >&*m* | write standard output to file descriptor *m* |
| >&- | close standard output |
| | |
| <*file* | read standard input from *file* |
| <&*m* | read standard input from file descriptor *m* |
| <&- | close standard input |
| <<*word* | read standard input from a "here document" |

Any of the file redirection syntaxes can be prefixed with a file descriptor to specify a file to be used in place of the default file for that syntax. For example, the following notation will redirect the standard error, rather than the standard output, to the file.

   2>*file*

You may also precede any of the file redirection syntaxes with the file descriptor for the default file for that syntax. The following list shows each of the redirection syntaxes along with an equivalent syntax that explicitly uses the file descriptor for the default file of that syntax.

| | |
|---|---|
| >*file* | 1>*file* |
| >>*file* | 1>>*file* |
| >&*n* | 1>&*n* |
| >&- | 1>&- |
| | |
| <*file* | 0<*file* |
| <&*n* | 0<&*n* |
| <&- | 0<&- |
| <<*word* | 0<<*word* |

A file descriptor must be a number in the range 0 to 9. File descriptors 0, 1, and 2 are the standard file descriptors described in the previous section; the section "Opening Files," later in this chapter, describes how to open new files and assign them to file descriptors.

The file redirection syntax can be put anywhere on the command line, but in practice, it is almost always placed at the end of the command line.

   *command parm1* ... *parmn* >/dev/null

The file redirection syntax is evaluated from left to right; therefore, if one notation is dependent upon another, you must ensure that they are specified in the proper order. For example, if you want to discard both standard output and standard error, you could write a command such as this:

   *command* >/dev/null 2>&1

This command says to redirect the standard output to `/dev/null`, and then to redirect standard error to the same file as the standard output.

If you inadvertently reversed these two specifications, as in the next example, you would not get what you expected. The following statement says to redirect the standard error to the same file as the standard output, probably the terminal, and then redirect the standard output to `/dev/null`. That is, the standard error is redirected to where the standard output was before the standard output was redirected.

```
command 2>&1 >/dev/null        # Probably wrong
```

The shell performs variable substitution before these syntaxes are applied; therefore, file names and file descriptors can be specified in variables.

```
STDOUT=/dev/null
command >$STDOUT
```

## REDIRECTING OUTPUT

The standard output from a command is normally connected to the terminal, but it can be redirected to a file as shown below.

```
command >file
```

If the file already exists, it will be overwritten; otherwise the file will be created. When a file is overwritten, its length is truncated to zero and the file is rewritten. Since the file is not recreated, the file attributes, such as the access permissions and the owner, are not changed.

The standard output from a command can be appended to a file by using the following syntax. If the file does not exist, this notation will also cause the file to be created.

```
command >>file
```

Similarly, standard error can be redirected as shown in the next example.

```
command 2>file
command 2>>file
```

The following syntax can be used to associate one file with another, so that whenever you write to file descriptor *n* the information is actually written to file descriptor *m*. If *n* is omitted, the standard output is written to file descriptor *m*.

```
command n>&m
```

This is commonly used to write standard output to standard error and vice versa. For example, the `echo` command writes its output to standard output. If you want to write a message to standard error, you could redirect the standard output of the `echo` command to the standard error as follows.

```
echo "Error message." 1>&2
```

Notice that the 1 in the redirection syntax is the file descriptor for the standard output. Since the standard output is the default for this redirection syntax, specifying the 1 is optional.

## REDIRECTING INPUT

The standard input of a command can be redirected so that the command reads information from a file rather than the terminal. For example:

*command <file*

You can also redirect the standard input of a command to read from an inline file using the following syntax. This type of redirection is called reading from a *here document* and is covered in more detail in the section "Here Documents," later in this chapter.

*command <<word*
*. . .*
*word*

The following syntax can be used to associate one file with another, so that whenever you read from file descriptor *n,* the information actually is read from file descriptor *m*. If *n* is omitted, the standard input is read from file descriptor *m*.

*command n<&m*

## REDIRECTING SHELL STATEMENTS

The file redirection syntaxes are normally used to redirect the standard input, standard output, and standard error of simple commands. You can also use these syntaxes to redirect the standard files of shell statements. However, in most shells, using file redirection with a shell statement will cause that statement to be executed in a subshell. This, in turn, has side effects that may be undesirable. The section "Reading Files" discusses these side effects and some alternatives in more detail.

The following examples show how you can use the redirection operators to redirect the standard input, standard output, and standard error of shell statements.

```
{
    command
    . . .
} <stdin >stdout 2>stderr

if command-list
then
    command
    . . .
fi <stdin >stdout 2>stderr

for variable [in word-list]
do
    command
    . . .
done <stdin >stdout 2>stderr

while command-list
do
    command
    . . .
done <stdin >stdout 2>stderr

case string in
    pattern ) command-list ;;
    . . .
esac <stdin >stdout 2>stderr
```

You can also connect shell statements in a pipeline so that their standard input or standard output will be read or written to a pipe. The following example shows a `while` loop that has both its standard input and standard output connected to a pipe.

```
command |
while command-list
do
    command
    . . .
done |
command
```

## OPENING FILES

The `exec` command is normally used to execute a command in place of the current shell without creating a new process. However, if the command line passed to the `exec` command does not contain a command, but it does contain file redirection syntaxes, the `exec` command will apply the file redirection to the current shell process. This allows you to redirect the standard input, standard output, and standard error of the current shell script regardless of where they were connected when the shell was invoked. For example:

```
exec <file              # Read stdin from file
exec 1>&2               # Write stdout to stderr
exec >/dev/null 2>&1    # Discard stdout and stderr
exec >>file             # Append stdout to file
```

While each of the standard files can be redirected using the `exec` command, the `exec` command is most frequently used to redirect the standard input of the shell script. This will be discussed in more detail in "Reading Files" later in this chapter.

The `exec` command can also be used to open arbitrary files. To open a file for writing, you can use one of the following statements. As you might expect, the first statement will overwrite the file if it exists or create it if it does not exist; the second statement will open a file so that information will be appended to the end of the file. In both cases, the open file is assigned to file descriptor *n*.

```
exec n>file
exec n>>file
```

The following example opens a file for reading and assigns the file to file descriptor *n*.

```
exec n<file
```

Similarly, you can open a here document for reading as shown in the next example. Again, the open file is assigned to file descriptor *n*.

```
exec n<<word
...
word
```

## WRITING FILES

Once a file has been opened for writing, you can redirect the output of any command to write to that file. The `echo` command is frequently used to write data from a shell script to a file. Since the output from the `echo` command is normally written to its standard output, you can redirect its output to an arbitrary file as shown below.

```
echo "Message" 1>&n
```

This example assumes that file descriptor *n* was opened for writing, as shown in the previous section.

When writing to a file, it is not usually necessary to open the file and then write to the file through a file descriptor, as described above. Instead, it is more common to simply redirect the output of one or more commands to write directly to the file as shown in the following example. The first command overwrites the file, and each subsequent command appends information to the file.

```
command >file
command >>file
command >>file
. . .
```

## READING FILES

The `read` command is usually used to read information from a file. This command is built into the shell; it was discussed briefly in Chapter 3.

To read an entire file, the `read` command is usually used in the conditional test in a `while` loop. Since the `read` command will return success until the end of the file is encountered, and the `read` command reads one line at a time, the `while` loop will execute once for each line in the file. By redirecting the standard input of the `while` loop, it can be used to read any file. This is shown in the following example:

```
while read LINE
do
    . . .
done  <file
```

The problem with this loop is that using file redirection causes the loop to be executed in a subshell.[1] Since a subshell is a separate process, it cannot make changes that affect the current process. Thus, any changes made to variables within the loop will be lost when the loop exits. If all the work can be done within the loop and there is no need to pass information outside the loop, then the above loop is sufficient.

However, if you make changes to variables inside the loop that you need after the loop exits, you can write the loop as shown in the next example. The `exec` command redirects the standard input of the current shell script, not just the `while` loop. Since the loop does not need a different standard input than the current shell, it is not executed in a subshell.

```
exec  <file
while read LINE
do
    . . .
done
```

---

[1] The Korn shell and the POSIX shell do not have this behavior; they do not create a subshell when the input or output of a shell statement is redirected.

This method also has a drawback—namely, the standard input has been changed; therefore, the shell script can no longer receive input from the user. To solve this, you can save the standard input before it is redirected and restore it after the loop is completed.

In the following example, the standard input is temporarily merged with file descriptor 3. After the loop completes, file descriptor 3 is moved back to the standard input, and file descriptor 3 is closed.

```
exec 3<&0 <file
while read LINE
do
      . . .
done
exec 0<&3 3<&-
```

Unless you are using a very old version of the shell, you can also redirect the standard input of the read command to read directly from an open file.[2] In the following example, the exec command is used to open a file for reading and assign it to file descriptor 3. Then the standard input of the read command is redirected to read from file descriptor 3. Thus, neither the standard input of the shell script nor the standard input of the while loop needs to be redirected.

```
exec 3<file
while read LINE 0<&3
do
      . . .
done
exec 3<&-
```

In "The read Command" in Chapter 3, it was discussed how the read command can automatically parse each line as it is read. When it parses each line, it normally uses whitespace as the delimiter. This causes the read command to remove whitespace from the beginning and end of each line as it is read, and also to replace tabs and consecutive whitespace characters within each line with a single space. Thus, if you are trying to copy a file, you will not get an exact copy of the file. In order to preserve the whitespace in the file when it is read with the read command, you can set the IFS variable to the empty string and read each line into a single variable, as shown below.

```
OLDIFS=$IFS
IFS=
while read LINE
do
      echo "$LINE"
done
IFS=$OLDIFS
```

---

[2] Very old versions of the shell did not allow the file redirection syntaxes to be used with built-in commands.

This example may still not produce an exact copy of the file because some implementations of the `read` command allow a backslash character to be used for quoting single characters and a backslash followed by a newline to be used for line continuation. In this case, processing these characters will introduce changes to the information as it is read from the file.

Notice that this example saves the value of the `IFS` variable before setting it to the empty string and it restores the previous value of the `IFS` variable after the file has been read. This is good practice since other features of the shell also use the value in the `IFS` variable. (See "The `IFS` Variable" in Chapter 8.)

## CLOSING FILES

The following syntaxes can be used to close the standard output and the standard input respectively.

```
exec >&-
exec <&-
```

The next two syntaxes are equivalent and can be used to close any file descriptor; simply replace *n* with the file descriptor that you want to close.

```
exec n>&-
exec n<&-
```

Be careful when closing the standard files of commands that you are about to execute. Closing a file is not the same as redirecting it to `/dev/null`. For example, if a command writes to a closed file descriptor, it is an error. If that command is not designed to handle the error, it may abort. If a command writes to `/dev/null`, the output is simply discarded. If you do not want the output from a command, you should redirect its standard output to `/dev/null`.

```
command >/dev/null
```

## TRUNCATING A FILE

Either of the following two commands can be used to reset a file so that its length is zero, or if the file does not exist, to create the file. If the file already exists, the attributes of the file, such as its access permissions, will not be changed.

```
>file
: >file
```

The *>file* notation is allowed without a command for this purpose. Some people prefer to use this notation in conjunction with the null command ( : ). They are equivalent and are both commonly used.

These commands are equivalent to executing the following command:

```
cat /dev/null >file
```

## HERE DOCUMENTS

The shell provides a mechanism that allows you to store the standard input for a command in the shell script along with the command, thus allowing the shell script to be self-contained. This mechanism is called a *here document,* presumably because the data is "here" in the shell script, and the data is usually used for information that could loosely be called a document. When the command is executed, the data in the here document is redirected to the standard input of the command.

The syntax for redirecting the standard input from a here document is:

<< [ - ] *word*

The << symbol is used to redirect the standard input from a here document. This symbol is followed by a word that, when seen again on a line by itself, marks the end of the here document. The word can be any sequence of nonblank characters. For example:

```
cat <<END
This is a here document.
END
```

This causes the lines between <<END and the delimiting string, END, to be written to the standard input of the `cat` command.

Variable and command substitution are performed in the here document before it is written to the standard input of the command. Quotes can be used in the here document to prevent this substitution, and quotes that are part of the here document must be quoted themselves or they will be removed. You can prevent variable and command substitution in the entire here document by quoting the delimiting string. This prevents the need to quote individual dollar signs and back quotes that you do not want evaluated in the here document. For example:

*command* <<\END
. . .
END

Or:

*command* <<'END'
. . .
END

If the << symbol is followed by a hyphen, <<-, leading tabs, *but not spaces,* will be removed from the lines in the here document and from the delimiting string. Without using the hyphen, each line of the here document and the delimiting string would need to begin at the left margin. In the following example, the here document is allowed to conform to the indentation to the surrounding code.

```
if ...
then
      command <<-END
            This is a here document.
      END
fi
```

The following example shows how a large message can be stored in a here document and printed to the standard error using the `cat` command. This example uses a shell function named `Usage` to print the message.

```
Usage() {
      cat 1>&2 <<-EOF
            Usage: $0 [-options][etc.]
                  .
                  .
                  .

      EOF
}
```

To use a here document at the same time as other file redirection, all of the redirection operators belong on the command line, not following the here document. For example:

```
command <<EOF >stdout 2>stderr
...
EOF
```

Or:

```
command1 <<EOF | command2
...
EOF
```

A here document can also be used to pass information to a command so that it will execute without reading from the terminal. The following example shows a simple, self-contained set of commands that will make the `ed` editor reverse the lines in a file and then save the file.

```
ed - file <<-!
g/^/m0
w
q
!
```

Notice that the word used to mark the end of the here document in this example is the exclamation character. Remember that the word used to mark the end of the here document can be any sequence of nonblank characters.

## EXAMPLES OF FILE REDIRECTION

Each command in a sequence of commands must specify its own file redirection. In the following example, redirecting the standard error of one command does not affect the standard error of the other command.

> *command* 2>*ErrorFile1* | *command* 2>*ErrorFile2*

Do not use the same file for standard input and standard output. Remember, the output redirection operator (>) causes the file to be overwritten. As shown in the following example, the file gets destroyed before the sed command gets a chance to read its contents.

```
$ echo "foo" >file
$ sed 's/foo/bar/' <file >file
$ cat file
$
```

The next example is an excerpt from a shell script used to print files to one of several printers on a network. Depending upon which printer is available, one of the first three lines will be uncommented, which in turn will cause one of the cases to be selected. The pr command writes the files listed on the command line ($*) to its standard output, which is piped to the standard input of the case statement. The standard input of the case statement is also the standard input of all of the commands executed within the case statement. When one of the cases is executed, the rsh command will copy its standard input to the remote host where it becomes the standard input of the lp command. Finally, the lp command prints its standard input to the appropriate device.

```
DEVICE=lj1
# DEVICE=lj2
# DEVICE=lj3
pr $* |
    case $DEVICE in
        lj1 ) rsh host1 lp -dlj1 ;;
        lj2 ) rsh host2 lp -dlj2 ;;
        lj3 ) rsh host3 lp -dlj3 ;;
    esac
```

The next example shows how to write some constant information to the standard input of a command and then resume reading from the original standard input. Braces are used to collect the standard output from several commands and pipe it to the standard input of another command. The `echo` command is used to write the constant strings, and the `cat` command is used to copy the standard input to the standard output following the constant strings.

```
{
    echo "line 1"
    echo "line 2"
    echo "line 3"
    cat -
} | command
```

The next example shows nested `while` loops, each with its own redirection of standard input. The outer loop reads a list of file names, while the inner loop reads each file one line at a time.

```
while read FILENAME
do
    while read LINE
    do
        . . .
    done <$FILENAME
done <file
```

To read from the terminal while the standard input is redirected to another file, you can read from the special file `/dev/tty`.

```
while read FILENAME
do
    echo "Do you want to purge $FILENAME?"
    read ANSWER </dev/tty
    . . .
done <file
```

# 5

## The Environment

## IDENTIFYING SHELL SCRIPTS

A shell script is usually executed by invoking its name. This requires that the system be able to identify the shell script as a shell script, and further, it needs to be able to determine which shell should be used to execute the script. This is done by beginning the shell script with the following line:

```
#!/bin/sh
```

The first two characters are a *magic number* that identify the file as an interpreted file, that is, a file that is executed by another program. When the system sees #! as the magic number, it takes the rest of the line as the name of the interpreter for the file.

The use of the #! to identify interpreted files was not always a part of UNIX.[1] On older systems, a colon on the first line was used to identify Bourne shell scripts. On modern systems, either method can be used.

To see how these lines identify shell files, it is easiest to describe the steps followed

---

[1] On systems that support the #! notation, you should be able to find it documented in the manual page for exec (2). On the SCO systems that I have used, the #! notation is an option that must be enabled by rebuilding the kernel. The name of this option is "Hash Pling."

by the shell when a shell script is executed. When any shell (Bourne shell, C shell, etc.) executes a command, it first tries to execute the command using the `exec` system call. If the command begins with the #! magic number, `exec` will execute the interpreter for the file. Otherwise, if the `exec` fails but the file has execute permission, the shell will assume it is a shell script. If the current shell is the Bourne shell, it simply creates a subshell and executes the script. If the current shell is the C shell, it will read the first character of the file. If this character is a #, the script is assumed to be a C shell script; if it is any other character, the script is assumed to be a Bourne shell script. Since a colon is the null command in the Bourne shell, it is a harmless character that serves to identify the file as a Bourne shell script.

This convention was originally adopted to allow the C shell to identify and execute Bourne shell scripts. Some newer shells may not interpret these characters in exactly this way; therefore, you should check the manual pages for the shells involved if you are having any problems.

You can force a shell script to be run by a particular shell by including one of the following lines as the first line of the file:

| | |
|---|---|
| `#!/bin/sh` | Bourne shell |
| `#!/bin/sh5` | Bourne shell (ULTRIX)[2] |
| `#!/bin/csh` | C shell |
| `#!/bin/ksh` | Korn shell |
| `:` | Bourne shell, if executed from the C shell |
| `#` | C shell, if executed from the C shell |

## ENVIRONMENT VARIABLES

The *environment* is a list of name-value pairs, or environment variables, that are passed to a process when it is created. Initially, the environment is a copy of the parent process's environment. When a shell script is executed, the shell copies each environment variable to a shell variable with the same name so that it will be accessible to the shell script while it is executing. Since these variables are copied from the environment, any changes you make to the variables will not change the environment.

The `set` command, without any parameters, can be used to print the name and value of the variables that are currently defined in the shell script. The `env` command (System V) or `printenv` command (BSD) can be used to print the environment variables that are currently defined.

There are not many variables in the initial environment of a process except those that you put there yourself. Most users define several variables in their shell's startup file, but these variables cannot be counted on to be consistent from one user to another.

---

[2] While `/bin/sh` is available on ULTRIX, it is a very old version of the shell that is missing many modern features. Thus, you may prefer to use the version of the shell that is in `/bin/sh5`.

## Changing the Child Environment

As stated above, changing the value of a shell variable will not cause it to be changed in the environment. If you want to add a variable to the environment so that it will be available to each new process, you can use the export command. This will link the variable to the environment so that any changes made to the variable will be reflected in the environment.

For example, the make command checks the environment for a variable named CFLAGS. The following example passes -g to the make command through the CFLAGS environment variable.

```
CFLAGS=-g
export CFLAGS
make
```

If you want to pass a variable to another command through the environment without affecting the current environment, you can set and export the variable from a subshell. Enclosing a command sequence in parentheses forces the commands to be executed as a subshell. For example:

```
(CFLAGS=-g; export CFLAGS; make)
```

You can also export variables to the environment of a command without changing the current environment by preceding the command with one or more variable assignments. The variable assignment must be on the same line as the command and it must be in front of the command. Be sure not to put a semicolon between the variable assignment and the command. The following example shows how this method is used to pass the CFLAGS variable to the make command.

```
CFLAGS=-g make
```

## Changing the Parent Environment

In general, you cannot change the environment of the parent process except through cooperation between the parent and child. When a new process is created, the environment of the current process is copied and made available as the environment for the new process. Since the environment is copied, changes to the environment made by the new process do not affect the environment of the parent process.

If you simply want to pass information between two processes, using a file is the typical mechanism. If the information is small and well defined, the child can simply write the information to its standard output. The parent can then capture this output in a variable by surrounding the command with back quotes. For example:

```
USER=`whoami`
```

"The `eval` Command" in Chapter 3 shows an example where a command writes a sequence of commands to its standard output. Then the parent process executes the standard output from the command.

You also may be able to use a statement such as the one below. This statement allows you to execute another shell script in the context of the current shell, that is, without creating a new process. While this does not let you execute arbitrary commands, it does let you execute code from another file. Naturally, the file must contain shell code.

> . *file*

## The `PATH` Variable

The `PATH` variable lists the directories that the shell will search in order to locate commands. Most shell scripts will simply inherit the value of the `PATH` variable from the parent process. However, there may be times when you want to add more directories to the `PATH` variable, or you may want to restrict the directories listed in the `PATH` variable.

The shell will only use the `PATH` variable to find a command if the command name does not contain a slash. Sometimes you will see commands from the `/bin` directory executed using their full names. This ensures that the correct command is executed rather than some other command with the same name, but in another directory.

> `/bin/rm` *file*

There are several commands in the `/bin` directory that are also built into the shell, such as the `cd`, `test`, and `echo` commands. If only the command name is used to execute one of these commands, the built-in version will be used. However, if the full path name is used, the actual command will be executed.

If there is a directory that contains commands used by your shell script, you can add that directory to the `PATH` variable to ensure that the commands will be found. When you add a directory to the `PATH` variable, it is not necessary to ensure that the directory is not already listed in the `PATH` variable (within moderation, of course). However, be careful when adding a directory to the `PATH` variable from within a shell function because it will be added repeatedly each time the function is called. It is also not necessary to ensure that a directory listed in the `PATH` variable is an existing directory.

If you write shell scripts that execute other shell scripts from the same directory, or that use the dot command to reference other files in the same directory, the following statement can be used to ensure that that directory is listed in the `PATH` variable. This prevents persons who periodically use the commands in that directory from needing to have that directory listed in their `PATH` variable.

> `PATH=$PATH:`dirname $0``

Since `$0` contains the name used to invoke the current command, `dirname` will return the path of the current command, which is then appended to the `PATH` variable. If there is no path component in `$0`, `dirname` will return . (the symbol for the current directory). If this occurs, it indicates that the path of the command is already listed in the PATH variable.

**Note:** In most cases, adding . to the PATH variable is neither useful nor harmful. However, some security-conscious users have policies against including . in the PATH variable because there is a potential for someone to attempt to cause a command to execute a bogus command from the current directory. Since . is added as the last directory in the list of directories to search, it should not normally be searched, but if you are writing shell scripts for a security-conscious user, you should avoid using this technique.

Also, if the command is executed by specifying a relative path name, the relative path will be added to the PATH variable. Thus, if the shell script changes directories while it executes, the path name will no longer be correct.

# USER AND SYSTEM INFORMATION

## Getting the Name of the User

One of the two variables USER or LOGNAME, depending upon the type of the system, is usually set to the user name of the current user. However, these variables can be changed by the user, and, therefore, their value is not reliable. Depending upon your purpose, this may be all you need.

There are also several commands that can be used to return the user name of the current user, namely the whoami, logname, id, and who commands. The main differences between these commands are which systems support them and what value they return after the su command has been used to change users.

The whoami command is available on BSD systems. Although it is not standard on System V systems, it is frequently available in a directory for unsupported utilities. The whoami command prints the user name of the current user. If the user uses the su command to change users, whoami will print the name of the user that you are su'd to.

```
USER=`whoami`
```

The logname command is available on System V systems and many BSD systems. It also prints the user name of the current user. However, it does not change when the user uses the su command unless the - option is used. That is, su *user* does not change the user name, but su - *user* does change the user name.

```
USER=`logname`
```

The id command is available on System V systems and many BSD systems. It prints the user name, user ID, group name, and group ID in the format shown below. If the user uses the su command to change users, id will print the information for the user that you are su'd to.

```
uid=0(root) gid=1(other)
```

The following code shows two `sed` filters that will extract the user name and the user ID from the output of the `id` command.

```
USER=`id | sed -e 's/.*(//' -e 's/).*//'`
UID=`id | sed -e 's/uid=//' -e 's/(.*//'`
```

The `who` command can be used to list who is on the system. The `am i` option of the `who` command lists information about the current user in the format shown below; however, some systems do not include the host name in the output. The `who am i` command will always return the original user name; it does not change when the user `su`'s to another user.

```
hostname!username     ttyp8     Jun 10 12:00
```

The user name can be extracted from the output of the `who am i` command using the following command. This command will work whether or not the host name is part of the output.

```
USER=`who am i | sed -e 's/ .*//' -e 's/.*!//'`
```

## Is the User the Superuser?

The user name of the superuser is `root`; however, on some systems there may be more than one user name for the superuser. Therefore, to determine if the current user is the superuser, it is more common to check that the user ID of the current user is zero, which is always the user ID of the superuser.

The following example shows how to test the output of the `id` command to determine whether or not the current user is the superuser:

```
if id | grep "^uid=0(" >/dev/null 2>&1
then
     echo "Is superuser"
else
     echo "Is not superuser"
fi
```

The next example shows a shell function that will return true (success) if the current user is the superuser; otherwise, it will return false (failure).

```
IsSuperuser() {
    case `id` in
        "uid=0("* ) return 0   ;;
        * )         return 1   ;;
    esac
}
```

### Getting the Name of the System

The `hostname` command is usually used to return the name of the current system. However, the `hostname` command is not standard on System V systems, even though it is usually available.

```
HOSTNAME=`hostname`
```

Some systems include the domain name in the value returned by the `hostname` command. The following command removes the domain name so that only the name of the system is returned. This command will work whether or not the domain name is part of the output.

```
HOSTNAME=`hostname | sed -e 's/\..*//'`
```

Another method of getting the name of the current system is to use the `uname` command. This command is probably more portable than using the `hostname` command, but in practice, most shell scripts use the `hostname` command anyway.

```
HOSTNAME=`uname -n`
```

## USING SIGNALS

Normally when a process receives a signal, the receiving process will be aborted. The shell provides the `trap` command to catch signals so that the process can do something other than a premature exit. Instead of aborting the process, the commands in a command list will be executed. The syntax of the `trap` command is shown below.

```
trap [command-list] signo ...
```

Depending upon the parameters to the `trap` command, it can be used to catch signals, ignore signals, or to reset signals to their default behavior. Each of these variations will be discussed in the sections that follow.

```
trap command-list signo ...      # Catch
trap '' signo ...                # Ignore
trap signo ...                   # Reset
```

The `trap` command can be placed anywhere in a shell script, but it is usually found near the beginning so that it will be executed before any signal is received.

The command list is executed when the shell script receives any of the signals listed. If the command list does not contain the `exit` command, the process will resume execution from where it was interrupted.

The signals that are of interest to shell programmers are 0, 1, 2, 3, 9, and 15.

0   Signal 0 is not a real signal; it is a convention implemented by the shell. When a shell command exits, either by executing the `exit` command or by executing through the end of the shell script, the shell sends itself a signal 0.

1   Signal 1 (SIGHUP) is signaled when the process receives a hang-up signal. The hang-up signal is usually received when you "hang up" the modem, disconnect your terminal, or close your X Window.

2   Signal 2 (SIGINT) is signaled when the process receives an interrupt signal. The interrupt signal is typically associated with the interrupt key entered from the keyboard. For example, control-C or the `DELETE` key are frequently configured as the interrupt key. See the manual page for the `stty` command.

3   Signal 3 (SIGQUIT) is signaled when the process receives a quit signal. The quit signal is typically associated with the quit key entered from the keyboard. For example, control-\ is frequently configured as the quit key. See the manual page for the `stty` command.

9   Signal 9 (SIGKILL) is used to kill processes, but it cannot be caught by the process. If signal 9 is specified to the `trap` command, it will be ignored.

15  Signal 15 (SIGTERM) is signaled when the process receives the terminate signal. This is the default signal sent to a process by the `kill` command.

## Catching Signals

The most common use of the `trap` command is to allow the shell script to regain control when a signal occurs so that it can clean up before it terminates. Such `trap` commands are usually set to catch signals 1, 2, 3, and 15. The following example shows a typical `trap` command used to remove temporary files when the command receives a signal.

```
trap 'rm -f /tmp/*.$$; exit 1' 1 2 3 15
```

The command list of the `trap` command is usually enclosed in single quotes. This prevents the shell from evaluating the command list when the `trap` command is executed. It simply removes the quotes and saves the command list until the signal is received. When the signal is received, the shell evaluates and executes the command list. Since the command list is no longer quoted, the shell performs variable substitution, command substitution, and so forth, at that time.

Notice in the previous example, the last command in the command list is the `exit` command. This is necessary to cause the shell script to terminate after the command list is executed. Without the `exit` command, the shell script would resume execution from where it was interrupted.

The command list is usually written on one line using semicolons to separate the commands. However, the command list could also be written over several lines as shown here:

```
trap 'command
      command
      ...' 1 2 3 15
```

## Ignoring Signals

When the command list is empty, the shell will ignore the signal if it is received. Remember, an empty command list is not the same as no command list at all.

```
trap '' signo ...
```

## Resetting Signals

When the command list is omitted, not just empty, the signals will be reset to their default action, which is to abort the process if the signal is received.

```
trap signo ...
```

## Examples of the `trap` Command

The following example shows how a function could be used to handle the clean-up tasks for both normal and abnormal termination. The function expects the exit status to be passed as a parameter, which it will pass on to the `exit` command. When Cleanup is called as the result of a signal, it is passed a one; when it is called for normal termination, it is passed a zero.

```
Cleanup() {
    rm /tmp/*.$$
    exit $1
}
trap 'Cleanup 1' 1 2 3 15
    .
    .
    .
Cleanup 0
```

The next example shows how a signal can be used to interrupt a long command and then resume executing the rest of the shell script. The shell script initially ignores signals 2 and 3 to prevent keyboard interrupts from aborting the process. When the shell script is about to copy a file to the user's terminal, signal 2 is enabled so that the user can enter a keyboard interrupt to stop the file from being copied to the terminal. Notice that the command list only contains the null command ( : ). It is sufficient in this case to interrupt the `cat` command and do nothing. When the process continues, it will continue at the statement following the `cat` command. After the `cat` command has finished, signal 2 is set to be ignored again.

```
trap '' 2 3
    .
    .
    .
trap ':' 2
cat file
trap '' 2
    .
    .
    .
```

In the next example, signal 2 or 3 is needed to stop a loop from repeating indefinitely. If either signal is received, the variable STOP is set to 1. An if statement at the
end of the loop checks the value of STOP before repeating the loop.

```
STOP=
trap 'STOP=1; trap 2 3' 2 3
while :
do
    ...
    if [ $STOP ]; then
        break
    fi
done
```

Notice that the command list of the trap command on the second line contains a
trap command that will reset the signals. This prevents the possibility of receiving another signal before the signals can be reset. If the signals are not reset until the loop is
complete, there is a small window where another signal could be received before the signals are reset. By resetting the signals in the command list of the trap command, this
window is closed. In most situations, this is not important; therefore, you will not normally see the signals reset in the command list of the trap command.

## REMOTE COMMAND EXECUTION

The remote shell command allows you to execute a command on another system. The
first thing you will need to do is determine the name of the remote shell command. The
command is usually called rsh, but it might also be called remsh (HP-UX), or rcmd
(SCO). You also need to be careful on SGI systems since /bin/rsh is the restricted
shell and /usr/bsd/rsh is the remote shell. All of the examples in this section will
use rsh as the name of the remote shell command.

### Checking the Remote Connection

If you are writing a command that executes commands on a remote system, you may
want to perform some error checking to identify network problems. This may help prevent people from coming to you when your shell script fails, even though the problem is
actually something wrong with the network.

The `hostaddr` command in Chapter 10, "Examples of Shell Scripts," can be used to validate the name of a remote system. This command returns the IP address of a system by searching the `/etc/hosts` file. If the name of the system is not valid, the IP address will be empty. This command may not work correctly on systems that use YP, BIND, or some other network server, since those systems may not have a complete list of valid hosts in the `/etc/hosts` file.

The `CheckHostname` function in Chapter 9, "Examples of Shell Functions," is more reliable than the `hostaddr` command because it uses the `ping` command to verify the name of the system. However, this function has the disadvantage that on some systems the `ping` command may take a long time to return if the remote system is not responding.

Both of these functions only check that the name of the system is valid, not whether the system is available. In the discussion of the `CheckHostname` function, it discusses how you can modify that function so that it can be used to determine if the system is responding to network request.

If you want to check the remote connection but you are not ready to execute the remote command, one of the previous functions is probably what you need. For example, these examples can be used when checking configuration values. However, if you are ready to execute a remote command, you may as well let the `rsh` command check the connection for you.

Remote connection frequently fails, even though the physical connection to the system is functioning correctly. For example, the user may not have permission to execute commands on the system. You can ensure that the user executing the shell script has permission to access the remote system by executing a simple remote command that should not fail. For example, the following command executes a simple `echo` command on the remote system and discards the output.

```
rsh host "echo testing >/dev/null"
if [ $? -ne 0 ]; then
    echo "Connection to host failed." 1>&2
    exit 1
fi
```

## Executing Remote Commands

Executing a command on another system is remarkably similar to executing a command on the current system. The remote shell command automatically connects the standard input, standard output, and standard error of the current shell script to the remote command. In the following example, the `echo` command on another system is used to write a message to the standard output of the current shell script. While using the `echo` command on the current system would be much more efficient, this example shows how simple it is to execute a command on a remote system.

```
$ rsh host echo "Message to standard output."
Message to standard output.
$
```

However, a word of warning: when the standard input of the shell script is connected to the remote shell command, all of the standard input is copied to the remote command. When the remote command returns to the current system, the standard input will be empty. For example, you might expect the following command to read a file and write it to the standard output. Instead, it only writes the first line of the file to the standard output.

```
while read LINE
do
     rsh host echo "$LINE"
done <file
```

You can avoid this problem by redirecting the standard input of the remote command to /dev/null so that it will not be connected to the standard input of the current shell script. Since this problem is fairly common, some versions of the rsh command provide a -n option to do this for you.

When commands are executed on a remote system, they are executed by the login shell of the user. Since most people do not use the Bourne shell as their login shell, you can force the use of the Bourne shell as shown below. This command says to execute the sh command on the remote system, and the command that you want to execute, *command,* is passed as a string to the sh command.

```
rsh host "sh -c 'command'"
```

For simple command execution, it does not matter which shell executes the command. However, if you need to use a specific feature of the shell, such as an if statement, you will need to make sure that the correct shell is being used to execute the remote command.

## Getting Status from a Remote Command

When you test the execution status ($?) following a remote shell command, you are testing the status of the remote shell command, not the command that it executed remotely. This may not be what you want. For example, the following command tells you whether the rsh command was successful, not the rm command.

```
rsh host rm file
if [ $? -ne 0 ]; then
     echo "The rsh command failed."
fi
```

There is no straightforward way to retrieve the status of a command executed in a remote shell; you will have to take explicit actions to return the information. The most common way to get the status of a remote command is to save it in a file and retrieve the file when you return to the local system.

If the remote command does not use the standard output, it can be a convenient mechanism to transmit the status back to the local system. The following example uses the `echo` command to write the exit status of the `false` command to the standard output. Since the entire command is enclosed in back quotes, this value is captured in the variable `STAT`.

```
$ STAT=`rsh host "sh -c 'false; echo \\$?'"`
$ echo $STAT
1
$
```

## Using Quotes with a Remote Command

The problem with using quotes with the remote shell command is that the command line is evaluated more than once because more than one shell is involved—the current shell, the remote login shell, and the remote `sh` command. You may be able to execute simple commands without using any quotes.

```
rsh host echo foo
```

However, if any metacharacters are used, they will be interpreted by the current shell unless they are quoted. In the following example, the semicolon separating the two `echo` commands is enclosed in quotes so that it will be ignored by the current shell. If the quotes were not used, the second `echo` command would be executed on the current system.

```
rsh host "echo foo; echo bar"
```

Sometimes you will need more than one set of quotes. The outer set of quotes is processed and removed by the current shell. An inner set of quotes may be necessary when the command needs to be quoted when it is executed on the remote system. In the following example, the outer quotes prevent the current shell from removing the inner quotes. When the command arrives on the remote system, the asterisk is still quoted to prevent the shell on the remote system from expanding it into a list of file names.

```
rsh host "echo '*'"
```

When more than one set of quotes is needed, it is usually best to use double quotes as the outer quotes. Since the outer quotes will be processed by the current shell, this will permit the current shell to substitute variables into the command line. Since single quotes are ignored inside double quotes, the current shell will be able to substitute variables anywhere in the command line.

```
rsh host "sh -c 'command'"
```

You can use double quotes for both the outer quotes and the inner quotes, as shown below. When the current shell removes the outer quotes, it also removes the backslashes. Remember, a backslash can be used to quote a double quote inside double quotes.

rsh *host* "sh -c \\"*command*\\""

Variables that must be evaluated on the remote system pose a special quoting problem. It is best to avoid them whenever possible. For example, the previous example that retrieved the exit status of the remote command by accessing the variable $? could have been written to test the exit status of the remote command using an if, while, ||, or && statement and then return a value of your own choosing. The following example shows how this could have been done:

STAT=`rsh *host* "sh -c 'if *command*; then echo 0; else echo 1;fi;'"`

Or:

STAT=`rsh *host* "sh -c '(*command* && echo 0) || echo 1'"`

When you need to nest quotes indefinitely, you can use some number of backslashes to quote a double quote character. You will need to determine how many times the command line will be evaluated to determine how many backslashes to use. Every time the command line is evaluated, \\ will be changed to \ and \" will be changed to ". For example, \\\" becomes \". The following example shows this progression for command lines that are evaluated once, twice, and three times. The eval command is a command that is built into the shell and can be used to evaluate a command line and return the result.

```
$ echo \"                        # Evaluated once
"
$ eval echo \\\"                  # Evaluated twice
"
$ eval eval echo \\\\\\\"         # Evaluated three times
"
$
```

## Using File Redirection with a Remote Command

You may need to use quotes to indicate whether file redirection parameters are intended for the remote shell command or the command executed on the remote system. Remember, metacharacters that are not quoted will be evaluated by the current shell; otherwise, they will be evaluated by the remote shell. In the following example, since the file redirection is not quoted, it will be evaluated by the current shell. Thus, the standard output of the rsh command will be sent to *file* on the local system.

```
rsh host echo foo >file
```

In the next example, however, the file redirection will be passed as part of the command to the remote system. This will put the output of the echo command into *file* on the remote system.

```
rsh host "echo foo >file"
```

The next command copies a local file to the standard input of a remote lp command.

```
cat localfile | rsh host lp
```

The following example shows two ways to copy a local file to a remote file.

```
cat localfile | rsh host "cat - >remotefile"

rsh host "cat >remotefile" <localfile
```

And vice versa, this command copies a remote file to the local system.

```
rsh host cat remotefile >localfile
```

## Examples of Remote Commands

Another way to evaluate the success or failure of a remote command is to analyze the output that it returns. In this example, the error messages from the rsh command are merged with the standard output from the mt command. A case statement is used to identify certain error messages. When one of these messages is found, a customized message is printed, and the shell script is exited. Notice that the messages are abbreviated using wildcard characters so that only a unique portion of the message is needed in the pattern. This also makes the messages more portable since error messages vary slightly from one system to the next. Also, be sure to check the manual page for the mt command because it is also inconsistent from one version of UNIX to the next.

```
HOST=host
DEVICE=tapedevice
STATUS=`rsh $HOST mt -f $DEVICE status 2>&1`
case $STATUS in
    *nknown?host* )
        echo "The $HOST is not known." 1>&2
        exit 1
        ;;
    *ogin?incorrect* )
        echo "$LOGNAME cannot login to $HOST." 1>&2
        exit 1
```

```
            ;;
        *offline* )
            echo "$DEVICE is not online." 1>&2
            exit 1
            ;;
esac
```

The next example shows how to test whether or not a remote file is writable.

```
STATUS=`rsh host "sh -c 'if [ -w remotefile ]; then      \
                            echo OK;                     \
                    else;                                \
                            echo FAILED;                 \
                    fi;                                  \
            ' "`
if [ "$STATUS" = "OK" ]; then
    echo OK
fi
```

In the next example, a file on the local system is copied to a file on the remote system. The exit status from the `cat` command is passed back to the local system where it is tested.

```
STATUS=`cat localfile |
        rsh host   "sh -c 'cat - >>remotefile; echo \\$?'"`
if [ "$STATUS" != "0" ]; then
    echo "Remote cat failed ($STATUS)" 1>&2
    exit $STATUS
fi
```

The next example shows how you can use the `grep` command to examine a remote file. The output of the `grep` command is written to the remote standard output, which in turn is written to the local standard output; this is handled transparently by the remote shell command.

The example also shows several variables being substituted into the remote command. The variable substitution is performed by the local shell. Since the single quotes around the `grep` command are ignored until the double quotes are removed, they do not prevent the local shell from substituting values for PATTERN and FILE.

```
HOST=host
FILE=remotefile
PATTERN="search pattern"
rsh $HOST "sh -c 'grep -i \"$PATTERN\" $FILE'"
```

# 6

## Parsing Command
## Line Parameters

## THE COMMAND LINE

The command line consists of the command name followed by any number of parameters. It is usually terminated by the end of the line, but it may also be terminated by a command separator (see "Command Separators" in Chapter 1). The command name is the first *word* (string of characters separated by spaces or tabs) on the line. A parameter is any word following the command name on the command line.

In the following example, the command name is `mv`, and it is followed by two parameters, `abc` and `def`.

```
mv abc def
```

If a parameter contains whitespace, it must be quoted to prevent the shell from separating it into more than one parameter. For example:

*command* `"Hello world"`

A command may span multiple lines if the line to be continued ends with a backslash (see "Line Continuation" in Chapter 1). The following two commands are equivalent:

```
echo "Part one;" \
     "part two."

echo "Part one;" "part two."
```

## COMMAND LINE CONVENTIONS

Any command can be written to receive parameters from the command line. While you may write a command that receives its parameters any way you wish, the following syntax is recommended.

> *command* [*options*] [*parameters*]

This syntax uses options to request variations in the behavior of a command and parameters to pass information to the command. In this syntax, the options always precede the parameters.

An option consists of a single letter that is either specified or omitted. An option is distinguished from a parameter by preceding it with a hyphen. There must be no space between the hyphen and the option. For example:

> *command* *-a*

An option may also have a value that immediately follows it on the command line. For an option with a value, the value is not optional. That is, an option always has a value or it never has a value. Whitespace between the option name and the option value is allowed, but not required. For example:

> *command* *-aOptionValue*
> *command* *-a OptionValue*

Multiple options may be specified by separating them with whitespace and preceding each option with a hyphen. When more than one option is specified and neither has a value, they may be combined into a string of option letters, without spaces, following a single hyphen. For example:

> *command* *-a -b*
> *command* *-ab*

The special option `- -` is used to terminate the list of options. This is useful when a parameter may begin with the hyphen; once the options are processed, the remaining items on the command line are processed as parameters. For example:

> *command* `- -` *-parm*

The parameters are specified on the command line following the options. Any number of parameters may be specified on the command line; however, there may be a limit on the total length of the command line. When more than one parameter is specified, they are separated by whitespace. If a parameter contains whitespace, it must be quoted.

Most commands do not place any meaning on the order of the command options, but this is not always the case. For example:

*command  -a  -b*

is usually equivalent to

*command  -b  -a*

On the other hand, the parameters are often expected to be in a particular order. This allows the command to determine the meaning of each parameter by its location on the command line. For example, in the following command, all of the parameters are the same except the last parameter, which is the destination to which to copy the other files listed on the command line.

`cp` *file1*  [*file2* ...]  *target*

## PARSING OPTIONS

The following command definition will be used as an example in the next few sections to show various ways to parse command line options. This example defines two options, the f option that does not have a value, and the v option that does have a value.

*command*  [-f]  [-v *value*]

The parsing algorithms shown in the next few sections remove the options from the parameter list as they are processed so that when the parsing is complete, only the parameters to the command remain in the parameter list.

### Using the `getopts` Command

The `getopts` command simplifies the checking and parsing of the command options, and it ensures that the command conforms to the command line conventions described in the previous section. The following example shows how to use the `getopts` command to parse the options for the example command.

```
FLAG=FALSE
VALUE=
OPT=
while getopts fv: OPT
```

```
do
    case $OPT in
        f)  FLAG=TRUE
            ;;
        v)  VALUE=$OPTARG
            ;;
        \?) echo "Usage: ..." 1>&2
            exit 1
            ;;
    esac
done
shift `expr $OPTIND - 1`
```

The `getopts` command is passed a string of option characters followed by the name of a variable into which to return the next option. Notice that the variable passed to `getopts` is specified without the dollar sign; that is, the name of the variable is passed, not its value.

```
getopts fv: OPT
```

The string of option characters is the concatenation of the letter names of the options. If an option expects a value, its letter is followed by a colon. In this example, the option string `fv:` specifies two options, `f` and `v`. The `v` option expects a value, but the `f` option does not.

Each time the `getopts` command is called, it places the letter name of the next option in the variable that was passed to it (OPT). When there are no more options, `getopts` will return a nonzero exit status. The `getopts` command accepts the `--` option to indicate the end of the options.

If the option expects a value, `getopts` returns the value in the variable OPTARG.

The variable OPTIND will be set to the command line position of the next option. The OPTIND variable is usually used to shift the options from the command line after the options have been processed. You can see an example of this in the last line of the example.

If the `getopts` command detects an error, it returns the question mark character in place of the option name. Notice in the example that the question mark must be escaped when used as a case value since the question mark would otherwise be interpreted as a metacharacter that matches any single character.

The section "The `getopts` Command" in Chapter 12 discusses how to programmatically determine whether or not the `getopts` command is available, and if not, to use an alternate parsing technique.

## Using the `getopt` Command

The `getopt` command is available on some UNIX systems, but it has been superseded by the `getopts` command. It is discussed here because it is still used in many existing scripts, but when writing new scripts the `getopts` command should be used. The following example shows how to use the `getopt` command to parse the options for the example command.

```
FLAG=
VALUE=
OPT=
set -- `getopt fv: $*`
if [ $? != 0 ]
then
    echo "Usage: ..." 1>&2
    exit 1
fi
for OPT in $*
do
    case $OPT in
        -f )    FLAG=TRUE
                shift
                ;;
        -v )    VALUE=$2
                shift 2
                ;;
        -- )    shift
                break
                ;;
    esac
done
```

The `getopt` command is passed a string of option characters followed by all of the command line parameters.

```
getopt fv: $*
```

The string of option characters is the same as the string passed to the `getopts` command. It is the concatenation of the letter names of the options. If an option expects a value, its letter is followed by a colon. In this example, the option string `fv:` specifies two options, `f` and `v`. The `v` option expects a value, but the `f` option does not.

The `getopt` command reconstructs the parameter list to make it conform to a simpler subset of the command line syntax. It writes the reconstructed command line to its standard output, which is then reloaded into the positional parameters using the `set` command. The `--` option to the `set` command is necessary to prevent the `set` command from interpreting any of the options in the command line as one of its own options.

```
set -- `getopt fv: $*`
```

If the `getopt` command detects an error in the command line options, it returns a nonzero status.

The reconstructed command line ensures that:

- There are no invalid options or options with missing values.
- Each option is placed in its own positional parameter and is preceded by a hyphen. For example, `-ab` is changed to `-a -b`.
- If an option has a value, the value is in the next positional parameter.
- The `--` option is added to the command line (if it was not already there) to terminate the options.

**Note:** The above example of the `getopt` command is similar to the one in the manual page for the `getopt` command. However, this example does not correctly handle options or parameters that contain whitespace. Since the `getopt` command itself does not handle whitespace correctly, it does not matter that there are other places in the example that also have problems with whitespace. I do not recommend that you copy this example when writing a new shell script. In particular, you need to avoid the following problems:

- You should use `getopts` instead of `getopt`. The `getopt` command is provided to support existing code, but it should not be used for new development.
- You should use "`$@`" instead of `$*` to refer to the entire command line when one or more of the parameters may contain whitespace (see "Positional Parameters" in Chapter 2).
- You should omit the word list when using a `for` loop to process the positional parameters. If the word list is used, it is parsed into words using the characters in the `IFS` variable as delimiters. This may cause some of the parameters to be parsed differently than intended.

### When `getopts` Is Not Available

This section shows an example of how to parse the command line options without using `getopts` or `getopt`. The only significant deficiency in this example is that multiple options cannot be specified together. That is, you must specify

*command -a -b*

not,

*command -ab*

The following example shows how to parse the options for the example command when the `getopts` command is not available:

```
while [ $# -gt 0 ]
do
```

```
        case $1 in
          -f) FLAG=TRUE
              shift
              ;;
          -v) VALUE=$2
              shift 2
              ;;
          -v*)VALUE=`echo "$1" | sed 's/^..//'`
              shift
              ;;
          --) shift
              break
              ;;
          -*) echo "Usage: ..." 1>&2
              exit 1
              ;;
          *)  break
              ;;
        esac
    done
```

A `while` loop is used to examine the positional parameters until all of the options have been processed. The loop always examines the first positional parameter. After each option is processed, the positional parameters are shifted so that the first positional parameter is removed and the remaining positional parameters are moved up.

The end of the options is detected when either there are no more positional parameters or the next positional parameter does not begin with a hyphen.

The `case` statement inside the `while` loop has case values for the normal options of the command, `f` and `v`, and it has three other cases for special situations.

If an option has a value, it will have two entries in the `case` statement. The first case handles the option when there is a space between the option and its value. The second case handles the option when the space is omitted. For an example of this, see how the `v` option is processed in the above example.

The case value `- -` indicates the end of the options and terminates the loop.

The case value `- *` matches any option that is not handled by one of the previous case options. If this case value is executed, it implies that an undefined option was passed to the command.

The case value `*` matches any parameter that does not begin with a hyphen. This also indicates the end of the options and terminates the loop.

## Parsing Nonstandard Options

In many cases, the above algorithms are too complex for the task at hand. For example, the following command has just one option and a variable number of parameters.

*command* -v *parameter* ...

With something this simple you might find it easier to handle the option with a simple `if` statement as shown here:

```
if [ "$1" = "-v" ]; then
    VERBOSE=TRUE
    shift
fi
for parm
do
    ...
done
```

Once in a while you will see a command that accepts words for option names rather than letters. The following example shows a parser that allows you to specify a value for the DISPLAY variable using the `-display` option.

```
while [ $# -gt 0 ]
do
    case "$1" in
        -display )
            if [ $# -lt 2 ]; then
                echo "Missing parameter."
                exit 1
            fi
            DISPLAY=$2
            shift
            shift
            ;;
        -*) echo "Usage: ..." 1>&2
            exit 1
            ;;
        * ) break
            ;;
    esac
done
```

Notice in this example that the `shift` command is executed twice rather than passing it a shift count, as was done in the previous examples. Executing the command twice is actually the more common practice, and it may be slightly more portable, since the `shift` command in some older shells does not support the shift count as a parameter.

## PARSING PARAMETERS

After the options have been removed from the parameter list, only the parameters to the command, if any, are left in the parameter list.

After all of the options have been removed from the parameter list, it is usually a good time to check that the number of parameters remaining in the parameter list is the number of parameters that you expect. The variable $\$\#$ contains the number of parameters remaining in the parameter list.

The next example shows how you could process the parameters to a simple copy command.

```
copy source target
```

Since the parameters to this command are not optional, you could first check that there are exactly two parameters in the parameter list. Next, since the parameters are distinguished by their position in the parameter list, they can be accessed using the corresponding positional parameter. In this example, they are copied to variables with more descriptive names.

```
if [ $# -ne 2 ]; then
    echo "Usage: copy source target" 1>&2
    exit 1
fi
SOURCE=$1
TARGET=$2
```

When the parameters to a command are a list of similar items, such as a list of file names, some type of loop can be used to process the parameters. The next example shows how you could use a `while` loop to process a list of file names from the command line. During each pass of the loop, a file name is copied from the first positional parameter, then the `shift` command moves the next file name into the first positional parameter. When there are no more file names, the variable $\$\#$ will be zero, and the loop will terminate.

```
while [ $# -gt 0 ]
do
    FILE=$1
    shift
    . . .
done
```

The next example shows a `for` loop used to process a list of file names from the command line. When the `for` loop is used without a word list, the loop is executed once for each positional parameter. Each time the loop is executed, the next positional parameter is assigned to the loop variable (`FILE`). The loop continues until each parameter has been processed. Notice that this example does not use the `shift` command; therefore, unlike the previous example, the positional parameters are not destroyed by executing this loop.

```
for FILE
do
    . . .
done
```

Since the `for` loop does not destroy the parameter list when it scans the parameters, it can be used to access the parameters in any order. For example, the next example shows how to get the last parameter from the parameter list. When the loop is finished, the last parameter is in the variable LAST, and the positional parameters are unchanged.

```
for LAST
do
      :
done
```

# 7

# *Using Filters*

Filters are commands that get their data from the standard input, perform some transformation on the data, and then write the data to the standard output. More than one filter can be connected together to form a pipeline. By connecting several filters in a pipeline, you can perform complex transformations.

To combine more than one filter to form a pipeline, you simply string the commands together with the pipe symbol (|). In the following example, the `cat` command copies a file into a pipeline. The file is then processed by two filters before it is written to the standard input of a `while` loop where it is read one line at a time.

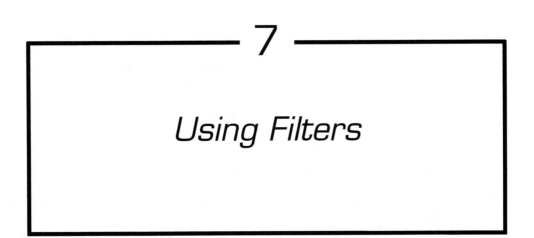

```
cat file        |
    filter_1    |
    filter_2    |
    while read LINE
    do
        ...
    done
```

The `cat` command is frequently used to copy a file into the beginning of a pipeline, as shown in this example; however, when there is only one file being `cat`'ed, it is more efficient to redirect the standard input of the first command in the pipeline, using the file redirection operator to read the file. Since the `cat` command has no other value, this would cause one less process to be used. For example, the above example could be rewritten to begin as follows:

*filter_1* <*file* | *filter_2* | . . .

## USING sed AS A FILTER

The design of the sed editor makes it an ideal tool for writing filters. It takes its input from the standard input and writes its output to the standard output, and the editing commands are entered on the command line. Since many of the examples in this book use sed, some of the special cases to watch for will be covered in this section rather than repeating them wherever they apply.

### Using Variables in sed Scripts

Some of the sed scripts shown in this chapter require you to provide some information. When this is necessary, the information that you provide is shown in italics. For example, in the filter to replace one text pattern with another (discussed later in this chapter), you are expected to replace the italicized words with the appropriate text.

    sed -e "s/*OldText*/*NewText*/g"

The filters in this chapter that require you to provide some information are written using double quotes around the sed script so that you can replace the italicized text with either a variable or a string of characters. For example, the following example shows the italicized text replaced with the variables OLD_TEXT and NEW_TEXT.

    sed -e "s/$OLD_TEXT/$NEW_TEXT/g"

When writing sed scripts that do not require you to provide any information, it is good practice to use single quotes around the sed script so that there is less chance that the characters in the script will be accidentally interpreted by the shell.

### Multiple Scripts

When consecutive sed commands are executed in a pipeline, you can pass all of the sed scripts to a single sed command. This can provide a considerable performance savings since sed will only execute once, processing all of the scripts in a single invocation. The effect will be the same as if separate sed commands were used to execute each script. When more than one script is passed to sed, you must precede each script with the -e option. (When there is only one script the -e is optional.) The following two examples are equivalent, except in the second example, only one sed process is used. Also, in the second example the `sed` command was written on two lines; therefore, a backslash was needed at the end of the first line to continue the command on the next line.

```
cat file |
    sed -e "s/OldText1/NewText1/g" |
    sed -e "s/OldText2/NewText2/g" |
    while read LINE
    do
        . . .
    done

cat file |
    sed -e "s/OldText1/NewText1/g" \
        -e "s/OldText2/NewText2/g" |
    while read LINE
    do
        . . .
    done
```

Most `sed` scripts in this chapter rely on the `sed` command to write the filtered information to the standard output. However, a few `sed` scripts use the `-n` option of `sed` to suppress this normal behavior. When the `-n` option is used, the `sed` script must explicitly write the information that it wants to the standard output, for example, by using the print command (`p`). The following `sed` command prints the second line from the file, but nothing else.

```
sed -n '2p' <file
```

Since the `-n` option may interfere with the way a `sed` script works, you should avoid combining `sed` scripts into a single invocation when some of the scripts need the `-n` option and others do not.

## Changing Delimiters

Several of the `sed` scripts in this chapter use the substitute command (`s`) of `sed` to replace one string with another. In these examples, the slash character (`/`) is used to delimit the new and old strings. If the text between the delimiters happens to contain a slash character, the `sed` command will get confused and probably print an error. To avoid this, you can use any other character as the delimiter as long as it is not contained in the text. For example, you will often see the % character used as the delimiter in `sed` scripts that process file names. Even though the % character can be used in a file name, it is much less likely to be used than the / character. For example, the following two `sed` commands are the same except for the choice of the delimiters.

```
sed -e "s/OldText/NewText/g"
sed -e "s%OldText%NewText%g"
```

It is difficult to write code that will work in all situations, but you can usually find a delimiter that will work for any particular situation.

## FILTERS FOR TEXT FILES

The rest of this chapter consists of a variety of examples of filters that can be used to process the information in test files.

### Replace Text

The following command searches each line for a pattern of characters that matches the *OldText*. Each instance of the text pattern that is found will be replaced with the *NewText*.

```
sed -e "s/OldText/NewText/g"
```

This sed script uses the substitute command (s) to replace the text. This is the basic format of the substitute command; you will see several variations of this command in the filters in this chapter.

The g at the end of this script says to replace the text wherever it is found in the line (globally). If the g is removed from the script, only the first instance of the text will be replaced on each line.

### Remove Text

The following command searches each line for a pattern of characters that matches the text. Each instance of the text pattern that is found will be removed.

```
sed -e "s/TextToRemove//g"
```

This variation of the substitute command (s) replaces the text with the empty string, which causes the text to be removed.

The g at the end of this script says to remove (replace with the empty string) the text wherever it is found in the line (globally). If the g is removed from the script, only the first instance of the text will be removed from each line.

### Remove Text from Front

The following command will remove the text from the beginning of any line that begins with the text:

```
sed -e "s/^TextToRemove//"
```

Removing text from the beginning of a line is the same as removing text in general, except that the search for the text is restricted to the beginning of the line. The caret character (^) immediately preceding the text is used to restrict the search to only match the characters if they are found at the beginning of a line.

### Remove Text from End

The following command will remove the text from the end of any line that ends with the text:

```
sed -e "s/TextToRemove\$//"
```

Removing text from the end of a line is the same as removing text in general, except that the search for the text is restricted to the end of the line. The \$ immediately following the text is used to restrict the search to match the characters only if they are found at the end of the line. The dollar sign is the symbol used by sed to indicate the end of the line. It is necessary to precede the dollar sign with a backslash to prevent the shell from interpreting it.

### Insert Text in Front

The following command will insert the text at the front of each line:

```
sed -e "s/^/TextToInsert/"
```

This variation of the substitute command replaces the beginning of the line with the text. The caret character (^) is the symbol used by sed to indicate the front of the line.

### Append Text to End

The following command will append the text to the end of each line:

```
sed -e "s/\$/TextToAppend/"
```

This variation of the substitute command replaces the end of the line with the text. The \$ is the symbol used by sed to indicate the end of the line. It is necessary to precede the dollar sign with a backslash to prevent the shell from interpreting it.

### Truncate

The following command searches each line from left to right for a pattern of characters that matches the pattern. If the pattern is found, this command will remove everything from the beginning of the pattern to the end of the line.

```
sed -e "s/Pattern.*//"
```

This sed script is similar to the script to remove text, except the pattern is immediately followed with the .* characters. The .* tells sed to match any characters. Thus, this command searches for the pattern followed by any characters and replaces it with the empty string.

In the following example, the string abc/def/ghi is passed through this filter to remove everything from the first slash to the end of the string. The result, abc, is assigned back to the variable STRING.

```
$ STRING=abc/def/ghi
$ PATTERN=/
$ STRING=`echo "$STRING" | sed -e "s%$PATTERN.*%%"`
$ echo "$STRING"
abc
$
```

You might also want to truncate a line so that it does not exceed a particular length. The following command will truncate the line so that it does not exceed the number of characters stored in the variable LEN.

```
cut -c1-$LEN
```

You could also use the following awk command to truncate lines to the length stored in the variable LEN.

```
awk '{printf "%-.'$LEN's\n",$0}'
```

This awk command takes each input line, $0, and formats it with awk's printf function. The sequence of characters following the printf function instruct it to format $0 as a string that is limited to the number of characters in the variable LEN.

For example:

```
$ LEN=10
$ awk '{printf "%-.'$LEN's\n",$0}' <file >newfile
$
```

## Downshift

This command downshifts the alphabetic characters in each line. Any upper case letter (A to Z) in the input will be changed to the corresponding lower case letter (a to z). Any other characters will not be affected.

```
tr '[A-Z]' '[a-z]'
```

## Upshift

This command upshifts the alphabetic characters in each line. Any lower case letter (a to z) in the input will be changed to the corresponding upper case letter (A to Z). Any other characters will not be affected.

```
tr '[a-z]' '[A-Z]'
```

## Change Tabs to Spaces

This command replaces every tab character with a space. The symbols *<space>* and *<tab>* represent a single space character and a single tab character, respectively.

```
sed -e 's/<tab>/<space>/g'
```

## Change Multiple Spaces to a Single Space

This command replaces strings of two or more spaces with a single space. The symbol *<space>* represents a single space character.

```
sed -e 's/<space><space>*/<space>/g'
```

Remember that * matches zero or more of the preceding characters; therefore, *<space>** means zero or more spaces and *<space><space>** means one or more spaces.

## Change Whitespace to a Single Space

This command combines the two previous commands to replace any whitespace with a single space. The symbols *<space>* and *<tab>* represent a single space character and a single tab character, respectively.

```
sed -e 's/[<space><tab>][<space><tab>]*/<space>/g'
```

## Delete Leading Whitespace

This command deletes spaces and tabs from the front of each line. The symbols *<space>* and *<tab>* represent a single space character and a single tab character respectively.

```
sed -e 's/^[<space><tab>]*//'
```

## Delete Trailing Whitespace

This command deletes spaces and tabs from the end of each line. The symbols *<space>* and *<tab>* represent a single space character and a single tab character, respectively.

```
sed -e 's/[<space><tab>]*$//'
```

## Delete Lines

This command deletes any line that contains the text.

```
sed -e "/Text/d"
```

The `grep` command is also frequently used to delete lines that contain a text pattern. The following command is equivalent to the previous command.

```
grep -v "Text"
```

## Delete Empty Lines

This command will delete empty lines. Notice that a line that contains spaces or tabs is not empty.

```
sed -e '/^$/d'
```

The characters `^$` is the symbol used by `sed` to mean the beginning of the line, immediately followed by the end of the line, or in other words, an empty line. Thus, this command will find empty lines and delete them (`d` is the delete command).

The following command will delete empty lines or lines that contain only whitespace. The symbols *<space>* and *<tab>* represent a single space character and a single tab character respectively.

```
sed -e '/^[<space><tab>]*$/d'
```

## Delete First Line

This command will delete the first line of the file and copy the rest of the file to the standard output.

```
sed -e '1d'
```

The first character in this `sed` script is the number one (i.e., not the letter ell), and it is the number of the line to delete. You could change this to delete any other line, or you could even change it to delete a range of lines. For example, the following command will delete lines one through four:

```
sed -e '1,4d'
```

## Delete Last Line

This command will delete the last line of the file and copy the rest of the file to the standard output.

```
sed -e '$d'
```

The dollar sign, when used as a line number, is the symbol used by `sed` to indicate the last line of the file. Thus, this command deletes the last line of the file. The `sed` command does not allow relative addressing; therefore, you cannot use something like `$-3,$d`, to delete the last four lines from the file.[1] To delete more than one line from the end of the file you can execute the command more than once.

## Print First Line

This command will print the first line from the standard input and ignore the rest.

```
sed -e '2,$d'
```

This command works by deleting the lines from the second line to the last line and writing the remaining lines (in this case, only the first line is left) to the standard output.

A more natural `sed` script to print the first line is shown in the following example. However, this script uses the `-n` option of `sed`. As stated earlier, when using the `-n` option, you should not combine multiple `sed` script into a single execution of `sed` unless you know that is what you want to do.

```
sed -n '1p'
```

This example can be generalized to print any single line, where *n* is the line number of the line to print.

```
sed -n 'np'
```

Or, you can print the first *n* lines as shown here:

```
sed -n '1,np'
```

Another more efficient method to print the first line is shown in the following command. This `sed` script uses the `q` command to quit `sed` after the first line is printed. Since the `q` command causes `sed` to quit, this script cannot be combined with other `sed` scripts in a single execution either. If you want to print the first line of a very large file, you may want to consider using this `sed` script, but for most situations, the increased efficiency will not be noticeable.

```
sed -e '1q'
```

---

[1] The `ed` editor does support this type of relative addressing, but it does not read its input file from the standard input and write the changed file to its standard output, which makes it difficult to use for writing filters.

### Print Last Line

This command will print the last line from the standard input and ignore the rest.

```
sed -n '$p'
```

### Delete Comments

In many ASCII files, such as shell scripts or configuration files, the pound sign (#) is used to indicate a comment. Depending upon the file, a comment may be required to begin in the first column, or in some files a comment can begin anywhere on a line.

The following command can be used to delete any line that begins with a pound sign.

```
sed -e '/^#/d'
```

The following command can be used to strip comments from the end of a line; however, if any comment begins in the first column, this command will leave a blank line in the file. You could use the previous filter followed by this filter, or some other combination of filters, to avoid leaving blank lines in the filtered output.

```
sed -e 's/#.*//'
```

When using a `while` loop to read a file, you can remove comments by using the pattern matching capability of the `case` statement. The following example shows how this might be done. Notice that in order to specify the pound sign as a pattern in the `case` statement, it must be quoted to prevent the shell from thinking it is a comment character.

```
while read LINE
do
    case $LINE in
        \#* )    continue    # Skip comment
                ;;

        * )      echo "$LINE"
                ;;
    esac
done
```

When the `read` command is used to process a file, as shown above, it will remove whitespace from the beginning and end of each line, and tabs and consecutive whitespace characters within each line will be replaced with a single space. ("The `read` Command" in Chapter 4 discusses this problem and ways to avoid it.)

## Delete Text Between Keywords

This command will delete the text between, and including, two keywords. Each keyword must be on a line by itself without leading or trailing whitespace.

```
sed -e "/^FirstKeyword\$/,/^SecondKeyword\$/d"
```

This `sed` command uses the delete command (d) to delete the unwanted lines; however, rather than specifying the lines to delete using line numbers, this command uses patterns to identify the lines to delete as shown in the following simplification. The lines that are not deleted are written to the standard output.

```
/StartingPattern/,/EndingPattern/d
```

The patterns used in the filter are the corresponding keywords, but they are also preceded with a ^ and followed by a \$. These characters indicate that the keywords must be at the beginning and the end of the line respectively; that is, they must be on a line by themselves.

The following example shows how you could use this filter to remove any text between the keywords `begin` and `end`.

```
$ KEYWORD1=begin
$ KEYWORD2=end
$ sed -e "/^$KEYWORD1\$/,/^$KEYWORD2\$/d" <file >newfile
$
```

## Extract Text Between Keywords

This filter is the reverse of the previous filter; it will extract the text between, and including, two keywords. In fact, the only difference between this filter and the previous filter is the exclamation mark (!) in front of the d command at the end of the filter. The exclamation mark reverses the sense of the match. Therefore, instead of finding and deleting all of the lines between the keywords, it finds and deletes all of the lines outside of the keywords.

As with the previous filter, each keyword must be on a line by itself without leading or trailing whitespace.

```
sed -e "/^FirstKeyword\$/,/^SecondKeyword\$/!d"
```

## Read a File Backwards

Once in a while you may need to read a file backwards; for example, you may want to read the most recent entries from a log file before reading the oldest entries. The following filter reverses the lines in a file so that they are written to the standard output last line first.

```
grep -n '.*' | sort -n -r | sed 's/^.*://'
```

This filter uses the `grep` command to number the lines in the file. The file is then sorted into reverse order, using the line number as the sort key. The reversed file is then passed through a `sed` script that removes the line numbers. Now the file is the same as it was, except that the lines are reversed.

The following example shows another way to reverse a file; it was presented earlier as an example of using a here document. It uses a series of commands to the `ed` editor to reverse the file. However, this command is not a filter; it reverses the file and writes it back over the original file rather than writing the file to its standard output. Also, this command does not work well for large files.

```
ed - file <<-!
g/^/m0
w
q
!
```

# Shell Utilities

## ARITHMETIC OPERATIONS

As stated in Chapter 2, shell variables only store strings of characters; the shell does not provide variables with numeric types. Numeric values are stored in variables as strings of numeric characters. In addition, the shell has no arithmetic operators; it relies on the `expr` command to add, subtract, multiply, and divide.

### Integer Arithmetic

The `expr` command can be used to perform integer arithmetic. The numbers passed to `expr` must consist solely of the digits zero to nine. The `expr` command supports addition, subtraction, multiplication, division, and modulus.

```
expr int1 + int2        # Add int2 to int1
expr int1 - int2        # Subtract int2 from int1
expr int1 * int2        # Multiply int1 by int2
expr int1 / int2        # Divide int1 by int2
expr int1 % int2        # Remainder of int1 divided by int2
```

For example:

```
$ expr 30 + 1
31
$ expr 30 - 1
29
$
```

If you use multiplication, you will need to quote the asterisk to prevent it from being interpreted by the shell.

```
$ expr 30 \* 2
60
$ expr 30 '*' 2
60
$
```

In the following example, a number is read from a file. The number is then incremented and written back into the file.

```
VERSION=`cat versionfile`
VERSION=`expr $VERSION + 1`
echo $VERSION >versionfile
```

## Relational Operations

The `test` command can be used to compare the value of two numbers.

```
test int1 -eq int2      # True if int1 is equal to int2
test int1 -ne int2      # True if int1 is not equal to int2
test int1 -lt int2      # True if int1 is less than int2
test int1 -le int2      # True if int1 is less than or equal to int2
test int1 -gt int2      # True if int1 is greater than int2
test int1 -ge int2      # True if int1 is greater or equal to int2
```

## Floating Point Arithmetic

The `bc`[1] command is an arbitrary precision arithmetic language processor that resembles the C language. It reads an expression either from its standard input or a file named on the command line. The result of the expression is written to its standard output.

The following examples show the floating point arithmetic operations. The value of *n* should be replaced with the number of decimal places that you want to the right of the decimal point.

---

[1] Some versions of the `bc` command may need the `-l` option to perform floating point arithmetic.

```
echo "scale=n; num1 + num2"  | bc      # Add num2 to num1
echo "scale=n; num1 - num2"  | bc      # Subtract num2 from num1
echo "scale=n; num1 * num2"  | bc      # Multiply num1 by num2
echo "scale=n; num1 / num2"  | bc      # Divide num1 by num2
```

In the following examples, the `echo` command is used to pass an expression to the standard input of the `bc` command.

```
$ echo "scale=2; 10 / 3" | bc
3.33
$ echo "scale=2; 3.33 * 3" | bc
9.99
$
```

## Hexadecimal Numbers

The following shell function uses the `dc` command to convert a hexadecimal number to a decimal number. The hexadecimal number should not include a `0x` or `0X` prefix.

```
hex2decimal() {
    NUM=`echo $1 | tr '[a-f]' '[A-F]'`
    echo 16i $NUM p | dc
}
```

The following shell function will convert a decimal number to hexadecimal:

```
decimal2hex() {
    echo 16o $1 p | dc
}
```

## Determine If a String Is Numeric

In the following example, the `expr` command is used to determine if a string is numeric by using it in an arithmetic expression. If the variable `NUMBER` contains a valid numeric string, the `expr` command will return 0 or 1; otherwise, it will return a larger value.

```
expr "$NUMBER" + 1 >/dev/null 2>&1
if [ $? -lt 2 ]; then
    echo "Numeric
else
    echo "Not numeric"
fi
```

The function `IsNumeric` in Chapter 9, "Examples of Shell Functions," shows how to write this example as a function.

### Adding a Column of Numbers

An easy way to add a column of numbers is to use a simple `awk` script. The following example adds the numbers in the fifth column from the output of the `ls` command. The fifth column contains the size of the file on System V systems; on BSD systems the fourth column should be used.

```
COLUMN=5
ls -l | awk '{total+=$'$COLUMN'} END {print total}'
```

The output from the `ls` command is passed to `awk` through a pipeline, and the column number is passed into the `awk` script through the variable `COLUMN`.

The `awk` script parses its input into fields, using whitespace as the delimiter. As each line is parsed, the field numbers, or positional parameters, are reset so that they can be treated as column numbers. After variable substitution, `$'$COLUMN'`, becomes `$5`. Thus, the fifth field is added to the value in `total` for each line of input.

After the last line is processed, the total is printed to the standard output.

The shell script `addcolumn` in Chapter 10, "Examples of Shell Scripts," shows how to write this example as a general purpose shell script.

## MANIPULATING STRINGS

### Using Filters on Strings

Filters are commonly used when processing information from text files; however, they can also be used to perform modifications on individual strings. Since the value of every variable is a string, using filters on strings provides a wide range of tools for manipulating the values of variables.

To use a filter on a string, the `echo` command is used to write the string to its standard output. The standard output of `echo` is then piped to a filter to form a pipeline. By enclosing the entire pipeline in back quotes, the output of the pipeline can be assigned back to a variable. When the `echo` command is used to write a string to the standard input of a filter, the string behaves as if it is a one-line file, which in fact it is.[2]

The following example replaces `def` with `xyz` in the string using a `sed` filter. This filter was discussed in "Replace Text" in Chapter 7.

```
$ STRING="abc def ghi"
$ STRING=`echo "$STRING" | sed -e "s/def/xyz/g"`
$ echo "$STRING"
abc xyz ghi
$
```

---

[2] If the string contains newline characters, then the filter will be applied to each line in the string, which may not be what you want.

## String Concatenation

Appending one string to another string is as simple as entering one string immediately followed by the other string. For example:

```
$ STRING1=abc
$ STRING2=def
$ VAR=$STRING1$STRING2
$ echo $VAR
abcdef
$
```

As you may recall from the discussion in "Using Variables" in Chapter 2, when a string is to be appended to the value of a variable, the variable name may be enclosed in braces to remove any ambiguity of where the variable name ends and where the string being appended to the value begins.

```
$ STRING=abc
$ VAR=${STRING}def
$ echo $VAR
abcdef
$
```

Here is one more example showing a string appended to the front of a variable.

```
$ STRING=def
$ VAR=abc$STRING
$ echo $VAR
abcdef
$
```

## Remove Extra Whitespace

Whitespace is frequently used to separate data items. Since whitespace can consist of any number of spaces and tabs strung together in any order, it is sometimes useful to convert whitespace to something more consistent. The following command removes leading and trailing whitespace and replaces imbedded whitespace with a single space.

```
STRING=`echo $STRING`
```

The value of the variable STRING is passed to the echo command. The shell parses the value of STRING into words, using whitespace to delimit the words. The echo command writes the words to its standard output with a single space between each word. The back quotes capture the standard output of the echo command and assigns it back to STRING.

Be sure not to quote the string, since that would prevent the shell from parsing it into words before passing it to the `echo` command.

## String Length

This statement returns the number of characters in the string.

```
expr "string" : '.*'
```

The `expr` command compares the string on the left side of the colon with the pattern on the right side of the colon and writes the number of characters that match to its standard output. The pattern . * matches everything; therefore, the `expr` command returns the length of *string*. If the command is enclosed in back quotes, the standard output can be captured and assigned to a variable. For example:

```
$ STRING=abcdefghijklmnopqrstuvwxyz
$ NUMCHARS=`expr "$STRING" : '.*'`
$ echo $NUMCHARS
26
$
```

If the string happens to be one character and that character is one of the operators of the `expr` command, this command will result in an error. If this situation is likely, you can use the following, slightly more complex, sequence to return the length of the string.

```
case "string" in
    ? ) echo 1 ;;
    * ) expr "string" : '.*' ;;
esac
```

In this example, if the string is a single character, the value of 1 is printed; otherwise, the previous command is used to print the number of characters in the string. To capture the length of the string in a variable, you can enclose the entire `case` statement in back quotes.

```
NUMCHARS=`case "string" in
            ? ) echo 1 ;;
            * ) expr "string" : '.*' ;;
        esac`
```

## Testing for a Substring

The `case` statement is a simple and powerful mechanism for pattern matching. If you specify a string as the case value, the patterns of the individual cases can use wildcard characters to check for a variety of substrings.

The following example shows a `case` statement used to test for a substring:

```
STRING="This is the string."
SUBSTR="substring"
case "$STRING" in
    *"$SUBSTR"* )    echo "Found it." ;;
    * )              echo "Not found."   ;;
esac
```

The first case pattern specifies the substring with an asterisk on each side. Since the asterisk matches any characters, this pattern will be selected if the substring is anywhere within the string. The second case pattern is an asterisk by itself, which will match anything. Thus, if the first pattern does not match, the second one will.

For more examples of pattern matching using the `case` statement, see "The `case` Statement" in Chapter 1.

Another common method of testing whether or not a string contains a substring is to use the `grep` command, as shown in the following example.

```
if echo "$STRING" | grep "$SUBSTRING" >/dev/null
then
    echo "Found it."
fi
```

## Extracting Substrings Using `expr`

This section shows how to extract a substring from a larger string using the matching operator (`:`) of the `expr` command. The following example shows the syntax of this command. The full string is specified on the left side of the colon and a regular expression that matches the string is specified on the right side of the colon. Then the portion of the regular expression that represents the substring to be extracted is enclosed between `\(` and `\)`. Each parenthesis used in the `expr` command must be preceded by a backslash character; this is necessary even though the expression is enclosed in quotes.

`expr` *"string"* : *"regexp\(regexp\)regexp"*

As you can see, the regular expression must separate the string into pieces so that parentheses can be put around the part to be extracted. Also, be sure to include at least one space or tab on each side of the colon.

The following subset of wildcard characters allow you to create regular expressions that match most substrings.

| | |
|---|---|
| .* | Matches any string including an empty string |
| . | Matches any single character |
| \. | Matches the period (.) |

You can use these characters to create patterns such as:

```
abc.*            Matches any string that begins with abc
.*abc            Matches any string that ends with abc
```

The following example shows an `expr` command that will extract the end of any string that begins with a pattern:

expr *"string"* : *"pattern*\(.*\)*"*

Conversely, the following command will extract the beginning of any string that ends with a pattern:

expr *"string"* : *"*\(.*\)*pattern"*

You can use a fixed number of periods in an expression to extract or remove characters at a particular location within a string. For example, the following expressions show how to extract or remove three characters from the beginning or end of a string.

```
expr "string" : '\(...\).*'       # Extract first three characters
expr "string" : '.*\(...\)'       # Extract last three characters
expr "string" : '...\(.*\)'       # Remove first three characters
expr "string" : '\(.*\)...'       # Remove last three characters
```

## Remove First Two Characters

This task is used frequently in code that parses command line options since the first two characters of an option are the hyphen and the letter that identifies the option. To get the option value, a code sequence, such as the one shown below, is used to remove the first two characters from the option.

```
STRING=`echo "$STRING" | sed -e 's/^..//'`
```

You could also use the `expr` command, as discussed in the previous section. The next example shows how to remove the first two characters from a string using `expr`.

```
STRING=`expr "$STRING" : '..\(.*\)'`
```

## Upshift the First Character

To upshift the first character in a string, you can separate the first character from the rest of the string, upshift the character, and reassemble the string. The following example shows how this can be done.

```
CHAR=`expr "$STR" : '\(.\).*'`      # Get the first character
CHAR=`echo $CHAR | tr [a-z] [A-Z]`  # Upshift the character
REMAINDER=`expr "$STR" : '.\(.*\)'` # Remove first character
STR="$CHAR$REMAINDER"               # Put it back together
```

The same statement can be written without temporary variables, but it is considerably more difficult to decipher.

```
STR=`expr "$STR" : '\(.\).*' |
     tr [a-z] [A-Z]``expr "$STR" : '.\(.*\)'`
```

# PARSING DATA

## The IFS **Variable**

IFS is a variable that is defined by the shell to store the internal field separator characters. These are the characters that are used as delimiters when separating the command line into parameters, parsing the word list of a for loop, and parsing the data read by the read command. Initially, the IFS variable contains a tab, space, and newline, which causes the data to be separated by whitespace.

You can set the IFS variable to another value to parse data that is not delimited by whitespace. Several of the examples in this section demonstrate how this is done. When changing the value of the IFS variable, you should restore its original value immediately after the new value is used so that it does not cause undesirable side effects when other commands are executed.

When the shell parses data using the characters in the IFS variable, it will ignore leading, trailing, and consecutive IFS characters. That is, they do not produce empty fields.

## Using the read **Command**

The read command allows you to parse each line of input automatically as it is read from the standard input. As each line is read, it is parsed into fields using the characters in the IFS variable as delimiters. The fields are then assigned to the variables listed on the read command line. If the line contains more fields than variables, the extra fields are all assigned to the last variable. When more than one field is assigned to the last variable, the fields will be separated by spaces. If there are more variables than fields, the unused variables are assigned the empty string.

```
while read field1 field2 field3 remainder
do
    ...
done
```

You can set the IFS variable to another value to parse data that is not delimited by whitespace. For example, to parse the fields in the password file, you can set the IFS variable to the colon character (:). The following example shows how to use this technique to produce a list of users from the password file:

```
OLDIFS=$IFS
IFS=:
while read USER PASSWD UID GUI GCOS REMAINDER
do
    echo "$USER $GCOS"
done </etc/passwd
IFS=$OLDIFS
```

## Using a for Loop

The for loop is typically used to process a list of words separated by whitespace. Each time the loop is executed, the next word in the list is assigned to the loop variable. The following example shows how a for loop can be used to parse the output of the date command:

```
$ for i in `date`
> do
>    echo $i
> done
Tue
Jan
1
00:00:01
PDT
1991
$
```

Again, you can set the IFS variable to another value to parse data that is not delimited by whitespace. For example, to parse a file name, you can set the IFS variable to the slash character (/) and then use the file name as the word list of the for loop. The following example shows how to use a for loop to parse a file name. Notice that leading, trailing, and consecutive IFS characters are ignored.

```
$ IFS=/
$ for i in /abc//def/
> do
>    echo $i
> done
abc
def
$
```

## Using the `set` **Command**

One of the functions of the `set` command is to reload the positional parameters with the information that is passed to it on the command line. Since the characters in the `IFS` variable are used to parse the command line into words, or parameters, you can use the `set` command to parse a string and load the pieces into the positional parameters. The variable $#$ will be set to the new number of positional parameters.

Be sure not to quote the string, since that would prevent the shell from parsing it into words. If you accidentally quote the string, the entire string will be treated as one parameter and loaded in to the first positional parameter.

Also, the `- -` option should be used to indicate that there are no options. This prevents a string beginning with a hyphen from being misinterpreted as an option to the `set` command. Some old versions of the shell do not support the `- -` option. "The `set` Command" in Chapter 13 discusses some alternatives for situations in which the `set` command does not support the `- -` option.

The following example shows how the `set` command can be used to parse the output of the `date` command. This example produces the same output as the `for` loop shown before.

```
$ set -- `date`
$ while [ $# -gt 0 ]
> do
>    echo $1
>    shift
> done
Tue
Jan
1
00:00:01
PDT
1991
$
```

The following example shows how to parse the output of the `date` command and reassemble it in a different format:

```
$ set -- `date`
$ echo "$2 $3, $6"
Jan 1, 1991
$
```

Initially, the positional parameters contain the parameters to the shell script. Since parsing data with the `set` command will cause the positional parameters to be reloaded, be sure to save the current value of any positional parameters that are still needed.

## Using the awk **Command**

The methods for parsing data shown so far are somewhat complicated if you want to extract only one or two fields from a string. The awk command is also useful for parsing and extracting fields from a string. The string is passed to awk through a pipeline. The awk command parses the string into fields separated by whitespace and loads the fields into variables that resemble the positional parameters. That is, the fields are loaded into variables named $1, $2, and so forth. The print command of awk is used to print the fields that you are interested in.

The following example uses awk to extract the second word from a string:

```
$ echo "abc def ghi" | awk '{print $2}'
def
$
```

The next example shows how to parse the output of the date command and reassemble it in a different format. This example produces the same output as the example using the set command in the previous section.

```
$ date | awk '{print "$2 $3, $6"}'
Jan 1, 1991
$
```

## Using the cut **Command**

The cut command is also useful for extracting fields from strings. The string is passed to cut through a pipeline. A field can be located either by parsing the string using a delimiter or by specifying the location of the field within the string.

The following example uses the cut command to print the second field from the string abc:def:ghi. The -d':' option instructs the cut command to use the colon character as a delimiter, and the -f2 option instructs the cut command to extract the second field.

```
$ echo "abc:def:ghi" | cut -d':' -f2
def
$
```

The cut command treats consecutive delimiters as empty fields; therefore, it is not useful for extracting fields that are separated by arbitrary whitespace.

The following example extracts the same field from the string, but specifies its location in the string as character positions 5 through 7.

```
$ echo "abc:def:ghi" | cut -c5-7
def
$
```

# INTERACTING WITH USERS

## Interactive Shells

An interactive shell is one in which the standard input and standard output are connected to a terminal. It is sometimes useful to be able to determine if the shell is interactive, for example, to determine whether or not to print a prompt or ask the user to enter a response to a question.

You can determine if a shell is interactive by checking for the i option in the variable $-. The variable $- contains letters that represent the options that are currently set in the shell; the letter i is present when the shell is interactive. For example:

```
case $- in
    *i* )   echo "The shell is interactive."      ;;
    * )     echo "The shell is not interactive."   ;;
esac
```

You can also use the -t option of the test command to determine whether the standard input or standard output is associated with a terminal. The -t option instructs the test command to return true if the file descriptor number following it is associated with a terminal and to return false otherwise.

The following if statement shows how to test whether or not the standard output is connected to a terminal. (File descriptor 1 is always the standard output, and file descriptor 0 is always the standard input.)

```
if [ ! -t 1 ]; then
    echo "Standard output is not connected to terminal." 1>&2
fi
```

## Printing Messages

By far, the simplest and most common method of writing information to the standard output is to use the echo command. It is usually best to enclose the message in double quotes; this prevents the shell from interpreting any metacharacters that might be in the message, but it allows you to include information stored in variables. For example:

```
$ FILE=/tmp/foo
$ echo "Cannot locate file $FILE"
Cannot locate file /tmp/foo
$
```

The normal output of the echo command is written to the standard output. You can redirect the output from the echo command to standard error as shown here:

```
echo "Error message." 1>&2
```

To write more than one line of output you can use separate `echo` commands for each line, or you can include newlines in the message as long as the message is enclosed in quotes.

```
$ echo "This is the first line.
> This is the second line."
This is the first line.
This is the second line.
$
```

To display a large message, you can also use a here document. A here document allows you to store a file inline in the shell script. The following example shows a message copied from a here document to the standard output. Here documents were discussed in "Here Documents" in Chapter 4.

```
cat <<-EOF
This is the first line.
This is the second line.
EOF
```

If you need to write variables into field positions, control the field width, or specify the justification within the field, you can use the `printf` function of the `awk` command. This function is similar to the `printf` library routine familiar to most C programmers.

The `printf` function is called with a format string followed by a list of strings to be substituted into the format string.[3] The format string contains message text and conversion specifications. There should be one conversion specification for each string following the format string. The conversion specification instructs `printf` how to format the corresponding string before substituting it into the format string. When all conversion specifications have been replaced, the message is printed to the standard output.

```
$ echo "abc" | awk '{printf("xxx%syyy", $1)}'
xxxabcyyy
$
```

A conversion specification begins with the % character. It can optionally be followed with a - and a number to indicate the minimum field width. Then the letter s must follow to indicate that the parameter is a string. The hyphen preceding the field width causes the string to be left justified within the field width; if the hyphen is omitted, the string will be right justified.

The following example shows how you can print items so that they line up to form

---

[3] The `printf` function supports data types other than strings, but since shell variables are always strings, the other data types are not discussed here.

vertical columns. Each line in the output contains the size and name of a file. The size is printed first in a field five characters wide (%5s). It is right justified in the field and followed by the label "Bytes." The name is separated from the size by two spaces. The \n character at the end of the format string is necessary to write the newline character at the end of each line.

```
for FILE in *
do
    SIZE=`wc -c <$FILE`
    echo $SIZE $FILE |
        awk '{printf("%5s Bytes  %s\n", $1, $2)}'
done
```

The fields to be printed are passed into awk through a pipeline. The awk command parses its input into fields separated by whitespace and loads the fields into the variables $1, $2, and so forth. Thus, in this example, $1 contains the value from SIZE and $2 contains the value from FILE.

## Printing a Prompt

A prompt is a line of output, usually in the form of a question, that is not followed by a newline. Since there is no newline, the cursor is waiting at the end of the line for an answer. A prompt is written using the echo command with an option that suppresses the newline. On System V systems, the \c character sequence is added to the end of the message to suppress the newline. On BSD systems, the -n option is used to suppress the newline.

```
echo "Would you like to ... [y/n]? \c"      # System V system

echo -n "Would you like to ... [y/n]? "      # BSD system
```

The following example shows a method that can be used on either System V or BSD systems. The if statement executes the echo command with the -n option and examines the result to see if it was interpreted as an option or if it was written as a parameter. Once the type of the echo command is determined, the variables C and N are initialized to appropriate characters to suppress the newline. Then these variables are included in the echo command line, as shown in the example. One of these variables will always be empty; therefore, that variable will disappear after it is substituted into the command line.

```
if [ "`echo -n`" = "-n" ]; then
    C='\c'
    N=
else
    C=
```

```
        N='-n'
fi
        .
        .
        .
echo $N "Would you like to ... [y/n]? $C"
```

Since this is not too elegant, you can write a shell function that hides the whole problem. The following function is also discussed in Chapter 9, "Examples of Shell Functions."

```
Prompt () {
    if [ "`echo -n`" = "-n" ]; then
        echo "$@\c"
    else
        echo -n "$@"
    fi
}
    .
    .
    .
Prompt "Would you like to ... [y/n]? "
```

## Asking Questions

You can ask a question from a shell script by prompting the user with a question, as described in the previous section, and then using the `read` command to read the answer from the standard input. The following example prompts the user using the System V `echo` command, described in the previous section. The `read` command will wait for the user to enter the answer. When the user enters the answer followed by the return key, the `read` command will store the answer in the variable ANSWER and the shell script will resume execution.

```
echo "Enter the name of ... \c"
read ANSWER
```

You can specify more than one variable after the `read` command, and each word in the answer will be stored in the corresponding variable; this is discussed in more detail in "The `read` Command" in Chapter 4. Since only one variable is used in the above example, the entire answer will be stored in the variable ANSWER.

When asking a yes or no question, the `read` command is usually followed by a `case` statement that matches the answer with the acceptable responses. In the next example, the answers y or yes are interpreted to mean yes and any other answer is interpreted to mean no.

```
echo "Would you like to ... [y/n]? \c"
read ANSWER
case "$ANSWER" in
    y | yes )   FLAG=TRUE    ;;
    * )         FLAG=FALSE   ;;
esac
```

The shell function `GetYesNo` in Chapter 9 shows a more complete example of processing yes or no questions. Using the `GetYesNo` function, you can ask questions in the following manner:

```
if GetYesNo "Would you like to ... [y/n]? "
then
    echo "Yes"
else
    echo "No"
fi
```

## Read a Single Character

The following example shows how to allow the user to enter a single character without requiring the return key to be pressed:

```
echo "Would you like to ... [y/n]? \c"
stty raw
ANSWER=`dd bs=1 count=1 2>/dev/null`
stty -raw
echo ""                      # Print a newline
case "$ANSWER" in
    [yY] )  FLAG=TRUE    ;;
    * )     FLAG=FALSE   ;;
esac
```

The System V `echo` command is used to write the question to the standard output, as discussed previously.

The `stty raw` command is used to prevent the normal processing of characters as they are received from the user's terminal. That is, the standard editing functions are disabled in raw mode, and the characters are not buffered into lines before being presented to the process.

The `dd` command reads a single character from the standard input and writes the character to its standard output. The standard output of the `dd` command is captured and assigned to the variable ANSWER.

After the character has been read, the `stty -raw` command is used to restore normal processing of characters from the user's terminal.

Then the echo command is used to write a newline to the standard output. This provides visual feedback so that the user knows the character has been read.

A case statement is then used to process the answer entered by the user.

### Read with a Time-out

When you read information from the standard input, the shell script will wait until the user presses the return key. If you do not want your program to wait forever, you can create an event that will interrupt the read command after some period of time.[4]

If the shell script receives a signal while the read command is waiting for input, the read command will be interrupted. When the shell script is resumed after processing the signal, it will be resumed at the statement following the read command.

The following example creates a background process that sleeps for a specified time interval (ten seconds in this example) and then uses the kill command to send signal 2 to the current process.

```
trap ":" 2
(sleep 10; kill -2 $$)&
echo "Would you like to ... [y/n]? \c"
read ANSWER
if kill -0 $! 2>/dev/null; then
    kill $!
fi
case "$ANSWER" in
    y | yes )    FLAG=TRUE    ;;
    *  )         FLAG=FALSE   ;;
esac
trap 2
```

The trap command is set to execute the null command (:) if signal 2 is received. This will interrupt the current process to do nothing, then continue executing the current process. Notice that a command must be executed when the signal is received because an empty command list passed to the trap command causes the signal to be ignored completely.

After the read is complete, the background process is killed. The variable $! contains the process ID of the process that was created earlier. The -0 option of the kill command is used to determine if the background process is still alive.

The final line of the example resets signal 2 to the default behavior.

### Conditional Output

If you would like to write messages that are printed only under certain conditions, you would normally print the message from inside an if statement.

---

[4] On HP-UX, the line command can be used to read the standard input. The -t option on this command lets you specify a time-out value. This is considerably simpler than the method shown in this section, but it is not portable to other systems.

```
if [ "$VERBOSE" = "TRUE" ]; then
    echo "Message"
fi
```

Another technique that can be used is to store the command that will be used to print the message in a variable. Then you can replace the command with the null command when the messages are not wanted. Since the command line is evaluated before it is executed, the variable containing the command name will be substituted into the command line before it is executed.

The following example uses the echo command to print messages when the verbose option is set, and it replaces it with the null command ( : ) when the verbose option is not set. The null command will ignore its parameters and do nothing.

```
if [ "$VERBOSE" = "TRUE" ]; then
    ECHO=echo
else
    ECHO=:
fi
    .
    .
    .
$ECHO "Message"
```

## Clear Screen

The tput command can be used to perform various terminal functions, one of which is to clear the terminal screen. To clear the terminal screen, you simply specify the clear option, as shown below.

```
tput clear
```

Unfortunately, the tput command is not available on many systems. Some systems have a clear command, but this is also not available on many systems.

One portable but crude way to clear the screen is to execute a command that causes the information on the screen to scroll away. The following sequence will print 24 blank lines.

```
for i in 1 2 3 4 5 6 7 8 9 10 1 2 3 4 5 6 7 8 9 20 1 2 3 4
do
    echo
done
```

If you are writing a shell script that will be executed on several different systems, it is often useful to hide portability problems in a shell function. The Clear function in Chapter 9, "Examples of Shell Functions," provides a portable solution to this problem. It first attempts to execute the clear command. If that fails, it executes the tput clear command. Finally, if that fails, it clears the screen by scrolling the information off the screen.

## The Terminal Bell

To ring the terminal bell (or make it beep) you can use the echo command to print the bell character to the standard output. However, depending upon whether the system is System V or BSD, the echo command works slightly differently.

The following command is used to print the bell character on System V systems. This command prints two characters. The first character is the character represented by 007 in the ASCII character set, the bell character. The second character, \c, is used to suppress the newline that the echo command normally appends to the output. Since the newline is suppressed, there is no visible output written to the standard output.

```
echo '\007\c'        # System V system
```

The following command is used to print the bell character on BSD systems. The ^G symbol, control-G, represents a single character that is generated by pressing the control key at the same time as the g character. Control-G is the representation used by the BSD echo command for the bell character. The -n option of the echo command suppresses the newline.

```
echo -n '^G'         # BSD system
```

## Turn Echo Off or On

If you want the user to enter information from the standard input, but you do not want it to be printed on the terminal screen as it is typed, use the following command:

```
stty -echo
```

To restore the echoing of characters after the user has finished entering the information, enter the following command:

```
stty echo
```

The following example requests a password. As the password is entered, nothing appears on the screen. Then after the password is entered, echoing is restored so that any further information will appear on the screen as it is entered.

```
stty -echo
echo "Enter your password followed by a carriage return."
read PASSWORD
stty echo
echo "Your password is $PASSWORD"
```

## PROCESS MANIPULATION

### Finding a Process by Name

Getting the process ID for a process, given its name, is typically done by parsing the output of the `ps` command. The following example will print a list of process IDs for all of the processes named *ProcessName*.

```
PID=`ps -ef            |
      grep "ProcessName"  |
      grep -v "grep"      |
      awk '{print $2}'`
```

In this example, the `ps` command is used to get a list of the current processes. On System V systems the `-ef` options are used with the `ps` command, but on BSD systems the `-auwx` options should be used.

The first `grep` command is used to remove any lines that do not contain the name of the process. However, since this command is executed as a pipeline, and the processes in a pipeline are executed in parallel, some of the commands from this command may show up in the output of the `ps` command. Therefore, the second `grep` command is needed to remove the first `grep` command. The first `grep` command will not remove itself from the output because it contains the name of the process as a parameter on its command line.

The `awk` command is used to print the second field from the lines that remain in the output. The second field contains the process ID on both System V and BSD systems.

### Killing a Process by Name

To write a command to kill a process by name, we can extend the example from the previous section.

```
PID=`ps -ef            |
      grep "ProcessName"  |
      grep -v "grep"      |
      awk '{print $2}'`
if [ "$PID" != "" ]; then
      kill $PID
fi
```

This example provides a simple "kill by name" command; however, it does not provide any error checking, and it does not distinguish between multiple processes with the same name. Compare this example with the more robust `Kill` command presented in Chapter 10, "Examples of Shell Scripts."

## PROCESSING MAIL

### Checking for New Mail

The following example can be used to write a message to the terminal whenever there is new mail in your mail box. It executes a continuous loop, once every sixty seconds. Each time the loop executes, it compares the size of the mail spool file with the size from the previous loop. If the mail spool file has grown, a message is printed to the standard output, informing you that new mail has arrived.

```
OLDSIZE=`ls -1 /usr/mail/$USER | awk '{print $5}'`
while :
do
    NEWSIZE=`ls -1 /usr/mail/$USER | awk '{print $5}'`
    if [ "$NEWSIZE" -gt "$OLDSIZE" ]; then
        echo "You have new mail."
    fi
    OLDSIZE=$NEWSIZE
    sleep 60
done
```

The mail spool files are located in the directory /usr/mail on System V systems and /usr/spool/mail on BSD systems. The name of a user's mail spool file corresponds to the user's login name. For example, the file /usr/mail/$USER is the name of the mail spool file for the current user on a System V system (assuming the variable USER has been initialized to the login name of the current user[5]). The example above uses the System V mail spool file location.

The size of the mail spool file is extracted from the output of the ls command. The file size is in the fifth field on System V systems and the fourth field on BSD systems.

### Counting Mail Messages

The mail spool file contains all of the messages currently being held for a particular user. There are several lines in a mail header that occur once and only once in every mail message. Therefore, by counting one of these lines, you can determine the number of messages in the mail spool file.

The following example counts the number of lines in the mail spool file that begin with the string "From:". Naturally, if the body of a mail message contains a line that begins with this string, this command will produce an inaccurate count. Since this is not likely and the consequences of the error are not severe, this possibility is ignored.

---

[5] The variable USER is automatically initialized to the login name of the user on many systems. If this is not the case on your system, you can use one of the methods discussed in the section "Getting the Name of the User" in Chapter 5.

```
echo "You have" \
    `grep -c "^From:" /usr/mail/$USER 2>/dev/null` \
    "messages."
```

The standard error of the `grep` command is redirected to `/dev/null` to discard the message that is printed if the spool file does not exist.

## Separating Mail Header and Body

The mail header is always separated from the body of the mail message by a blank line, and the header will not contain any other blank lines. Therefore, the following two filters can be used to separate the header and the body of a single mail message.

To get the header:

```
sed -e '/^$/,$d' <mailmessage
```

To get the body:

```
sed -e '1,/^$/d' <mailmessage
```

## Packaging Files for Mailing

There are a number of problems that you might encounter when sending mail using the normal UNIX sendmail. The next example shows a mail packaging command that avoids the following problems.

- **Sending several files:** When sending several files to someone else, it is simpler if they can be treated as a single "package." The following command collects all of the files in the package and creates a `tar` file to hold them. In addition to bundling the files into a single package, this also preserves the directory structure and the file attributes of each file.
- **Sending binary files:** Normally, only ASCII files can be sent through the mail. The following command uses the `uuencode` command to change the `tar` file into an ASCII file. The receiver of the file can restore it using the `uudecode` command. The `uuencode` and `uudecode` commands are very common and should be available on most systems.
- **Sending large files:** Large mail files will cause problems for some of the systems that may be used to route the mail message. The following command will divide the message into smaller files of 1000 bytes or less. Each of the smaller files will be prepended with a message indicating how to reconstruct the original file.

To use this command, you specify the mail address where you want the files sent, the name of the package, and the list of files that you want to send. For example, if the command is saved in a file named `MailPkg`, then to send all of the files in the current directory to a user named `john`, you would enter the following command:

```
MailPkg john BunchOfFiles *
```

The source to the shell script `MailPkg` follows:

```
#!/bin/sh
#
# SYNOPSIS
#    MailPkg address package file ...
#
ADDRESS=$1
PACKAGE=$2
shift 2

tar -cf /tmp/package.$$ $*

mkdir /tmp/split.$$
cd /tmp/split.$$
compress /tmp/package.$$ |
    uuencode $PACKAGE.tar.Z | split -1000

PARTNUM=1
MESSAGE=/tmp/message.$$
set x*
TOTAL=$#
while [ $# -gt 0 ]
do
    cat <<-EOF >$MESSAGE
    This is part $PARTNUM of $TOTAL of a compressed and
    uuencoded tar file.
    - File: $PACKAGE.tar.Z
    - Part: $PARTNUM
    ----- Cut Here -----
    EOF

    cat $1                         >>$MESSAGE
    echo "----- Cut Here -----" >>$MESSAGE

    mail $ADDRESS <$MESSAGE

    shift
    PARTNUM=`expr $PARTNUM + 1`
done
rm /tmp/package.$$
rm /tmp/message.$$
rm -rf /tmp/split.$$
```

## FILES AND DIRECTORIES

### Parsing File Names

The `basename` command can be used to return the last component of a file name. The last component is everything that follows the rightmost slash character (/).[6] If the file name does not contain a slash, the whole name is returned.

```
$ echo `basename abc/def`
def
$
```

The `dirname` command returns the directory path portion of a file name. This is everything to the left of the rightmost slash character. If the file name does not contain a slash, the string . / is returned, which is the relative name of the current directory.

```
$ echo `dirname abc/def`
abc
$
```

For a more general method of parsing a file name you can use one of the methods for parsing data shown earlier in this chapter. The following example is similar to the example for parsing data with a `for` loop. The slash character is assigned to the `IFS` variable so that the word list of the `for` loop will be parsed, using the slash character as a delimiter. Then by specifying a file name as the word list, each component of the file name can be processed individually. There is another example of using this technique in the `MkDir` command in Chapter 10, "Examples of Shell Scripts."

```
$ IFS=/
$ for f in abc/def
> do
>    echo $f
> done
abc
def
$
```

### Determining Full Path Name

The typical way to get the full path name for a directory is to use the `cd` command to move to the directory and then use the `pwd` command to get the full name of the directory. For example:

---

[6] A slash character is not allowed as a characters in a file name; it is only used in file names as a separator between the components of the directory hierarchy.

```
cd directory
FULLNAME=`pwd`
```

To prevent the side effect of changing the current directory, this command is usually executed in a subshell, as shown below.

```
FULLNAME=`(cd directory; pwd)`
```

To get the full name of a file, rather than a directory, you need to first separate the directory name from the file name. After the directory name has been expanded, the directory name and the file name are reassembled. For example:

```
cd `dirname file`
FULLNAME=`pwd`/`basename file`
```

The function `FullName` in Chapter 9, "Examples of Shell Functions," is an example of a function that will return the full name of either a directory or a file.

## Listing Files

The `find` command is indispensable for tasks that involve traversing a directory hierarchy. This section has several examples that use the `find` command to produce different lists of file names.

The following command will print the names of all files under the current directory:

```
find . -print
```

The file names listed by this command will be relative to the current directory. To produce the same list, but to list the full names of the files, use the following command:

```
find `pwd` -print
```

You can add the `-type f` option to only print the names of ordinary files or `-type d` to only print the names of directories. For example:

```
find . -type f -print    # Print the names of files.
find . -type d -print    # Print the names of directories.
```

The `-name` option can be used to restrict the list of files to files with a particular name or to files with a name that matches a pattern. For example, the following command lists all files in the current directory that end in the `.c` suffix. If the value for the name option contains wildcard characters, be sure to enclose the value in quotes. In this case, the wildcard characters must be processed by the `find` command, not the shell.

```
find . -type f -name "*.c" -print
```

The `find` command also allows you to reverse the sense of any option by preceding it with the exclamation point (!). Be sure to leave a space between the ! and the option. In the following example, the names of all the files under the current directory, except files named `core` or `tmp`, will be printed.

```
find . -type f ! -name core ! -name tmp -print
```

The `find` command has many other options that allow you to build complex commands for processing the files in a directory. It is worthwhile to periodically review the manual page for this command.

## Searching Directories

The following command will search the current directory for a file with a particular name. If the file is found, its name relative to the current directory is printed.

```
find . -type f -name "file" -print
```

In this example, the file name is enclosed in quotes. This allows the file name to contain wildcard characters so that the command will list all of the files that match a pattern.

The `findfile` command in Chapter 10, "Examples of Shell Scripts," shows a more complete example of this command.

If you want to search the current directory for all the files that contain a particular string, you can use the following command:

```
find . -type f -exec grep "pattern" {} /dev/null \;
```

This command uses the `find` command to pass the names of all the files under the current directory to the `grep` command, which then searches the files and lists the lines that contain the pattern.

The `findstr` command, also in Chapter 10, shows a more complete example of this command.

## Copying Directories

The simplest way to copy a directory is to use the `cp -r` command. The destination directory and any subdirectories will be created automatically. (In fact, the destination directory should not exist before this command is executed.) The `-r` option of the `cp` command may not be available on older System V systems. Another disadvantage of this command is that file access permissions and file modification times of the copied files are not preserved.

```
cd SourceDirectory
cp -r . DestinationDirectory
```

The following command is more complex, but it preserves the file access permissions and file modification times of the copied files:

```
cd SourceDirectory
find . -depth -print | cpio -pdmu DestinationDirectory
```

Before executing this command you must ensure that the destination directory already exists, but subdirectories beneath the destination directory will be created automatically. The `find` command is used here to create the list of files to be copied. It is important that this command be executed from the source directory so that the names printed by the `find` command will be relative file names. The `cpio` command reads the names from the `find` command and copies the files to the destination directory.

The next example shows yet another way to copy a directory. This command creates a `tar` file containing all the files to be copied. The `tar` file is passed through a pipeline to another command that unpacks the `tar` file in the destination directory. This command preserves the file access permissions and file modification times of the copied files, but it is not as fast as the command in the previous example.

```
(cd SourceDirectory; tar cf - .)|(cd DestinationDirectory; tar xf -)
```

A similar command can be used to copy directories from one system to another.

```
(cd LocalDirectory; tar cf - .)|rsh host "cd RemoteDirectory; tar xf -"
```

The `dircopy` command in Chapter 10, "Examples of Shell Scripts," shows a complete example of a shell script that will copy directories.

## Comparing File Dates

The following code will print the name of the newer (more recently modified) of two files:

```
ls -t file1 file2 | sed -n '1p'
```

The `ls` command lists the names of the two files, with the more recently modified file listed first. The `sed` command is used to print only the first of the two lines listed by the `ls` command. The string `1p` in the `sed` command is the number one (not the letter ell), followed by the letter `p`.

Another way to compare the modification dates of two files uses the `find` command. The following command will print the name of *file1* if it is newer than *file2*, otherwise it will not print anything.

```
find file1 -newer file2 -print
```

The above command can be used in an `if` statement to compare the modification dates of two files by examining its output to see whether or not it is empty. This technique is shown in the example below, and it is also used in the `IsNewer` shell function presented in Chapter 9, "Examples of Shell Functions."

```
if [ -n "`find file1 -newer file2 -print`" ]
then
     echo "Yes; file1 is newer than file2."
else
     echo "No; file1 is not newer than file2."
fi
```

You can compare the modification time of a file with an arbitrary time by creating a temporary file with the desired date and then using one of the above code sequences. For example, the following code creates a temporary file using the `touch` command. The date specification of the `touch` command is in the format *mmddhhmm* [*yy*], where the first *mm* is the month.

```
touch date-time /tmp/tmp.$$
if [ -n "`find file1 -newer /tmp/tmp.$$ -print`" ]
then
     echo "Yes; file1 is newer than date-time."
else
     echo "No; file1 is not newer than date-time."
fi
```

The following command can be used to produce a list of the names of all the files in the current directory that are newer than *file*.

```
find . -newer file -print
```

## Determine File Size

There are several ways to determine the size of a file. The first example below is the most portable method, but it actually counts the number of bytes in the file; therefore, it can be very slow when used with large files.

```
wc -c file | awk '{print $1}'
```

The `ls` command reads the file size from the directory entry for the file; therefore, it is faster than the previous example. However, the size of the file is located in a different field in the output of the `ls` command, depending upon the type of system. On System V systems, the file size is in the fifth field, but on BSD systems, the file size is in the fourth field. For example:

```
ls -l file | awk '{print $5}'        # System V system

ls -l file | awk '{print $4}'        # BSD system
```

## Determining Space Availability

This section shows how to determine how much space is available in a particular directory. Actually, this is the amount of space available in a file system, but in these examples, the name of any directory in the file system can be used to identify the file system.

The df command is used to display the amount of space available in a directory. Unfortunately, the format of the information displayed by the df command is different, depending upon the manufacturer of the system. Thus, this section will show different methods of parsing the output of the df command that cover a variety of systems. At the end of the section, there is a shell function that encapsulates the complexity of determining the type of system and the selection of one of the parsing techniques.

The examples in this section will report the amount of free space in thousands of bytes.

On Sun BSD systems, the following command can be used to determine the amount of space available. The output of the df command is piped to a sed filter that removes the title line from the output. The output is then passed to awk, which extracts the fourth field.

```
df directory | sed -n '2p' | awk '{print $4}'
```

On Sun Solaris, the same command is used, but the -k option is needed with the df command to display the information in kilobytes rather than blocks.

```
df -k directory | sed -n '2p' | awk '{print $4}'
```

On Digital Equipment's OSF based systems, you can use the same command as Sun Solaris.

On Digital Equipment's ULTRIX systems, the df command prints a two-line title instead of one. Thus, this command is similar to the command for Sun BSD, except the sed filter has been modified to only print the third line from the output of the df command.

```
df directory | sed -n '3p' | awk '{print $4}'
```

On SGI systems, the -k option is passed to the df command to display the information in kilobytes rather than blocks. The df command on SGI systems has a one-line title, but the amount of free space is in the fifth field rather than the fourth.

```
df -k directory | sed -n '2p' | awk '{print $5}'
```

On HP-UX, it is a little more difficult. The `df` command expects the name of a file system, not a directory. Most HP-UX systems have the command `/etc/devnm`[7] that will provide this conversion for you.

```
FILESYS=`/etc/devnm directory | awk '{print $1}'`
```

Now the name of the file system can be passed to the `df` command. The next problem is that the output of the `df` command is not partitioned into predictable fields. The following command uses a somewhat more complicated `sed` filter to extract the number of free blocks from the output of the `df` command.

```
BLOCKS=`df $FILESYS | sed -e 's/.*: *//' -e 's/ .*//'`
```

Next, the output of the `df` command is reported in blocks, not kilobytes. Since there are 512 bytes in a block, the number of blocks is divided by 2 to get the number of kilobytes.

```
expr $BLOCKS / 2
```

In order to write portable shell code it is often desirable to encapsulate portability problems. The following shell function will return the amount of space available in a directory for a variety of systems. The function `SystemType` is called to get a string that identifies the current system. The function `SystemType` is presented in Chapter 9, "Examples of Shell Functions."

```
SpaceAvail() {
    DIRECTORY=$1
    SYSTEM=`SystemType`
    case $SYSTEM in
        ULTRIX) SPACE=`df $DIRECTORY |
                    sed -n '3p' |
                    awk '{print $4}'`
            ;;
        SUNBSD) SPACE=`df $DIRECTORY |
                    sed -n '2p' |
                    awk '{print $4}'`
            ;;
        SOLARIS | DECOSF)
            SPACE=`df -k $DIRECTORY |
                    sed -n '2p'    |
                    awk '{print $4}'`
            ;;
```

---

[7] The `devnm` command is in the `/usr/sbin` directory on SVR4 systems, which includes HP-UX, beginning with their 10.0 release.

```
           SGI) SPACE=`df -k $DIRECTORY |
                         sed -n '2p' |
                         awk '{print $5}'`
                 ;;
           HP) FILESYS=`/etc/devnm $DIRECTORY | awk '{print $1}'`
               BLOCKS=`df $FILESYS |
                         sed -e 's/.*: *//' -e 's/ .*//'`
               SPACE=`expr $BLOCKS / 2`
                 ;;
           * ) echo "Unexpected system type." 1>&2
               exit 1
                 ;;
        esac

        echo $SPACE
    }
```

## Determining Space Usage

The `du -s` command will tell you the amount of space used in a directory. Unfortunately, on some systems, this command reports the amount of space used in kilobytes, and others report it in blocks of 512 bytes. The following shell function will return the amount of space used in a directory for a variety of systems. As in the previous example, the function `SystemType` is called to get a string that identifies the current system.

```
    SpaceUsed() {
        DIRECTORY=$1
        SYSTEM=`SystemType`
        case $SYSTEM in
            SUNBSD | ULTRIX )
                SPACE=`du -s $DIRECTORY`
                ;;
            HP | SGI | SOLARIS | DECOSF )
                SPACE=`du -s $DIRECTORY`
                SPACE=`expr $SPACE / 2`
                ;;
            * ) echo "Unexpected system type." 1>&2
                exit 1
                ;;
        esac

        echo $SPACE
    }
```

---

# 9

*Examples of Shell Functions*

---

The following shell functions are presented in this chapter:

| | |
|---|---|
| CheckHostname | Determine if a host name is valid |
| Clear | Clear the terminal screen |
| DownShift | Downshift the alphabetic characters in a string |
| FullName | Return the full name of a file or directory |
| GetYesNo | Ask a question that requires a yes or no answer |
| IsNewer | Compare the modification dates of two files |
| IsNumeric | Determine if a string contains a numeric value |
| IsSystemType | Determine if a string matches the current system |
| Prompt | Print a message to the standard output without a newline |
| Question | Ask a question |
| StrCmp | Compare two strings |
| SystemType | Return a string that identifies the type of the system |

## CHECKHOSTNAME FUNCTION

```
 1
 2  #
 3  # File: CheckHostname.sh
 4  #
 5
 6  CheckHostname() {
 7       #
 8       # NAME
 9       #    CheckHostname - determine if a host name is valid
10       #
11       # SYNOPSIS
12       #    CheckHostname [hostname]
13       #
14       # DESCRIPTION
15       #    This function will return true (0) if the host
16       #    name is valid; otherwise, it will return
17       #    false (1).  If the host name is omitted, the
18       #    current host is checked.
19       #
20       _PING=                          # Customized ping command
21       _HOST=${1:-`hostname`}  # Name of the host to check
22
23       case `uname -s` in
24            OSF1)    _PING="ping -c1 $_HOST"    ;;   # DEC OSF
25            HP-UX )  _PING="ping $_HOST 64 1"   ;;
26            IRIX )   _PING="ping -c1 $_HOST"    ;;   # SGI
27            SunOS )  _PING="ping $_HOST"        ;;   # BSD and
28                                                     # Solaris
29       * )               return 1                ;;
30       esac
31
32       if [ `$_PING 2>&1 | grep -ci "Unknown host"` -eq 0 ]
33       then
34            return 0
35       else
36            return 1
37       fi
38  }
```

This function checks that the name of the host is valid. The `ping` command is used to check the name, but the implementation of the `ping` command varies slightly from one system to the next. This function hides the complexity of determining the correct options to the `ping` command.

Even though the `ping` command tests the connection to the remote system, any error other than an unknown host is ignored. At the end of this discussion, there is an example of how to modify this function to use it to determine if the remote system is responding to network requests.

On some systems the `ping` command may take a long time to return if the remote system is not responding. You can set your own time-out to interrupt the `ping` command if you want to shorten the delay. (The section "Read with a Time-out" in Chapter 8 shows how to create a subshell that interrupts a command after a time-out has expired.)

Lines 20 and 21 define the variables that are used in this function. It is not necessary to define a variable before it is used, but it is a common practice to list the significant variables near the beginning of the function with a simple comment describing their purpose.

Line 21 copies the command line parameter to the variable _HOST. This line uses one of the variable initialization syntaxes; if $1 is not empty, it is assigned to _HOST; otherwise, the `hostname` command is executed and its standard output is assigned to _HOST.

Line 23 begins a `case` statement that determines the type of the current system by examining the string returned by the `uname` command. Each case value will assign the correct `ping` command for that system into the variable _PING.

Line 29 will be executed if this function is executed on any system other than one of the systems accounted for in the `case` statement. If this statement is executed, the function will return a status that indicates the system is not responding; this is not ideal, but it is probably acceptable in most cases.

Line 32 executes the `ping` command that is stored in the variable _PING. The standard error of the `ping` command is merged into its standard output so that a pipe can be used to pass it on to the `grep` command. The `grep` command examines the output of the `ping` command for the string Unknown host and writes the number of matches to its standard output.

The `if` statement compares the number written by the `grep` command with zero to determine whether or not the string was found. If the string was not found, a successful exit status is returned from line 34; otherwise, a failed status is returned from line 36.

As stated earlier, this function can be modified so that it will determine if the remote system is responding to network request. To do this, you simply replace lines 32–37 with the following line:

```
32        return $_PING >/dev/null 2>&1
```

This line executes the `ping` command stored in the variable _PING and returns the exit status of the `ping` command as the exit status of the function. Both the standard output and the standard error of the `ping` command are discarded.

## CLEAR FUNCTION

```
 1
 2   #
 3   # File: Clear.sh
 4   #
 5
 6   Clear() {
 7           #
 8           # NAME
 9           #     Clear - clear the terminal screen
10           #
11           # SYNOPSIS
12           #     Clear
13           #
14           # DESCRIPTION
15           #     This function will clear the terminal screen using
16           #     either the clear command or the tput command.  If
17           #     neither of these commands are available, 40 blank
18           #     lines will be printed to clear the screen.
19           #
20           { clear;        } 2>/dev/null  ||
21           { tput clear;   } 2>/dev/null  ||
22           for i in 1 2 3 4 5 6 7 8 9 10 \
23                    1 2 3 4 5 6 7 8 9 20 \
24                    1 2 3 4 5 6 7 8 9 30 \
25                    1 2 3 4 5 6 7 8 9 40
26           do
27                   echo
28           done
29   }
```

This function hides the complexity of finding a portable solution to the problem of clearing the terminal screen. It attempts to execute three different methods to clear the terminal screen. Each method is tried until one of them is successful. The last method will always work, but it is the least desirable solution.

The commands on lines 20 and 21 are enclosed in braces so that the standard error can be redirected to /dev/null. The braces are necessary because if the command is not found, the error is printed by the current shell. In the normal situation, when braces are not used, redirecting the standard error only redirects the messages that are printed by the command. In this case, the command fails before the new process is created, and, therefore, the message is printed by the current shell.

Lines 22–28 will be executed if both of the previous commands are unsuccessful. The echo command is used to print a blank line for each word in the word list of the `for` loop. Since the words are not actually used, I have chosen words that make it easier to see how many words are in the word list.

## DOWNSHIFT FUNCTION

```
 1
 2   #
 3   # File: DownShift.sh
 4   #
 5
 6   DownShift() {
 8       # NAME
 9       #    DownShift - downshift the characters in a string
10       #
11       # SYNOPSIS
12       #    DownShift string
13       #
14       # DESCRIPTION
15       #    This function will downshift the alphabetic
16       #    characters in the string.  Nonalphabetic
17       #    characters will not be affected.  The downshifted
18       #    string will be written to the standard output.
19       #
20
21       echo "$@" | tr '[A-Z]' '[a-z]'
22   }
```

This example shows how you can use a function as an alias. Using a function in this way allows you to assign a descriptive name to a sequence of commands. Without using this mechanism, it would be more difficult for those unfamiliar with the commands to understand their purpose. For example, compare the following two statements to see how much easier it is to understand the purpose of the statement when the `DownShift` function is used.

```
STRING=`DownShift "$STRING"`

STRING=`echo "$STRING" | tr '[A-Z]' '[a-z]'`
```

Notice that it is not necessary to check the number of parameters passed to this function; it behaves as you would expect whether there are zero, one, or many parameters passed to this function.

Line 21 performs the downshift. The `echo` command is used to copy the command line, "`$@`", to the standard input of the `tr` command where the characters in the range A–Z are replaced with the corresponding character in the range a–z.

## FULLNAME FUNCTION

```
1
2    #
3    # File: FullName.sh
4    #
5
6    FullName() {
7         #
8         # NAME
9         #     FullName - return full name of a file or directory
10        #
11        # SYNOPSIS
12        #     FullName file | directory
13        #
14        # DESCRIPTION
15        #     This function will return the full name of the
16        #     file or directory (the full name begins at the
17        #     root directory).  The full name will be written
18        #     to the standard output.  If the file or directory
19        #     does not exist, the name will be returned
20        #     unchanged.
21        #
22        _CWD=`pwd`              # Save the current directory
23
24        if [ $# -ne 1 ]; then
25             echo "Usage: FullName filename | directory" 1>&2
26             exit 1
27        fi
28
29        if [ -d $1 ]; then
30             cd $1
31             echo `pwd`
32        elif [ -f $1 ]; then
33             cd `dirname $1`
34             echo `pwd`/`basename $1`
35        else
36             echo $1
37        fi
38
39        cd $_CWD
40   }
```

Any script that changes directories after it begins execution will need to ensure that the file names and directory names it uses are full path names. This function can be used to convert either file names or directory names to their full name.

Lines 22 and 39 save and restore the current directory. Remember that if the output of the function is not redirected, this function will be executed in the current shell, and changing the directory could cause a potentially undesirable side effect for the calling code.

Lines 24–27 ensure that exactly one parameter is passed to this function. If this check fails, a message is printed and function exits.

If this function is executed in a subshell, remember that the `exit` command will behave like a `return` command; it will not exit the command file. This is not the desired behavior for this situation, but since this error should only occur if the function is executed incorrectly, it should only be encountered during the development of the shell script, and, thus, not cause any serious problems.

Lines 29–37 perform the actual work of the function. An `if` statement is used to separate the task into three cases:

- If the parameter is the name of a directory, this function will change to the directory and use the `pwd` command to get the full name of the directory.
- If the parameter is the name of a file, the name will first be parsed into its directory and file components. Then the directory name will be expanded by changing to the directory and using the `pwd` command as above. Then the full directory name and the file name will be reassembled.
- If the parameter is not the name of an existing file or directory, it will be returned without making any changes.

## GETYESNO FUNCTION

```
 1
 2    #
 3    # File: GetYesNo.sh
 4    #
 5
 6    GetYesNo() {
 7         #
 8         # NAME
 9         #    GetYesNo - ask a yes or no question
10         #
11         # SYNOPSIS
12         #    GetYesNo message
13         #
14         # DESCRIPTION
15         #    This function will prompt the user with the
16         #    message and wait for the user to answer "yes" or
17         #    "no". This function will return true (0) if the
18         #    user answers yes; otherwise, it will return
19         #    false (1).
20         #
21         #    This function will accept y, yes, n, or no, and it
22         #    is reasonably tolerant of upper and lower case
```

```
23      #      letters; any other answer will cause the question
24      #      to be repeated.
25      #
26      _ANSWER=                    # Answer read from user
27
28      if [ $# -eq 0 ]; then
29              echo "Usage: GetYesNo message" 1>&2
30              exit 1
31      fi
32
33      while :
34      do
35              if [ "`echo -n`" = "-n" ]; then
36                      echo "$@\c"
37              else
38                      echo -n "$@"
39              fi
40              read _ANSWER
41              case "$_ANSWER" in
42                      [yY] | yes | YES | Yes)  return 0  ;;
43                      [nN] | no  | NO  | No )  return 1  ;;
44                      * ) echo "Please enter y or n."    ;;
45              esac
46      done
47  }
```

This is an example of a frequently used code sequence that is easily encapsulated. This function can be used to ask questions that are answered by yes or no. Later in this chapter, the function Question shows how to ask questions that expect answers other than yes or no.

Here is an example of how you might call this function:

```
if GetYesNo "Remove file $FILE?"; then
    rm $FILE
fi
```

Lines 28–31 ensure that the function is called with the correct number of parameters. If there are no parameters, it is an error, but any other situation will be handled as you would expect.

Line 33 is the beginning of an infinite loop. This function will loop until it gets an answer that it expects. The only way to end this loop is to execute the return command on line 42 or 43.

Lines 35–39 print the message each time the loop is executed. The message will be printed without a newline so that the cursor remains at the end of the message waiting for the user to enter an answer. Since the method for suppressing the newline is different on different systems, line 35 performs a test to see which of two methods to use.

Line 40 reads the standard input for the user's answer. The current process will block until the user enters an answer and presses the return key. When the process resumes, the answer will be in the variable _ANSWER.

Lines 41–45 are a `case` statement that selects one of three options depending upon the answer. Lines 42 and 43 match the answer with a variety of patterns. These patterns take into account all of the answers the user is likely to enter. Depending upon the answer, a different exit status is returned.

The default case on line 44 will be executed if the answer does not match any of the patterns. In this case, the user is instructed how to enter the answer, and the question is repeated.

## ISNEWER FUNCTION

```
1
2    #
3    # File: IsNewer.sh
4    #
5
6    IsNewer() {
7            #
8            # NAME
9            #     IsNewer - compare the dates of two files
10           #
11           # SYNOPSIS
12           #     IsNewer file1 file2
13           #
14           # DESCRIPTION
15           #     This function will return true (0) if file1 has
16           #     been modified more recently than file2; otherwise,
17           #     it will return false (1).
18           #
19           if [ $# -ne 2 ]; then
20                   echo "Usage: IsNewer file1 file2" 1>&2
21                   exit 1
22           fi
23
24           if [ ! -f $1 -o ! -f $2 ]; then
25                   return 1        # No
26           fi
27
28           if [ -n "`find $1 -newer $2 -print`" ]; then
29                   return 0        # Yes
30           else
31                   return 1        # No
32           fi
33   }
```

This function compares the modification dates of two files. For example:

```
if IsNewer file1 file2
then
        echo "Yes; file1 is newer than file2."
fi
```

Notice that if *file1* is not newer than *file2*, it does not necessarily follow that *file2* is newer than *file1*. The files may be the same, one of the files may not exist, or one of the files may not be an ordinary file.

Lines 19–22 ensure that exactly two parameters are passed to this function. If this check fails, a message is printed and the function exits.

Lines 24–26 ensure that the names passed to this function are the names of files. If they are not, this function does not treat it as an error; it simply returns false.

On line 28, the find command with the -newer option is used to compare the modification dates of the two files. It will print the name of *file1* if it is newer than *file2*, otherwise, it will not print anything.

The if statement on line 28 examines the output of the find command using the -n option of the test command. This option causes the test command to return success if the output is not empty.


## ISNUMERIC FUNCTION

```
 1
 2   #
 3   # File: IsNumeric.sh
 4   #
 5
 6   IsNumeric() {
 7           #
 8           # NAME
 9           #     IsNumeric - determine if a string is numeric
10           #
11           # SYNOPSIS
12           #     IsNumeric string
13           #
14           # DESCRIPTION
15           #     This function will return true (0) if the string
16           #     contains all numeric characters; otherwise, it
17           #     will return false (1).
18           #
19           if [ $# -ne 1 ]; then
20                   return 1
21           fi
22
```

```
23        expr "$1" + 1 >/dev/null 2>&1
24        if [ $? -ge 2 ]; then
25              return 1
26        fi
27
28        return 0
29  }
```

Since all variables in the shell contain strings, there is no type checking to ensure that a variable that should contain a number does, in fact, contain a number. This function will test the value of a variable by performing an arithmetic operation on it to see if it causes an error. For example:

```
NUMBER=123456
if IsNumeric $NUMBER
then
    echo "$NUMBER is numeric."
fi
```

Lines 19–21 ensure that only one parameter is passed to this function. However, rather than treating the wrong number of parameters as an error, this function treats it as a non-numeric value and returns false. This allows the function to return the correct answer, for example, if the value contains whitespace, but the caller did not quote the value on the command line.

Line 23 uses the `expr` command to add zero to the value. If one of the characters in the value is not a digit between 0 and 9, the `expr` command will return a value of 2 or greater in its exit status. Notice that the `expr` command uses its exit status to return information about the expression; therefore, the normal values of zero for success and not zero for failure do not apply.

Since the output from the `expr` command is not needed, both the standard output and standard error are discarded by redirecting them to `/dev/null`.

Lines 24–28 translate the exit status from the `expr` command into the success or failure value returned by this function.

## ISSYSTEMTYPE FUNCTION

```
1
2   #
3   # File: IsSystemType.sh
4   #
5
6   IsSystemType() {
7         #
8         # NAME
9         #    IsSystemType - compare string with current system
```

```
10      #
11      # SYNOPSIS
12      #     IsSystemType string
13      #
14      # DESCRIPTION
15      #     This function will return true (0) if the string
16      #     matches one of the values returned by the uname
17      #     command; otherwise, it will return false (1).
18      #
19      if [ $# -ne 1 ]; then
20              echo "Usage: IsSystemType string" 1>&2
21              exit 1
22      fi
23
24      if [ "$1" = "`uname -s`" ]; then
25              return 0
26      elif [ "$1" = "`uname -m`" ]; then
27              return 0
28      else
29              case `uname -r` in
30                      "$1"* ) return 0 ;;
31              esac
32      fi
33      return 1
34  }
```

This function allows you to conditionally execute nonportable commands by comparing a string with one of the values returned by the `uname` command. This is similar to using the `ifdef` capability of the C preprocessor. For example:

```
if IsSystemType "HP-UX"
then
        ...
fi
```

The function `SystemType`, shown later in this chapter, shows another way to identify systems so that commands can be conditionally executed.

Lines 19–22 ensure that exactly one parameter is passed to this function. If this check fails, a message is printed and the function exits.

Lines 24–32 compare the string with the various outputs from the `uname` command. If a match is found, a successful exit status is returned. If no match is found, line 33 returns an unsuccessful status.

Lines 24 and 26 check for an exact match with the name of the operating system and the model name of the computer hardware.

Lines 29–31 check to see if the string matches the beginning of the version string returned by the `uname -r` command. This check assumes the most significant information is at the front of this string.

## PROMPT FUNCTION

```
 1
 2   #
 3   # File: Prompt.sh
 4   #
 5
 6   Prompt() {
 7         #
 8         # NAME
 9         #    Prompt - print a message without a newline
10         #
11         # SYNOPSIS
12         #    Prompt [message]
13         #
14         # DESCRIPTION
15         #    This function prints the message to the standard
16         #    output without a newline at the end of the line.
17         #
18         #    If the message is not passed, ">" will be
19         #    printed.
20         #
21         if [ "`echo -n`" = "-n" ]; then
22               echo "${@:-> }\c"
23         else
24               echo -n "${@:-> }"
25         fi
26   }
```

The `Prompt` function prints a message to the standard output without a newline. That is, after the message is printed, the cursor remains at the end of the message. This is done by using the `echo` command and specifying an option to suppress the newline. The problem is that on different systems, a different method is used to suppress the newline:

- On System V systems, the `\c` character sequence is added to the end of the message to suppress the newline.
- On BSD systems, the `-n` option is used to suppress the newline.

Line 21 determines which of these methods should be used to suppress the newline. The output of the `echo -n` command is compared with the string `-n`. If they are equal, then the `echo` command did not interpret the `-n` as an option and, therefore, must be using the other method to suppress the newline.

On lines 22 and 24, the message is echoed using the appropriate method to suppress the newline. The variable `$@` is used to pass all of the command line parameters (that is, the message) to the `echo` command. The code sequence `${@:-> }` is a little cryptic, but it is one of the variable initialization syntaxes. It instructs the shell to use the value of the variable $@ if it is not empty, otherwise use the string "> ". This is how the default message gets passed to the echo command if no message is passed to Prompt.

## QUESTION FUNCTION

```
 1
 2  #
 3  # File: Question.sh
 4  #
 5
 6  Question() {
 7      #
 8      # NAME
 9      #     Question - ask a question
10      #
11      # SYNOPSIS
12      #     Question question default helpmessage
13      #
14      # DESCRIPTION
15      #     This function will print a question and return the
16      #     answer entered by the user in the global variable
17      #     ANSWER.  The question will be printed to the
18      #     standard output.  If a default answer is supplied,
19      #     it will be enclosed in square brackets and
20      #     appended to the question.  The question will then
21      #     be followed with a question mark and printed
22      #     without a newline.
23      #
24      #     The default answer and the help message may be
25      #     omitted, but an empty parameter (i.e.,"") must
26      #     be passed in their place.
27      #
28      #     The user may press enter without entering an
29      #     answer to accept the default answer.
30      #
31      #     The user may enter "quit" or "q" to exit the
32      #     command file. This answer is not case sensitive.
33      #
34      #     The user may enter a question mark to receive a
35      #     help message if one is available. After the help
36      #     message is printed, the question will be printed
37      #     again.
38      #
39      #     The user may enter !command to cause the UNIX
```

```
40    #     command to be executed.  After the command is
41    #     executed, the question will be repeated.
42    #
43    #     The answers -x and +x cause the debugging option
44    #     in the shell to be turned on and off respectively.
45    #
46    #     For "yes and no" questions, "yes", "y", "no", or,
47    #     "n" can be entered.  This response is not case
48    #     sensitive.
49    #
50    #     The answer will be returned exactly as the user
51    #     entered it except "yes" or "no" will be returned
52    #     for yes or no questions, and the default answer
53    #     will be returned if the user enters a return.
54    #
55    if [ $# -ne 3 ]; then
56         echo "Usage: Question question"\
57              "default helpmessage" 1>&2
58         exit 1
59    fi
60    ANSWER=          # Global variable for answer
61    _DEFAULT=$2      # Default answer
62    _QUESTION=       # Question as it will be printed
63    _HELPMSG=$3      # Text of the help message
64
65    if [ "$_DEFAULT" = "" ]; then
66         _QUESTION="$1? "
67    else
68         _QUESTION="$1 [$_DEFAULT]? "
69    fi
70
71    while :
72    do
73         if [ "`echo -n`" = "-n" ]; then
74              echo "$_QUESTION\c"
75         else
76              echo -n "$_QUESTION"
77         fi
78         read ANSWER
79         case `echo "$ANSWER" | tr [A-Z] [a-z]` in
80              "" ) if [ "$_DEFAULT" != "" ]; then
81                        ANSWER=$_DEFAULT
82                        break
83                   fi
84                   ;;
85
86              yes | y )
87                   ANSWER=yes
```

```
 88                        break
 89                        ;;
 90
 91           no | n )
 92                   ANSWER=no
 93                   break
 94                   ;;
 95
 96           quit | q )
 97                   exit 1
 98                   ;;
 99
100           +x | -x )
101                   set $ANSWER
102                   ;;
103
104           !* ) eval `expr "$ANSWER" : "!\(.*\)"`
105                   ;;
106
107           "?" )echo ""
108                   if [ "$_HELPMSG" = "" ]; then
109                           echo "No help available."
110                   else
111                           echo "$_HELPMSG"
112                   fi
113                   echo ""
114                   ;;
115
116           * ) break
117                   ;;
118           esac
119    done
120  }
```

This is the granddaddy of all question and answer functions. It incorporates just about every feature you can imagine. One of the disadvantages of providing so many options in a function such as this is that a legitimate answer entered by the user might accidentally have a special meaning to the function. You might want to use this function as a template of what is possible and create your own function that only has the features that you need.

This function is designed to give the user a lot of flexibility in answering the question. A default answer is provided and help text is available if the user does not understand the question. If the user is really lost, they can enter `quit` to leave the shell script entirely.

When this function is called, it must be passed exactly three parameters. Be sure to quote the parameters since, in all likelihood, they will contain whitespace. The first parameter is the question to be asked. The second parameter is the default answer. This answer will be returned if the user enters return without an answer. The third parameter is a message that will be printed if the user enters a question mark. This is intended to be a helpful message that will provide more information to help the user answer the question.

For example:

```
FILENAME=core
QUESTION="Remove $FILENAME"
DEFAULT="yes"
HELPMSG="The file $FILENAME is going to be
removed.  Is that OK?"

Question "$QUESTION" "$DEFAULT" "$HELPMSG"
if [ "$ANSWER" = "yes" ]; then
    . . .
fi
```

Lines 55–59 ensure that exactly three parameters are passed to this function. If this check fails, a message is printed and the function exits.

Lines 60–63 define the variables that are used in this function. It is not necessary to define a variable before it is used, but it is a common practice to list the significant variables near the beginning of the function with a simple comment describing their purpose.

Lines 61 and 63 copy the default answer and the help message from the positional parameters to variables with more descriptive names.

Lines 65–69 copy the question to the variable _QUESTION. If a default answer was passed to this function, it is enclosed in brackets and appended to the question. Then a question mark and a space are appended to the question.

Line 71 begins a loop that will be repeated until the function gets an answer. The conditional test is the null command (:), which always returns true. Therefore, this loop can only be terminated by executing a break, exit, or return command somewhere in the loop.

Lines 73–77 print the message each time the loop is executed. The message will be printed without a newline so that the cursor remains at the end of the question waiting for the user to enter an answer. Since the method for suppressing the newline is different on different systems, line 73 performs a test to see which method to use. These lines could be replaced with the Prompt function discussed earlier in this chapter.

Line 78 reads the standard input for the answer. The current process will block until the user enters an answer and presses the return key. When the process resumes, the answer will be in the variable ANSWER.

Line 79 begins a case statement that evaluates the answer. This statement also downshifts the answer so that if the user enters an answer that has special meaning to this function, the case of that answer can be ignored. For example, quit, QUIT, or Quit can be entered to exit the command file.

Lines 80–84 will be executed if the user presses the enter key without entering an answer. This function interprets this action to mean that the user accepts the default answer. If the function was passed a default answer, it is copied to the variable ANSWER and the `break` statement terminates the loop. If a default answer was not provided, the loop will continue and the question will be repeated.

  Lines 86–89 and 91–94 process the answer if the user enters yes, y, no, or n. When this function is used for yes or no questions, ANSWER will be set to yes or no, regardless of how the answer was entered. For example, if the user enters "Y", the answer returned by this function will be yes. Notice that if the user pressed return to accept the default answer, the default answer is returned unaltered. Therefore, to simplify testing the answer, be sure to specify the default answer for yes or no questions as yes or no, rather than y or Yes, etc.

  For yes or no questions, you can also use the GetYesNo function presented earlier in this chapter.

  Lines 96–98 exit the shell script if the user enters q or quit. This causes the entire shell script to be exited. If there is cleanup to be performed, you can set a trap handler to catch signal 0. (See "Using Signals" in Chapter 5 for more information on processing signals.)

  Lines 100–102 are used to enable (-x) and disable (+x), the debugging option of the shell. When one of these options is entered, it is simply passed on to the set command to set the corresponding option in the shell. After setting the option, the question is repeated.

  Lines 104–105 allow the user to enter UNIX commands. The leading ! is removed from the answer, and the remainder of the answer is executed by the shell as a command. Do not forget that the shell script may have changed directories, set the PATH variables, or altered the environment in some way. For example, if the shell script has changed directories, and the user enters an ls command, the user may be confused by the output. After the UNIX command is executed, the question is repeated.

  Lines 107–114 print the help message if the user enters a question mark. If the shell script did not pass a help message to this function, the message "No help available." is printed. Notice that the question mark on line 107 must be quoted to prevent it from being interpreted as a pattern matching character. After printing the help message, the question is repeated.

  Line 116 is executed if none of the previous cases are satisfied. This is the case that is normally executed. That is, this case is executed when the user enters an answer to the question. Since the answer is already in the variable ANSWER, there is nothing to do but exit the loop and return to the caller.

## STRCMP FUNCTION

```
1
2   #
3   # File: StrCmp.sh
4   #
5
6   StrCmp() {
```

```
 7      #
 8      # NAME
 9      #     StrCmp - compare two strings
10      #
11      # SYNOPSIS
12      #     StrCmp string1 string2
13      #
14      # DESCRIPTION
15      #     This function returns -1, 0, or 1 to indicate
16      #     whether string1 is lexicographically less than,
17      #     equal to, or greater than string2. The return
18      #     value is written to the standard output, not the
19      #     exit status.
20      #
21      if [ $# -ne 2 ]; then
22              echo "Usage: StrCmp string1 string2" 1>&2
23              exit 1
24      fi
25
26      if [ "$1" = "$2" ]; then
27              echo "0"
28      else
29              _TMP=`{ echo "$1"; echo "$2"; }|sort|sed -n '1p'`
30
31              if [ "$_TMP" = "$1" ]; then
32                      echo "-1"
33              else
34                      echo "1"
35              fi
36      fi
37  }
```

This function can be used to compare two strings lexicographically. It is similar to the strcmp routine in libc.a. The following example shows how you could use this function:

```
case `StrCmp "string1" "string2"` in
    -1 )    echo "string1 is less than string2."       ;;
     0 )    echo "string1 is equal to string2."        ;;
     1 )    echo "string1 is greater than string2."    ;;
     * )    echo "StrCmp failed."                       ;;
esac
```

Lines 21–24 ensure that the function is called with the correct number of parameters. If this check fails, a message is printed and the function exits.

Since the return value of this function is written to its standard output, it will probably be executed in back quotes so that the standard output can be captured in a variable.

Remember that most versions of the shell will execute this function in a subshell (see "Function Execution" earlier in Chapter 3) so the `exit` statement will behave the same as a `return` statement in this situation. Therefore, the example above includes a case value to catch values other than -1, 0, and 1. If there is an error, the error message will be written to the standard error and the standard output will be empty.

Line 26 tests to see if the strings are equal. If they are, line 27 writes the number 0 to the standard output.

If the strings are not equal, lines 29 to 35 will be executed.

Line 29 uses the `sort` command to sort the strings so that the string that is lexicographically less than the other will be the first line in the output from the `sort` command. The output of the `sort` command is piped to a `sed` filter that is used to print only the first of the two lines written by the `sort` command. The string `1p` in the `sed` command is the number one (not the letter ell) followed by the letter p.

The entire pipeline on line 29 is enclosed in back quotes so that its standard output can be captured in the variable _TMP.

Line 31 compares the string stored in the variable _TMP with the first string. If they are equal, the first string is lexicographically less than the second string. In this case, line 32 writes the number -1 to the standard output. Otherwise, line 34 writes the number 1 to the standard output.


## SYSTEMTYPE FUNCTION

```
1
2  #
3  # File: SystemType.sh
4  #
5
6  SystemType() {
7         #
8         # NAME
9         #     SystemType - return the type of the system
10        #
11        # SYNOPSIS
12        #     SystemType
13        #
14        # DESCRIPTION
15        #     This function determines the type of the system on
16        #     which it is executing and returns one of the
17        #     following strings:
18        #
19        #         AIX        DECOSF   HP         SCO
20        #         SGI        SOLARIS  SUNBSD     ULTRIX
21        #
22        #     ULTRIX is returned for Digital Equipment's older
23        #     BSD systems and DECOSF is returned for their OSF
```

```
24      #       based systems.
25      #
26      #       SUNBSD is returned for Sun BSD systems (versions
27      #       4.*) and SOLARIS is returned for Sun System V
28      #       systems (versions 5.*).
29      #
30      #       If this function is unable to determine the type
31      #       of the system, it will return an empty string.
32      #
33      _HOSTNAME=`hostname | sed 's/\..*//'`
34
35      case `uname -s` in
36          AIX )           echo AIX                    ;;
37          HP-UX )         echo HP                     ;;
38          IRIX )          echo SGI                    ;;
39          OSF1 )          echo DECOSF                 ;;
40          ULTRIX )        echo ULTRIX                 ;;
41          SunOS )         case `uname -r` in
42                              4*)   echo SUNBSD   ;;
43                              5*)   echo SOLARIS  ;;
44                          esac
45                          ;;
46          $_HOSTNAME )    case `uname -m` in
47                              IP*)    echo SGI   ;;
48                              i386)   echo SCO   ;;
49                          esac
50                          ;;
51      esac
52  }
```

This function is the reverse of the `IsSystemType` function discussed earlier. Instead of the caller specifying a string and the function checking it, this function returns a string and the caller checks it. For example,

```
case `SystemType` in
    HP )        ... ;;
    SGI )       ... ;;
    SOLARIS )   ... ;;
    * ) echo "Unexpected type of system." 1>&2
        exit 1
        ;;
esac
```

The strings returned by `uname` are frequently changed by the vendors so that they accurately reflect information describing the current system. Thus, this function has the advantage over the `IsSystemType` function that the dependency on the strings returned by `uname` is centralized. In addition, the criteria for identifying the system can be tailored to your specific needs.

Line 33 uses the `hostname` command to get the name of the current system. On some systems, the value returned by `hostname` also contains the domain name. Therefore, a `sed` script is used to remove anything following and including a period.

The value returned by the `uname -s` command is used to make the first attempt at identifying the system. On line 35, this value is used in a `case` statement to select one of several systems. If it is `AIX`, `HP-UX`, `IRIX`, `OSF1`, or `ULTRIX`, then we can identify the system and return the proper string.

However, if the value is `SunOS`, we need to determine whether the system is a Sun BSD system or a Sun Solaris system. Lines 41–45 check the revision number of the operating system. Beginning with revision 5.0, SunOS changed from BSD based system to System V (Solaris) based system.

Also, some systems return the name of the current system rather than the name of the operating system for the `-s` option of `uname`. The field is supposed to be the "system name," which is somewhat ambiguous. Most vendors interpret the "system name" to be the name of the operating system and the "node name" to be the name of the system as defined by the user. I have seen two systems that return the name of the system as defined by the user for the command `uname -s`:

- SGI's IRIX version 3.3 and before; newer versions of IRIX return the string `IRIX` for the command `uname -s`.
- As of version 3.2 of SCO's operating system, it still returned the name of the system as defined by the user for `uname -s`.

Lines 46–50 are executed if this problem occurs. In this case, these two systems are distinguished using the machine hardware name that is returned by `uname -m`.

# 10

# *Examples of Shell Scripts*

This chapter shows several examples of complete shell scripts. These examples range from simple scripts, such as the `Cat` command, to fairly complex scripts, such as the `Kill` command.

The names of some of the commands in this chapter contain upper case letters. While this is not common practice on UNIX systems, these commands resemble some other UNIX command with a similar name. The similarity in names is intended to draw attention to the UNIX commands they resemble.

| | |
|---|---|
| `Cat` | Concatenate files |
| `DirCmp` | Compare the files in one directory with those in another |
| `Kill` | Kill a process (send signal) by name |
| `MkDir` | Create a directory and any missing path components |
| `Shar` | Create a shell archive |
| `Wc` | Recursive version of the `wc` command |
| `addcolumn` | Add a column of numbers |
| `dircopy` | Copy the contents of a directory |
| `findcmd` | Search the directories in the `PATH` variable for a command |
| `findfile` | Recursively search for a file |

findstr          Recursively search for files that contain a string
hostaddr         Return the IP address for a system
ptree            Print a process tree

## CAT COMMAND

```
 1   #!/bin/sh
 2   #
 3   # NAME
 4   #    Cat - concatenate files
 5   #
 6   # SYNOPSIS
 7   #    Cat [file ...]
 8   #
 9   # DESCRIPTION
10   #    This command concatinates the files by reading each
11   #    file in sequence and writing it to the standard output.
12   #
13   # RETURN VALUE
14   #    0    Successful completion
15   #    1    One or more files were not found
16   #
17   ##############################################################
18   ERROR=0                # Has there been an error (0=no, 1=yes)
19   LINE=                  # Line read from file
20
21   while [ $# -gt 0 ]
22   do
23       if [ ! -r "$1" ]; then
24           echo "Cannot find file $1" 1>&2
25           ERROR=1
26       else
27           IFS=
28           while read LINE
29           do
30               echo "$LINE"
31           done <"$1"
32       fi
33       shift
34   done
35
36   exit $ERROR
```

This command is similar to the UNIX cat command. The command has little
practical value, but it is included here because it is a simple shell script, and, therefore, it
is a good place to discuss some of the basics concepts of the shell script.

Line 1 contains the string that must begin all shell scripts to ensure that they are executed by the program /bin/sh, which is the Bourne shell. This line was discussed in "Identifying Shell Scripts" in Chapter 5.

Lines 2–17 are comments that describe the shell script. The format of the information is similar to a manual page. It contains a simple description, a description of the syntax, a detailed description, and the meaning of the status returned by the shell script. Since the comment is stored in the front of the shell script, it will never become lost or separated from the shell script.

Lines 18 and 19 define the variables that are used in the shell script. It is not necessary to define a variable before it is used, but it is a common practice to list the variables in the beginning of the shell script with a simple comment describing their purpose. The IFS variable is not defined here because it is predefined by the shell in every shell script.

Lines 21–34 are a while loop that is executed once for each file name that was entered on the command line. The variable $# contains the number of parameters, or in this case, the number of file names. The variable $1 contains the name of the file currently being processed. After each file is copied, the shift, on line 33, deletes the first positional parameter and decrements $#. This moves the next file name to $1.

Notice that $1 is quoted in lines 23 and 31. This is just a precaution in case the file name contains an unusual character such as a space or tab.

Line 23 checks that file is readable. If it is not, a message is printed to the standard error and the variable ERROR is set to one to record the error. Rather than exiting the shell script when there is an error, the shell script skips the file and continues with the next file.

On line 27, the IFS variable is set to be empty. This prevents the read command from interpreting the information as it is read from the file. While not always necessary, it is good practice to restore the IFS variable immediately after you have used it. Since it is not necessary in this example, it has been left out.

Lines 28–31 are a loop that reads the file one line at a time. On line 31, the standard input of the loop is redirected to the file named in $1. The read command will return a successful exit status until the end of the file is reached. On line 30, each line is written to the standard output using the echo command.

Line 36 exits the shell script and sets the command exit status to the value stored in the variable ERROR. This variable is initially set to zero, but it will be set to one if any file is not found or cannot be read.

## DIRCMP COMMAND

```
1  #!/bin/sh
2  #
3  #  NAME
4  #     DirCmp - compare the files in two directories
5  #
```

```
 6  # SYNOPSIS
 7  #     DirCmp [-v] dir1] dir2
 8  #
 9  # DESCRIPTION
10  #     This command compares the files in two directories and
11  #     lists the files that are not the same.  There will be
12  #     three separate lists for:
13  #
14  #     1. Files not in the first directory, but in the second
15  #     2. Files not in the second directory, but in the first
16  #     3. Files in both directories, but not the same
17  #
18  #     -v  Verbose option.  This option prints the lines that
19  #         are different, rather than just the name of the
20  #         file when the file is in both directories, but the
21  #         files are not the same.
22  #
23  # RETURN VALUE
24  #     0   The directories are the same
25  #     1   Usage error or abnormal termination
26  #     2   The directories are not the same
27  #
28  ################################################################
29  CMDNAME=`basename $0`
30  USAGE="Usage: $CMDNAME [-v] [dir1] dir2"
31
32  CURDIR=`pwd`                      # Current directory
33  DIR1=                             # Source directory
34  DIR2=                             # Target directory
35  DIR1_FILES=/tmp/files1.$$         # Files in dir1
36  DIR2_FILES=/tmp/files2.$$         # Files in dir2
37  ALL_FILES=/tmp/allfiles.$$        # Files in dir1 or dir2
38  COMMON_FILES=/tmp/comfiles.$$ # Files in dir1 and dir2
39  TMP=/tmp/tmp.$$                   # Temporary file
40  FOUND=FALSE                       # Differences found?
41  FIRST=
42  VERBOSE=FALSE
43
44  trap 'rm -f /tmp/*.$$; exit 1' 1 2 3 15
45
46  #
47  # Parse the command options.
48  #
49  while :
50  do
51      case $1 in
52              -v)  VERBOSE=TRUE
```

```
53                     shift
54               ;;
55          --)  shift
56               break
57               ;;
58          -*)  echo "$USAGE" 1>&2
59               exit 1
60               ;;
61          *)   break
62               ;;
63     esac
64 done
65
66 #
67 # Get command line parameters.
68 #
69 if [ $# -eq 1 ]; then
70      DIR1="."
71      DIR2="$1"
72 elif [ $# -eq 2 ]; then
73      DIR1="$1"
74      DIR2="$2"
75 else
76      echo "$USAGE" 1>&2
77      exit 1
78 fi
79
80 #
81 # Check the directories.
82 #
83 if [ ! -d $DIR1 ]; then
84      echo "$DIR1 is not a directory." 1>&2
85      exit 2
86 fi
87
88 if [ ! -d $DIR2 ]; then
89      echo "$DIR2 is not a directory." 1>&2
90      exit 2
91 fi
92
93 #
94 # Find the files to compare.
95 #
96 cd $DIR1
97 find . \( -type f -o -type l \) -print | sort >$DIR1_FILES
98 cd $CURDIR
99
```

```
100  cd $DIR2
101  find . \( -type f -o -type 1 \) -print | sort >$DIR2_FILES
102  cd $CURDIR
103
104  #
105  # Build a list of all files.
106  #
107  cat $DIR1_FILES $DIR2_FILES | sort | uniq    >$ALL_FILES
108  cat $DIR1_FILES $DIR2_FILES | sort | uniq -d >$COMMON_FILES
109
110  #
111  # Print the files that are in dir2, but not in dir1.
112  #
113  cat $DIR1_FILES $ALL_FILES | sort | uniq -u >$TMP
114  if [ -s $TMP ]; then
115       FOUND=TRUE
116       echo ""
117       echo "Files missing from $DIR1:"
118       for f in `cat $TMP`
119       do
120             f=`expr $f : '..\(.*\)'`
121             echo "   $f"
122       done
123  fi
124
125  #
126  # Print the files that are in dir1, but not in dir2.
127  #
128  cat $DIR2_FILES $ALL_FILES | sort | uniq -u >$TMP
129  if [ -s $TMP ]; then
130       FOUND=TRUE
131       echo ""
132       echo "Files missing from $DIR2:"
133       for f in `cat $TMP`
134       do
135         f=`expr $f : '..\(.*\)'`
136         echo "   $f"
137       done
138  fi
139
140  #
141  # Print the files that are in dir1 and dir2, but are not
142  # the same.
143  #
144  FIRST=TRUE
145  for f in `cat $COMMON_FILES`
```

```
146  do
147        cmp -s $DIR1/$f $DIR2/$f
148        if [ $? -ne 0 ]; then
149              FOUND=TRUE
150              f=`expr $f : '..\(.*\)'`
151              if [ "$FIRST" = "TRUE" ]; then
152                    FIRST=FALSE
153                    echo ""
154                    echo "Files that are not the same:"
155              fi
156
157              if [ "$VERBOSE" = "TRUE" ]; then
158                    echo ""
159                    echo "File: $f"
160                    diff $DIR1/$f $DIR2/$f
161              else
162                    echo "     $f"
163              fi
164        fi
165  done
166
167  rm -f /tmp/*.$$
168  if [ $FOUND = TRUE]; then
169        exit 2
170  else
171        echo "The directories are the same."
172        exit 0
173  fi
```

You can use this command to compare two directories to see what changes have been made. For example, you can use this command to compare two versions of a product installation.

In lines 29–42, assign initial values to the significant variables used in this shell script and provide a brief comment describing the purpose of each variable.

Lines 29 and 30 define the usage message for this command. Line 29 gets the name of this command from the command line. This is used to keep the usage message accurate even if this command is renamed.

On lines 35–39, the names of the temporary files are appended with the suffix $$. The $$ will be replaced with the process ID of this command when it is executed. This ensures that the temporary file names will be unique so that two simultaneous executions of this shell script will not use the same temporary files.

Shell scripts that use resources that need to be released when the shell script exits must ensure that the resources are released even when the shell script exits unexpectedly. Line 44 uses the `trap` command to specify the commands that are to be executed if signal

1, 2, 3, or 15 is received. This command will ensure that any files in the /tmp directory that end with the process ID of the current process are removed before this process exits.

Lines 49–64 parse the command options. This is the parsing technique that was described in "When getopts Is Not Available" in Chapter 6. The DirCmp command only has one option, -v, but this section of code also parses the standard options as well.

Lines 69–78 process the command line parameters. The calling sequence for the command is very simple; there will either be one or two parameters. If there are two parameters, they are the names of the first and second directories, respectively. When there is only one parameter, the current directory is the first directory and the parameter is the name of the second directory.

Lines 83–91 ensure that both directories exist.

Lines 96–102 generate a sorted list of the files in each directory. It is necessary to change the current directory to each directory before generating the list so that the find command will print the relative names of the files in each directory. This is necessary so that the names of the corresponding files in the two directories will be listed the same. After the lists of file names are generated, the command returns to the original directory.

Lines 107–108 generate two new lists—a list of all the files in either directory and a list of the files that are in both directories. The cat command is used to merge the file names from both directories. Since the uniq command only examines adjacent lines, the input to uniq must be sorted. On line 107, the uniq command filters the list of files so that we have a list of files that are in either directory. On line 108, the -d option of the uniq command is used to list the names of each file name that is not unique; that is, it is in both directories.

Lines 113–123 print the names of the files that are in the second directory but not in the first directory. This is done by comparing the file names in the first directory with the names of all the files and listing the files that are only listed once using the -u option of the uniq command. The file names found are written to a temporary file. If the temporary file is not empty, a heading is printed followed by the file names. Line 120 removes the first two characters from the file name before it is printed. When the names were generated by the find command, they were prefixed with the directory name, which was ./ at the time.

Lines 128–138 print the names of the files that are in the first directory but not in the second directory.

Lines 144–165 print the names of the files that are in both directories but are not the same. The list of files that are in both directories was created in line 108. Line 145 is a for loop that is executed once for each of the files. The corresponding file in each directory is compared using the cmp command on line 147. If the files are not the same, an unsuccessful status will cause lines 148–164 to be executed. These lines print a heading and the name of the files that are not the same. If the verbose option is used, the diff command is used to print out the differences between the files.

Line 167 removes all temporary files created by this command.

Lines 168–173 exit with the proper message and exit status, based on whether or not any differences were found.

## KILL COMMAND

```
 1  #!/bin/sh
 2  #
 3  # NAME
 4  #     Kill - kill a process (send a signal) by name
 5  #
 6  # SYNOPSIS
 7  #     Kill [-signal] ProcessName
 8  #
 9  # DESCRIPTION
10  #     This command will send a signal to any process with the
11  #     name ProcessName.  The user will be asked for
12  #     conformation before sending the signal to the process.
13  #
14  #     -signal
15  #          Specifies the signal to send to the process.  Any
16  #          value that is accepted by the kill(1) command may
17  #          be specified.  For example, either -9 or -KILL can
18  #          be used to send signal nine to the process.  If
19  #          this option is not used, signal 15 (TERM) will be
20  #          sent to the process.
21  #
22  # RETURN VALUE
23  #     0     Successful completion
24  #     1     Usage error or abnormal termination
25  #
26  ##############################################################
27  PATH=$PATH:`dirname $0`
28
29  . SystemType.sh
30  . GetYesNo.sh
31
32  CMDNAME=`basename $0`
33  USAGE="Usage: $CMDNAME [-signal] ProcessName"
34  OLD_IFS=$IFS            # Original value of IFS variable
35  SIGNAL=                 # Optional signal; see kill(1)
36  NAME=                   # Name of process to kill
37  PID=                    # PID of process being checked
38  PROCNAME=               # Name of process being checked
39  OWNER=                  # Owner of process being checked
40  PS_OPTS=                # Options for ps command
41  PROCESS_LIST=/tmp/list.$$ # Output of ps command
42  TITLE_PRINTED=FALSE     # Title printed? (TRUE or FALSE)
43  FOUND=FALSE             # Found matching process?
44  LINE=                   # Single line of output from ps
45  COL=                    # Column where process name begins
46  SYSTEM= `SystemType`    # String identifying the system
```

```
47
48   trap 'rm -f /tmp/*.$$; exit 1' 1 2 3 15
49
50   #
51   # Get and check the command line parameters.
52   #
53   case $1 in
54        --)  shift
55             ;;
56        -*)  SIGNAL=$1      # Leave the hyphen
57             shift
58             ;;
59   esac
60   if [ $# -ne 1 ]; then
61        echo "$USAGE" 1>&2
62        exit 1
63   fi
64
65   NAME=$1           # Get the name of the process to kill.
66
67   #
68   # Determine which options to use with the ps command.
69   #
70   case $SYSTEM in
71        SUNBSD | ULTRIX )   PS_OPTS="-auxw"     ;;
72        * )                 PS_OPTS="-ef"       ;;
73   esac
74
75   #
76   # Get a list of the current processes and filter out the
77   # lines that do not contain the process we are looking for.
78   #
79   ps $PS_OPTS               |
80        sed '1d'             |      # Remove the title line
81        grep "$NAME"         |      # Eliminate the chaff
83        grep -v "$0"         |      # Eliminate this process
83        grep -v "ps $PS_OPTS"    >$PROCESS_LIST
84
85   #
86   # Check each process.
87   #
88   exec <$PROCESS_LIST
89   IFS=
90   while read LINE
91   do
92        IFS=$OLD_IFS
93        #
94        # Get the owner, PID, and name of the process.
```

```
 95        #
 96        set $LINE
 97        OWNER=$1
 98        PID=$2
 99
100        #
101        # Determine the column where the process name begins.
102        #
103        case $SYSTEM in
104              AIX | HP | SGI | SOLARIS )    COL=48 ;;
105              SUNBSD | DECOSF )             COL=57 ;;
106              ULTRIX )                      COL=51 ;;
107              * )  echo "Unexpected system type." 1>&2
108                     exit 1
109                     ;;
110        esac
111
112        LINE=`echo "$LINE" | cut -c$COL-`
113        set dummy $LINE
114        shift
115        PROCNAME=$1
116
117        if [ "$PROCNAME" = "$NAME" -o \
118              "`basename $PROCNAME`" = "$NAME" ]; then
119
120              FOUND=TRUE
121
122              #
123              # Print title.
124              #
125              if [ "$TITLE_PRINTED" = "FALSE" ]; then
126                     echo "PID Owner     Process"
127                     TITLE_PRINTED=TRUE
128              fi
129
130              #
131              # Ask user.
132              #
133              if GetYesNo \
134                  "$PID  $OWNER  $PROCNAME (y/n)? "  </dev/tty
135              then
136                     kill $SIGNAL $PID
137              fi
138        fi
139        IFS=
140   done
141
142   if [ "$FOUND" = "FALSE" ]; then
```

```
143        echo "Process \"$NAME\" not found."
144  fi
145
146  rm -f /tmp/*.$$
147  exit 0
```

This command has been written many times in slightly different variations. A simplified version of this command was shown in "Killing a Process by Name" in Chapter 8.

Line 27 adds the directory where this shell script is stored to the PATH variable. This is a technique that was discussed in "Reusing Functions" in Chapter 3. It is used in this shell script to allow it to include the files SystemType.sh and GetYesNo.sh on lines 29 and 30.

Lines 29 and 30 use the dot command to include the declarations for the System-Type function and the GetYesNo function. These functions are described in Chapter 9.

Lines 32–46 assign initial values to the significant variables used in this shell script and provide a brief comment describing the purpose of each variable.

Lines 32 and 33 define the usage message for this command. Line 32 gets the name of this command from the command line. This is used to keep the usage message accurate even if this command is renamed.

On line 41, PROCESS_LIST is assigned the name of a temporary file that will be used to hold the output from the ps command. The $$ suffix on the file name will be substituted with the process ID of this command when it is executed. This creates a unique temporary file name so that two simultaneous executions of this command will not use the same temporary file.

On line 46, SYSTEM is assigned the string returned by the function SystemType. This function was defined on line 29 by executing the file SystemType.sh.

Shell scripts that use resources that need to be released when the shell script exits must ensure that the resources are released even when the shell script exits unexpectedly. Line 48 uses the trap command to specify the commands that are to be executed if signal 1, 2, 3, or 15 is received. This command will ensure that any files in the /tmp directory that end with the process ID of the current process are removed before the process exits.

Lines 53–59 process the command line options. The calling sequence for this command is similar to the UNIX kill command. Other than the -- option, the only option that is allowed is the name or number of the signal to send to the process. If an option other than -- is passed to this command, it must be the signal; therefore, it will be saved in the variable SIGNAL so that it can be passed on to the kill command later in the shell script.

Once the command option has been removed from the command line, lines 60–63 ensure that there is exactly one parameter on the command line, namely, the name of the process to kill.

Line 65 copies the name of the process from the command line to the variable NAME. This is a more descriptive name for the variable, and it also allows the positional parameters to be reused later in the shell script.

Lines 70–73 determine which options should be used with the ps command. If the system is a BSD system (SUNBSD or ULTRIX), the -auwx options are used with the ps command; otherwise, the -ef options are used. These options are saved in the variable PS_OPTS.

Lines 79–83 use the ps command to get a list of the processes that are currently executing on the system. The output of the ps command is piped to several filters that remove most of the lines that do not contain the name of the process to kill. The purpose of these filters is to remove as much of the output from the ps command as possible because these filters are much faster than the while loop that processes the rest of the output.

Line 80 deletes the first line of the output, which is the title line from the ps command.

Line 81 removes any line that does not contain the name of the process.

Line 82 removes the line for the current process to prevent this shell script from being able to kill itself. The name of the current process is actually /bin/sh, but the name of the shell script, saved in $0, is also listed in the output of the ps command.

Line 83 removes the line for the ps command, which sometimes shows up in its own output. This is also the final stage in the pipeiine. The output of the pipeline is written to a temporary file, the name of which is stored in the variable PROCESS_LIST.

Line 88 causes the standard input of the shell script to be redirected to the file just created. This technique was discussed in "Reading Files" in Chapter 4. It is used here, rather than redirecting the standard input of the while loop in lines 90–140, so that the loop will not be executed in a subshell. This, in turn, is necessary so that the value of the variable FOUND is not lost after the loop completes.

Line 89 sets the IFS variable to be empty. This forces the read command to read the standard input without removing any whitespace from the line. This is necessary in order to be able to locate the process name. The number of fields before the process name is not always the same, but the process name always starts in a particular column.

Line 90 begins a while loop that reads the standard input one line at a time.

Line 92 restores the original value of the IFS variable so that other commands inside the while loop will not be adversely affected. On line 139, the IFS variable will be set to empty again, just before the next line is read.

Line 96 uses the set command to parse the line that was just read and loads the fields into the positional parameters. The only fields that are needed are the process ID and the owner. The process name cannot be extracted using a field position because the process name is not always in the same field position. This happens because the fields in the output of the ps command sometimes run together without leaving interleaving whitespace.

Lines 97 and 98 get the owner and the process ID of the process. These values are always in the first two fields in the output of the ps command.

Lines 103–110 determine where the name of the process begins in the output from the ps command. The case statement is used because, depending upon the type of the system, the process name begins in a different column.

Line 112 removes the front of the line so that the process name is moved to the front.

Line 113 uses the `set` command to parse the rest of the line. Since the fields in the line are separated by whitespace, each field will be loaded into the corresponding positional parameter. The "dummy" parameter is used here in case the name of the process begins with a hyphen. This technique is discussed in "The `set` Command" in Chapter 12; it is a portable method to prevent the `set` command from interpreting a value beginning with a hyphen as an option. The `shift` command following the `set` command removes the dummy parameter.

Line 115 copies the process name to the variable `PROCNAME`.

Lines 117 and 118 compare the name of the process with the name of the process to kill. Line 118 allows the user to specify the simple file name of the process to kill even if the name of the process is a full path name.

Line 120 sets a flag variable to record whether the process was found. This is used later in lines 142–144 to determine whether or not to print a message.

Lines 125–128 print a title line for the confirmation question. The whitespace between the words in the title are tab characters. The variable `TITLE_PRINTED` is used to prevent the title from being printed more than once if more than one process is found.

Line 133 uses the `GetYesNo` function to ask the user to confirm that the process should be killed. The `GetYesNo` function was defined on line 30 by executing the file `GetYesNo.sh`. Notice that the standard input of the function is redirected to `/dev/tty`. This is necessary since the standard input of the current process was redirected on line 88 to read from the temporary file that contains the output of the `ps` command. The device `/dev/tty` is a generic device that refers to the user's terminal.

The whitespace between the process ID, owner, and process name are tab characters. This causes these values to line up with the labels in the title line.

If the user answers yes to the question, line 136 kills the process. Since the `kill` command uses the same signal option as this command, the value of `SIGNAL` is passed to the `kill` command. Since `SIGNAL` is not quoted, it will disappear after the variable is substituted into the command line if its value is empty. The other parameter to the `kill` command is the process ID of the process to kill. This value was saved in the variable `PID` on line 98.

Line 139 sets the `IFS` variable to be empty again. This is necessary since the `read` command is about to be executed to read the next line from the file.

Lines 142–144 print a message if the process to kill was not found.

Line 146 removes the temporary file created by this process.

## MKDIR COMMAND

```
1  #!/bin/sh
2  #
3  # NAME
4  #    MkDir - create a directory and missing path components
5  #
6  # SYNOPSIS
```

```
 7  #     MkDir directory
 8  #
 9  # DESCRIPTION
10  #     This command will create the directory and any missing
11  #     path components leading up to the directory.
12  #
13  # RETURN VALUE
14  #     0     Successful completion
15  #     >0    Usage error or error status returned from the
16  #           mkdir command
17  #
18  ##################################################################
19  CMDNAME=`basename $0`
20  if [ $# -ne 1 ]; then
21          echo "Usage: $CMDNAME directory" 1>&2
22          exit 1
23  fi
24
25  case $1 in
26          /*)  DIR=        ;;
27          *)   DIR=.       ;;
28  esac
29
30  IFS=/
31  for d in $1
32  do
33          DIR="$DIR/$d"
34          if [ ! -d "$DIR" ]; then
35                  mkdir "$DIR"
36                  if [ $? -ne 0 ]; then
37                          exit $?
38                  fi
39          fi
40  done
41
42  exit 0
```

You may occasionally want to create a directory whose parent does not exist. On many systems, the `-p` option to `mkdir` provides this functionality. However, if you are on a system that does not have this capability, you can use this command.[1]

Since this command uses the `mkdir` command to create each missing directory in the hierarchy, the normal file system protection behaves as you would expect. Similarly, if this command fails, the error message will be printed by `mkdir`, and the status returned by this command will be the status returned from `mkdir`.

---

[1] On some systems, the `mkdir -p` command does not work on NFS mounted directories.

Lines 20–23 ensure that exactly one parameter is passed to this command. Line 19 gets the name of this command from the command line. This is used to keep the usage message accurate even if this command is renamed.

Lines 25–28 determine if the directory name begins at the root directory (/) or the current directory. This information is used to determine the initial value of DIR.

Line 30 changes the IFS variable to contain the slash (/) character. This will cause the for statement on line 31 to parse the word list into words, using a slash as the delimiter. Since the word list ($1) is a path name, the words processed by the for statement will be the components of the path.

Line 31 uses a for statement to parse the directory name. Since the word list is parsed into words separated by slashes, the variable d will be set to the next node in the directory path during each successive iteration of the loop.

On line 33, the current node, d, is appended to the portion of the path that has already been checked, DIR.

On line 34, the new path is tested to see if it exists as a directory. If it does not, it is created using the mkdir command. If mkdir fails, any message that it prints is printed to the standard error of the shell script, and the shell script exits using the status returned by mkdir.

When the for loop finishes, each node will have been tested and created if necessary.

## SHAR COMMAND

```
 1  #!/bin/sh
 2  #
 3  # NAME
 4  #    Shar - create a shell archive
 5  #
 6  # SYNOPSIS
 7  #    Shar file ...
 8  #
 9  # DESCRIPTION
10  #    This command creates a shell archive that contains the
11  #    files listed on the command line.  The shell archive
12  #    is written to the standard output.  To unpack the
13  #    archive, enter the following command, where archive is
14  #    the name of the shell archive.
15  #
16  #         sh archive
17  #
18  # RETURN VALUE
19  #    0    Successful completion
20  #    1    Usage error
21  #
22  ################################################################
23  CMDNAME=`basename $0`
```

```
24  if [ $# -lt 1 ]; then
25          echo "Usage: $CMDNAME file ..." 1>&2
26          exit 1
27  fi
28
29  echo "#!/bin/sh"
30  echo "# This is a shell archive; to unpack:"
31  echo "# 1. Remove everything before the \"#!/bin/sh\"."
32  echo "# 2. Save the rest of the archive."
33  echo "# 3. Execute the archive by entering \"sh archive\"."
34  echo "#"
35  echo "# This archive contains the following files:"
36  echo "#"
37
38  for FILE
39  do
40          echo "#      $FILE"
41  done
42
43  for FILE
44  do
45          echo ""
46          echo "if [ -f $FILE ]; then"
47          echo "    echo The file $FILE already exists."
48          echo "else"
49          echo "    echo Extracting $FILE"
50          echo "    sed 's/^X//' >$FILE  <<\EOF"
51          sed 's/^/X/' <$FILE
52          echo "EOF"
53          echo "fi"
54  done
55  echo "exit 0"
56
57  exit 0
```

This is a very simple version of the UNIX shar command, which is used to create shell archives. A shell archive is a collection of files that have been packed together into a single file, or shell archive. It is called a shell archive, because the archive can be unpacked to produce the original files by simply executing the following command.

```
sh archive
```

That is, it is created in such a way that it itself is a shell command that when executed will unpack itself. Shell archives are frequently used to send one or more files to another user via electronic mail.

Lines 24–27 ensure that at least one file name is passed to this command. Line 23 gets the name of this command from the command line. This is used to keep the usage message accurate even if this command is renamed.

Lines 29–36 write a standard comment into the front of the archive. This comment tells the user how to unpack the archive.

Lines 38–41 add the names of the files inside the archive to the comment at the front of the archive.

Lines 43–54 copy each file named on the command line into the archive.

Line 45 puts a blank line before each file in the archive.

Lines 46–50 put some shell commands in front of each file in the archive. These commands will be executed when the archive is unpacked. These commands will ensure that the file being unpacked does not already exist, and they will print the name of the file as it is being unpacked.

Line 50 puts a `sed` command into the archive that will copy the file from the archive. When the file is copied into the archive on line 51, each line is prefixed with an X. The purpose of this is to prevent the mail system from interpreting any of the lines in the file as a mail header directive. The `sed` command on line 50 removes the X from the beginning of each line as the file is copied from the archive.

Line 50 copies the file into the archive.

Line 52 puts a string that marks the end of the file, EOF, into the archive.

Line 53 puts the end of the `if` statement, started on line 46, into the archive.

Line 55 puts an `exit` statement into the archive.


## WC COMMAND

```
 1  #!/bin/sh
 2  #
 3  # NAME
 4  #    Wc - recursive version of the wc command
 5  #
 6  # SYNOPSIS
 7  #    Wc [-c][-1][-w] [file | directory ...]
 8  #
 9  # DESCRIPTION
10  #    This is a recursive version of the wc command.  This
11  #    command counts the lines, words, and characters in the
12  #    files similar to the wc command, however, this command
13  #    also searches subdirectories for files to include in
14  #    the counts.
15  #
16  #    If a file name on the command line contains wildcard
17  #    characters, it must be quoted so that the wildcard
18  #    characters can be processed inside this shell script
19  #    rather than being expanded into file names on the
20  #    command line.  For example:
```

```
21  #
22  #          Wc "directory/*.c"
23  #
24  #     will search "directory" and its subdirectories for
25  #     files that end in ".c" and count the lines, words, and
26  #     characters in those files.
27  #
28  #     -c   Count characters
29  #
30  #     -1   Count lines
31  #
32  #     -w   Count words
33  #
34  # RETURN VALUE
35  #     0    Successful completion
36  #     1    Usage error
37  #
38  ################################################################
39  CMDNAME=`basename $0`
40  USAGE="Usage: $CMDNAME [-c][-1][-w] [file | directory ...]"
41  TMP=/tmp/Wc.$$          # Temporary file for output of wc
42  LINE=                   # Line read from file
43  DIR=                    # Top level directory
44  PATTERN=                # File name matching pattern
45  C=                      # Suppress newline of echo (Sys V)
46  N=                      # Suppress newline of echo (BSD)
47  COUNT_LINES=FALSE       # Display the number of lines?
48  COUNT_WORDS=FALSE       # Display the number of words?
49  COUNT_CHARS=FALSE       # Display the number of characters?
50  LINES=0                 # Cumulative line count
51  WORDS=0                 # Cumulative word count
52  CHARS=0                 # Cumulative character count
53
54  trap 'rm -f /tmp/*.$$; exit 1' 1 2 3 15
55
56  #
57  # Parse command options.
58  #
59  while :
60  do
61      case $1 in
62          -c)  COUNT_CHARS=TRUE
63               shift
64               ;;
65          -1)  COUNT_LINES=TRUE
66               shift
67               ;;
68          -w)  COUNT_WORDS=TRUE
```

```
69                     shift
70                     ;;
71           --)    shift
72                  break
73                     ;;
74           -*)    echo "$USAGE" 1>&2
75                  exit 1
76                     ;;
77           *)     break
78                     ;;
79      esac
80 done
81
82 #
83 # Set default.
84 #
85 if [ $COUNT_LINES = FALSE -a \
86        $COUNT_WORDS = FALSE -a \
87        $COUNT_CHARS = FALSE ]
88 then
89      COUNT_LINES=TRUE
90      COUNT_WORDS=TRUE
91      COUNT_CHARS=TRUE
92 fi
93
94 #
95 # Set the options for echo.
96 #
97 if [ "`echo -n`" = "-n" ]; then
98      C='\c'
99 else
100     N='-n'
101 fi
102
103 for parm in "${@:-.}"
104 do
105     if [ -d "$parm" ]; then
106           DIR="$parm"
107           PATTERN="*"
108     else
109           DIR=`dirname "$parm"`
110           PATTERN=`basename "$parm"`
111     fi
112
113     for d in `find $DIR -type d -print | sort`
114     do
115             #
116             # The standard error of wc is sent to /dev/null to
```

```
117                 # discard the message that is printed when there
118                 # is no file that matches the pattern.
119                 #
120                 wc $d/$PATTERN 2>/dev/null |
121                     grep -v "total$" >$TMP
122
123             exec  <$TMP
124             while read LINE
125             do
126                     set -- $LINE
127
128                     if [ "$COUNT_LINES" = "TRUE" ]; then
129                         LINES=`expr $LINES + $1`
130                         echo $N "    $1$C"
131                     fi
132                     shift
133
134                     if [ "$COUNT_WORDS" = "TRUE" ]; then
135                         WORDS=`expr $WORDS + $1`
136                         echo $N "    $1$C"
137                     fi
138                     shift
139
140                     if [ "$COUNT_CHARS" = "TRUE" ]; then
141                         CHARS=`expr $CHARS + $1`
142                         echo $N "    $1$C"
143                     fi
144                     shift
145
146                     echo "    $@"
147             done
148         done
149 done
150
151 #
152 # Print totals.
153 #
154 if [ "$COUNT_LINES" = "TRUE" ]; then
155     echo $N "  $LINES$C"
156 fi
157
158 if [ "$COUNT_WORDS" = "TRUE" ]; then
159     echo $N "  $WORDS$C"
160 fi
161
162 if [ "$COUNT_CHARS" = "TRUE" ]; then
163     echo $N "  $CHARS$C"
164 fi
```

```
165
166   echo "  Total"
167
168   rm -f /tmp/*.$$
169   exit 0
```

This command is similar to the UNIX `wc` command except that this command is recursive. This command uses the `find` command to get a list of directories. Then it uses the `wc` command on the files in each directory. The results of the `wc` command are added to the totals for all of the directories.

Lines 39–52 assign initial values to the significant variables used in this shell script and provide a brief comment describing the purpose of each variable.

Lines 39 and 40 define the usage message for this command. Line 39 gets the name of this command from the command line. This is used to keep the usage message accurate even if this command is renamed.

On line 41, `TMP` is assigned the name of a temporary file that will be used to hold the output from the `wc` command. The `$$` suffix on the file name will be replaced with the process ID of this command when it is executed. This creates a unique temporary file name so that two simultaneous executions of this command will not use the same temporary file.

Shell scripts that use resources that need to be released when the shell script exits must ensure that the resources are released even when the shell script exits unexpectedly. Line 54 uses the `trap` command to specify the commands that are to be executed if signal 1, 2, 3, or 15 is received. This command will ensure that any files in the `/tmp` directory that end with the process ID of the current process are removed before this process exits.

Lines 59–80 parse the command options. This is the parsing technique that was described in "When getopts Is Not Available" in Chapter 6. This method is more portable than using `getopts`, but it has the disadvantage that you cannot specify more than one option behind a single hyphen. For example, you cannot specify all the options to this command as `-lwc`.

It would be more friendly to use the `getopts` command to parse the parameters in this command, but since this command is usually used without options or with just one option, this is a good time to show an example of this parsing technique.

If the user does not specify any options to this command, lines, words, and characters will be counted. Lines 85–92 set all of the options to `TRUE` if no options were specified.

This command uses the `echo` command to write information to the standard output. Since the information is not all written to standard output all at once, this command must be able to suppress the newline that the `echo` command normally appends to each message. Lines 97–101 determine the method used by the `echo` command on the current system to suppress the newline. This technique was discussed in "Printing a Prompt" in Chapter 8. One of the variables `N` or `C` will contain the appropriate option, and the other will be empty. These variables are used with the `echo` command whenever it is necessary to suppress the newline.

Line 103 begins a `for` loop that is executed once for each parameter on the command line. The code sequence $\${@:-.}$ says to use $\$@$ if it is not empty; otherwise, use dot (.), which is the symbol that represents the current directory. Thus, the word list of the `for` loop will be the names from the command line or dot.

Lines 105–111 check the parameter to see if it is a directory name or a file name. This information is used to determine how to parse the parameter into the correct directory name, `DIR`, and file name, `PATTERN`.

Line 113 begins another `for` loop that is executed once for each of the subdirectories of the current parameter. The word list for this `for` loop is created by using the `find` command to get a list of the subdirectories of the directory `DIR`. This list is sorted alphabetically and entered as the word list for the `for` loop.

Line 120 uses the `wc` command to count the lines, words, and characters in the files in the directory. The standard error of the `wc` command is discarded in case there are no files to count. The standard output of the `wc` command is filtered by the `grep` command to remove the line that gives the totals for the files counted by the `wc` command. The remainder of the output is then written to a temporary file.

Line 123 causes the standard input of the shell script to be redirected to the temporary file just created. This technique was discussed in "Reading Files" in Chapter 4. It is used here, rather than redirecting the standard input of the `while` loop in lines 124–147, so that the loop will not be executed in a subshell. This in turn, is necessary so that the variables `LINES`, `WORDS`, and `CHARS` can be changed inside the loop and used outside the loop.

Line 124 begins a `while` loop that reads the temporary file one line at a time.

Line 126 uses the `set` command to parse each line from the `wc` command. Lines 128–146 add the totals for the current file to the cumulative totals and print the totals for the current file to the standard output. The totals for the current file are printed without a newline so that the line can be conditionally composed depending upon the options that were used to execute the command.

Line 146 prints the name of the file and ends the line with a newline.

Lines 154–166 print the cumulative totals for all of the files processed.

Line 168 removes the temporary file that was used to hold the output of the `wc` command.

**Note:** The whitespace inside the quoted strings on lines 130, 136, 142, 146, 155, 159, 163, and 166 are tab characters. Spaces can be used, but the output will not line up as nicely.

## ADDCOLUMN COMMAND

```
1   #!/bin/sh
2   #
3   # NAME
4   #     addcolumn - add a column of numbers
5   #
6   # SYNOPSIS
7   #     addcolumn [column]
```

```
 8   #
 9   #  DESCRIPTION
10   #      This command will read its standard input and add the
11   #      numbers in the specified column.  If column is omitted,
12   #      the first column is added.
13   #
14   #  RETURN VALUE
15   #      0    Successful completion
16   #      1    Error condition occurred
17   #
18   ###################################################################
19   CMDNAME=`basename $0`
20   if [ $# -gt 1 ]; then
21         echo "Usage: $CMDNAME [column]" 1>&2
22         exit 1
23   fi
24
25   COLUMN=${1:-1}
26
27   expr "$COLUMN" + 1 >/dev/null 2>&1
28   if [ $? -ge 2 ]; then
29         echo "Usage: $CMDNAME argument is not numeric." 1>&2
30         exit 1
31   fi
32
33   awk '{total+=$'$COLUMN'} END {print total}'
```

This command is useful for adding a column of numbers. The following example shows this command being used to add the fifth column from the output of the `ls` command. On System V systems, this column is the size of the file; on BSD systems, the size of the file is in the fourth column.

```
ls -l *.c | addcolumn 5
```

Lines 20–23 ensure that at most one parameter is passed to this command. Line 19 gets the name of this command from the command line. This is used to keep the usage message accurate even if this command is renamed.

Line 25 initializes the variable COLUMN with the parameter from the command line. The code sequence `${1:-1}` says to assign `$1` to COLUMN if it is not empty; otherwise, assign 1 to COLUMN. This is how the column variable is set to one, the default, if the parameter to this command is omitted.

Lines 27–31 ensure that the column number is a numeric value. This technique was discussed in "Determine If a String Is Numeric" in Chapter 8. Even in simple commands such as this, it is better to add as much checking as you can. It not only helps others who use the command, but it also helps prevent them from coming to you for help when the command does not work.

Line 33 is a simple `awk` command that does the actual work of the shell script. It has the same standard input and standard output as the shell script.

The `awk` script parses its input into fields using whitespace as the delimiter. As each line is parsed, the field numbers, or positional parameters, are reset so that they can be treated as column numbers. The column number is passed into the `awk` script through the variable COLUMN. After variable substitution, $'$COLUMN', becomes $n, where n is the number of the field to be added to the value in `total` for each line of input.

After the last line is processed, the total is printed to the standard output.

## DIRCOPY COMMAND

```
 1  #!/bin/sh
 2  #
 3  # NAME
 4  #     dircopy - copy the contents of a directory
 5  #
 6  # SYNOPSIS
 7  #     dircopy directory1 directory2
 8  #
 9  # DESCRIPTION
10  #     This command will copy the contents of one directory
11  #     to another.  The destination directory and any
12  #     subdirectories will be created as needed.
13  #
14  # RETURN VALUE
15  #     0    Successful completion
16  #     1    Usage error
17  #
18  ##############################################################
19  CMDNAME=`basename $0`
20  CURDIR=`pwd`                    # Current directory
21  TARGET=                         # Destination directory
22
23  if [ $# -ne 2 ]; then
24      echo "Usage: $CMDNAME directory1 directory2" 1>&2
25      exit 1
26  fi
27
28  if [ ! -d "$1" ]; then
29      echo "$1 is not a directory." 1>&2
30      exit 1
31  fi
32
33  if [ -f "$2" ]; then
34      echo "$2 is not a directory." 1>&2
35      exit 1
```

```
36   fi
37
38   if [ ! -d "$2" ]; then
39        mkdir -p "$2"
40   fi
41
42   cd "$2"
43   TARGET=`pwd`
44   cd $CURDIR
45
46   cd "$1"
47   find . -depth -print        |
48        cpio -pdmu $TARGET 2>&1 |
49        grep -iv "blocks"
```

This is one of those commands that is not complicated, but it is difficult to remember exactly what to do without seeing an example.

Lines 19–21 initialize the variables used in this shell script. Line 19 gets the name of this command from the command line. This is used to keep the usage message accurate even if this command is renamed.

Lines 23–26 ensure that the correct number of parameters are passed to this command.

Lines 28–31 ensure that the first directory exists and that it is a directory.

Since the second directory does not need to exist before this command is executed, lines 33–36 only check to ensure it is not an ordinary file. That is, if it exists it must be a directory.

Lines 38–40 ensure that the destination directory exists. The -p option to the mkdir command is used to create any missing directories in the path of the destination directory as well as the directory itself. This option may not be available on all systems. If it is not available, this command will only create the destination directory and its subdirectories, not the directories leading up to the destination directory. You can also use the MkDir command presented earlier in this chapter.

Lines 42–44 get the full name of the second directory. This is done by changing to the directory and capturing the standard output of the pwd command in the variable TARGET.

Line 47 copies the directory. The find command is used to produce the list of files to be copied. It is important that this command be executed from the source directory so that the names printed by the find command will be relative file names. The cpio command reads the names from the find command and copies the files to the destination directory.

The standard error of the cpio command is merged with its standard output to allow the number of blocks copied message to be removed from the output without losing any other error messages.

Since there is no exit statement, the exit status of the shell script will be the exit status of the find command.

# FINDCMD COMMAND

```
 1  #!/bin/sh
 2  #
 3  # NAME
 4  #     findcmd - search for a command
 5  #
 6  # SYNOPSIS
 7  #     findcmd command
 8  #
 9  # DESCRIPTION
10  #     This command searches the directories listed in the
11  #     PATH variable for the command.  It makes a reasonable
12  #     attempt to find the same command as would be found by
13  #     the shell, except that it does not find functions or
14  #     built-in commands:
15  #
16  #     1. If the command name contains a /, the PATH variable
17  #        is not used.
18  #     2. The directories in the PATH variable are searched in
19  #        order, from left to right.
20  #     3. Files without execute access are ignored even if the
21  #        file name matches the command name.
22  #     4. The search concludes when the first match is found.
23  #
24  # RETURN VALUE
25  #     0     Command was found
26  #     1     Usage error
27  #     2     Command was not found
28  #
29  ###############################################################
30  CMDNAME=`basename $0`
31  if [ $# -ne 1 ]; then
32      echo "Usage: $CMDNAME command" 1>&2
33      exit 1
34  fi
35
36  FOUND=FALSE
37  COMMAND=$1
38
39  case $COMMAND in
40      */* )       if [ -x "$COMMAND" -a ! -d "$COMMAND" ]; then
41                      echo "$COMMAND"
42                      FOUND=TRUE
43                  fi
44                  ;;
45
46      * )         IFS=:
```

```
47                      for dir in `echo "$PATH"              |
48                              sed -e 's/^:/.:/'            \
49                                  -e 's/::/:.:/g'          \
50                                  -e 's/:$/:./'`
51              do
52                      if [ -x "$dir/$COMMAND" -a !    \
53                              -d "$dir/$COMMAND" ]
54                      then
55                              echo "$dir/$COMMAND"
56                              FOUND=TRUE
57                              break
58                      fi
59              done
60                      ;;
61      esac
62
63      if [ "$FOUND" = "FALSE" ]; then
64              echo "$COMMAND not found"
65              exit 2
66      else
67              exit 0
68      fi
```

This shell script is useful for locating executable files or commands. It looks for the command in each directory specified in the PATH variable. It performs a search similar to the one the shell uses to locate commands. If the command is found, the path name of the command is printed.

This command is similar to other commands that are available on some systems such as the which command or the whence command that is built into the Korn shell.

Lines 31–34 ensure that only one parameter is passed to this command. Line 30 gets the name of this command from the command line. This is used to keep the usage message accurate, even if this command is renamed.

Line 36 initializes a variable that keeps track of whether or not the command has been found.

Line 37 copies the command name from the first positional parameter to the variable COMMAND to give it a more descriptive name.

Line 39 begins a case statement that determines whether or not the command name contains a slash (/).

Lines 40–44 are executed if the command name contains a slash. In this case, the directories in the PATH variable are not searched. The command name is simply tested to determine if it is the name of an executable file.

Lines 46–60 are executed if the command name does not contain a slash. Line 47 begins a for loop that is executed once for each directory in the PATH variable.

Line 46 changes the IFS variable to contain the colon (:) character. This will cause the following for statement to parse the word list into words using a colon as the delimiter. Since the word list is a list of directory names separated by colons, the words processed by the `for` statement will be the directories listed in the PATH variable.

Line 47 uses a `for` statement to parse the PATH variable. Since the word list is parsed into words separated by colons, the variable `dir` will be set to the next directory in the PATH variable during each successive iteration of the loop.

A `sed` script is used to preprocess the contents of the PATH variable before it is used as the word list of the `for` loop. Since the syntax of the PATH variable allows an empty directory name to indicate the current directory, the `sed` script is used to replace any empty directory name with a dot ( . ), the symbol for the current directory. The `sed` command on lines 48–50 consists of three separate scripts that replace an empty directory at the beginning of the PATH variable, in the middle of the PATH variable, and at the end of the PATH variable, respectively.

The body of the `for` loop in lines 52–58 will be executed once for each directory in the PATH variable. The `if` statement on line 52 tests each directory to see if it contains the command and if it is executable. If the command is found, the name of the command is printed to the standard output, the variable FOUND is set to TRUE, and the `break` command is executed to terminate the `for` loop.

You can modify this shell script so that it will find all occurrences of a command by removing the `break` command on line 57.

Line 63 tests the variable FOUND to see if the command has been found so that it can set the correct exit status and print a message if necessary.


## FINDFILE COMMAND

```
 1  #!/bin/sh
 2  #
 3  # NAME
 4  #     findfile - recursively search for a file
 5  #
 6  # SYNOPSIS
 7  #     findfile filename [directory ...]
 8  #
 9  # DESCRIPTION
10  #   This command searches the directories and their
11  #   subdirectories for the file.  If no directories are
12  #   listed on the command line, the current directory is
13  #   searched.  If the file is found, the path name of the
14  #   file is printed.
15  #
16  #   If the file name contains wildcard characters, it must
17  #   be quoted so that the wildcard characters can be
18  #   processed inside this shell script rather than being
19  #   expanded into file names on the command line.
20  #
21  # RETURN VALUE
```

```
22  #      0     Successful completion
23  #      1     Usage error
24  #
25  ##############################################################
26  CMDNAME=`basename $0`
27  if [ $# -eq 0 ]; then
28          echo "Usage: $CMDNAME filename [directory ...]" 1>&2
29          exit 1
30  fi
31
32  NAME=$1
33  shift
34
35  find "${@:-.}" -name "$NAME" -print
```

This is another one of those tasks that is not complicated, but encapsulating it in a shell script makes it easier to remember how to find files. For example, the following example shows how to use this command to find all files named core in the current directory:

```
findfile core
```

Or, the following example will find all files named core in the /usr directory:

```
findfile core /usr
```

Lines 27–30 ensure that at least one parameter is passed to this command. Line 26 gets the name of this command from the command line. This is used to keep the usage message accurate even if this command is renamed.

Line 32 copies the file name from the first positional parameter to the variable NAME. The shift command removes this parameter from the command line so that the remaining parameters are the names of the directories to search.

Line 35 uses the find command to search the directories for the file. The first parameter to the find command, "${@:-.}", is a variable initialization syntax that says to use the value of the variable $@ if it is not empty, otherwise to use dot (.). Thus, if any directories are listed on the command line, they will be passed to the find command; otherwise, the current directory will be searched.

## FINDSTR COMMAND

```
1  #!/bin/sh
2  #
3  # NAME
4  #     findstr - recursively search for a string
5  #
```

```
 6  # SYNOPSIS
 7  #     findstr [-iv] string [filename]
 8  #
 9  # DESCRIPTION
10  #     This command searches the files in the current
11  #     directory and its subdirectories for the string.  The
12  #     name of each file that contains the string is listed.
13  #
14  #     The string may be a simple string or it may be any
15  #     regular expression accepted by the grep command.  If
16  #     the string contains whitespace or any other
17  #     metacharacter, it must be quoted.
18  #
19  #     The search can be restricted to files with a particular
20  #     name by specifying the file name parameter.  This
21  #     parameter may contain wildcard characters to restrict
22  #     the search to file names that match a pattern, but the
23  #     file name must be quoted so that the wildcard
24  #     characters can be processed inside this command file
25  #     rather than being expanded into file names on the
26  #     command line.
27  #
28  #     -i   Ignore the case of the string.
29  #
30  #     -v   Verbose; list the lines that contain the string.
31  #          Without this option, only the names of the files
32  #          containing the string will be printed.
33  #
34  # RETURN VALUE
35  #     0    Successful completion
36  #     1    Usage error
37  #
38  ##################################################################
39  CMDNAME=`basename $0`
40  USAGE="Usage: $CMDNAME [-iv] string [filename]"
41  STRING=                       # String to search for
42  FILENAME=                     # Name of the files to check
43  I=                            # Option for grep; Ignore case
44  L=-1                          # Option for grep; List names only
45
46  #
47  # Parse command options.
48  #
49  if [ "$OPTIND" = 1 ]; then
50      while getopts iv OPT
51      do
52          case $OPT in
```

```
53                    i)   I=-i         # Ignore case
54                         ;;
55                    v)   L=           # Verbose
56                         ;;
57                    \?)  echo "$USAGE" 1>&2
58                         exit 1
59                         ;;
60              esac
61        done
62        shift `expr $OPTIND - 1`
63   else
64        USAGE="Usage: $CMDNAME [-i][-v] string [filename]"
65        while :
66        do
67              case $1 in
68                    -i)  I=-i         # Ignore case
69                         shift
70                         ;;
71                    -v)  L=           # Verbose
72                         shift
73                         ;;
74                    --)  shift
75                         break
76                         ;;
77                    -*)  echo "$USAGE" 1>&2
78                         exit 1
79                         ;;
80                    *)   break
81                         ;;
82              esac
83        done
84   fi
85
86   #
87   # Make sure the number of parameters is reasonable.
88   #
89   if [ $# -lt 1 -o $# -gt 2 ]; then
90        echo "$USAGE" 1>&2
91        exit 1
92   fi
93
94   STRING=$1
95   FILENAME=${2:-"*"}
96
97   find . \( -type f -o -type l \) -name "$FILENAME" -print |
98        xargs -e grep $I $L -- "$STRING" /dev/null
99
100  exit 0
```

This command allows you to use `grep` to search all the files in a directory hierarchy rather than just the files listed on the command line. This is probably one of the most frequently written shell scripts; everyone seems to have a version of this command in one form or another.

The normal behavior for this command is to list the names of the files that contain the string. If you want to see the individual lines that contain the string you need to use the `-v` option.

Lines 39–44 assign initial values to the significant variables used in this shell script and provide a brief comment describing the purpose of each variable.

Lines 39 and 40 define the usage message for this command. Line 39 gets the name of this command from the command line. This is used to keep the usage message accurate even if this command is renamed.

Lines 49–84 parse the `i` and `v` options from the command line. This is an example of a very friendly and portable parsing algorithm. It uses the `getopts` command to parse the options if it is available; otherwise, it has its own parsing code.

On systems that support `getopts`, the variable OPTIND is initially set to one. This fact is used in line 49 to determine which method to use to parse the options. Lines 50–62 are used to parse the options if `getopts` is available. Lines 64–83 are used to parse the options if `getopts` is not available. Both of these methods are discussed in Chapter 6.

Lines 89–92 check that there is either one or two parameters on the command line. This is an important check in this command because one of the most common mistakes is to forget to quote a file name that contains wildcard characters. When this happens, the shell will expand the file name into a list of file names that will be detected as too many parameters.

Lines 94 and 95 copy the string and file name from the positional parameters to variables with more descriptive names. Since the file name is an optional parameter, a variable initialization syntax is used to assign the value to FILENAME. It will assign $2 to FILENAME if it is not empty; otherwise, * will be assigned to FILENAME.

Lines 97–98 are where the real work of this shell script is performed.

The `find` command is used to generate a list of the files to search. The dot (.) following the `find` command indicates that the search should start in the current directory. The `-type f -o -type l` specifies that only ordinary files and symbolic links are to be searched. The `-name "$FILENAME"` tells the `find` command to only look at files with names that match the value contained in the FILENAME variable. The FILENAME variable needs to be quoted so that wildcard characters are not expanded by the shell. The `-print` option says to print the names of the files that are found.

The names of the files are piped to the `xargs` command. This command is used to gather parameters into groups that are then passed to another command. This avoids creating a process to execute the command for each parameter. This usually results in a significant performance improvement.

Unfortunately, `xargs` is not available on all systems. If `xargs` is not available on your system, lines 97–98 can be replaced with the following lines. This will create a more portable but less efficient version of this shell script.

```
97   find . -type f -o -type 1 -name "$FILENAME" \
98        -exec grep $I $L -- "$STRING" {} /dev/null \;
```

The names of the files are then passed to the `grep` command.

The value in the variables I and L may contain options to be passed on to the `grep` command. If either of these variables is empty, it will disappear after it is substituted in the command line.

The `--` option is used to ensure that if the string begins with a hyphen, it is not interpreted as an option to the `grep` command.

The file `/dev/null` is always passed as the last file name to `grep` because whenever `grep` has two or more file name parameters, it will prefix its output with the name of the file that it is searching.


## HOSTADDR COMMAND

```
1    #!/bin/sh
2    #
3    # NAME
4    #      hostaddr - return the IP address for a system
5    #
6    # SYNOPSIS
7    #      hostaddr [hostname]
8    #
9    # DESCRIPTION
10   #      This command writes the IP address for the system to
11   #      the standard output.  If the host name is not passed,
12   #      the IP address of the current system is returned.  If
13   #      the host is not found, nothing will be written to the
14   #      standard output.
15   #
16   #      Since this command searches the /etc/hosts file to find
17   #      the IP address for the system, this command may not
18   #      work on systems that use a network server to manage the
19   #      names of the hosts on the network, such as YP or BIND.
20   #
21   #################################################################
22
23   HOST=${1:-`hostname`}
24   HOST=`echo $HOST | sed -e 's/\..*//'`
25
26   cat /etc/hosts                          |
27       sed  -e 's/#.*//'                   \
28            -e 's/        /  /g'           \
29            -e 's/ */ /g'                  \
30            -e 's/ *$//g'                  \
```

```
31                  -e 's/^ *//g'                               \
32                  -e "s/ $HOST[. ].*/ $HOST/g"                |
33          sed     -n "/ $HOST$/p"                             |
34          sed     -e 's/ .*//'
35
36    exit 0
```

This command finds the line in the /etc/host file for a particular host and extracts the IP address from that line. This is a good example of combining several filters to locate and extract a particular field from a file.

Line 23 copies the command line parameter to the variable HOST. This line uses one of the variable initialization syntaxes; if $1 is not empty, it is assigned to HOST; otherwise, the hostname command is executed and its standard output is assigned to HOST.

Line 24 uses a sed filter to remove the domain name from the host if it is present.

Lines 26–34 form a pipeline. This pipeline is a series of filters that progressively eliminate information until all that is left is the IP address of the host. The output of the pipeline is written to the standard output of the shell script.

On line 26, the cat command copies the /etc/host file to its standard output to start the pipeline.

Lines 27–32 form a single sed command that executes several sed scripts. Line continuation is used so that each sed script can be written on a separate line.

Line 33 is another sed command, but it uses the -n option, which is not compatible with the previous sed command. Therefore, a separate sed command is used to execute this script.

Similarly, line 34 executes another sed command that cannot use the -n option; therefore, it is also executed as a separate command.

Line 27 removes comments from each line. This filter may leave empty lines or lines with only whitespace in the file.

Line 28 replaces all tabs with spaces. The whitespace in this sed script is shown symbolically below:

   -e 's/<tab>/<space>/g'

Line 29 replaces multiple spaces with a single space.

   -e 's/<space><space>*/<space>/g'

Line 30 removes trailing spaces from each line.

   -e 's/<space>*$//g'

Line 31 removes leading spaces from each line.

   -e 's/^<space>*//g'

Line 32 truncates any line that contains the host name so that the host name is the last word on the line. If the host name contains the domain name, the domain name is also removed.

```
-e "s/<space>$HOST[.<space>].*/<space>$HOST/g"
```

Line 33 removes all lines except the line that ends with the name of the system we are looking for. This should result in a single line being printed.

```
-n "/<space>$HOST$/p"
```

Line 34 truncates the line at the location of the first blank character. Since the IP address is the first field on the line, this should leave only the IP address.

```
-e 's/<space>.*//'
```

## PTREE COMMAND

```
 1  #!/bin/sh
 2  #
 3  # NAME
 4  #     ptree - print a process tree
 5  #
 6  # SYNOPSIS
 7  #     ptree [-n] [pid]
 8  #     ptree [-n] [pid] [level] [datafile]
 9  #
10  # DESCRIPTION
11  #     This command will print the process tree for the
12  #     process identified by pid.  When called by the user,
13  #     only the first format shown should be used.  If the
14  #     process ID (pid) is not passed, process 1 is assumed.
15  #
16  #     The second format of this command is only used when
17  #     this command calls itself recursively to print the next
18  #     level of the process tree.
19  #
20  #     -n   Do not recurse
21  #
22  # RETURN VALUE
23  #     0    Successful completion
24  #     1    Usage error
25  #
26  #############################################################
27  PATH=$PATH:`dirname $0`
```

```
28
29    . SystemType.sh
30
31    CMDNAME=`basename $0`
32    USAGE="Usage: $CMDNAME [-n] [pid]"
33    RECURSIVE=TRUE          # List processes recursively
34    PROCESS=                # PID of the starting process
35    LEVEL=                  # Indentation level (num parents)
36    DATAFILE=               # Reformatted output from ps
37    PSFILE=/tmp/ps.$$       # Output from the ps command
38    PS_OPTS=                # Options for the ps command
39    OLD_IFS=$IFS            # Original value of IFS variable
40    SYSTEM=`SystemType`     # String identifying the system
41
42    #
43    # Temporaries
44    #
45    PID=                    # Process ID
46    PPID=                   # Process ID of the parent process
47    OWNER=                  # Owner of the process
48    NAME=                   # Name of the process
49    LINE=                   # Line from the data file
50    OUTLINE=                # Line of output
51    INDENT=                 # Column number where line begins
52
53    trap 'rm -f /tmp/*.$$; exit 1' 1 2 3 15
54
55    FillLine() {
56          #
57          # SYNOPSIS
58          #     FillLine line column
59          #
60          _LINE="$1"
61          _COLUMN=$2
62          _LEN=`expr "$_LINE" : '.*'`
63          while [ $_LEN -lt $_COLUMN ]
64          do
65                _LINE="$_LINE "
66                _COLUMN=`expr $_COLUMN - 1`
67          done
68
69          echo "$_LINE"
70    }
71
72    while :
73    do
74          case $1 in
75                -n ) RECURSIVE=FALSE
```

```
76                      shift
77                         ;;
78          -- )  shift
79                 break
80                    ;;
81          -* )  echo "$USAGE" 1>&2
82                 exit 1
83                    ;;
84          * )  break
85                    ;;
86       esac
87  done
88
89  #
90  # Make sure the number of parameters is reasonable.
91  #
92  if [ $# -eq 0 ]; then
93       PROCESS=1
94       LEVEL=0
95       DATAFILE=/tmp/ptree.$$
96  elif [ $# -eq 1 ]; then
97       PROCESS=$1
98       LEVEL=0
99       DATAFILE=/tmp/ptree.$$
100 elif [ $# -eq 3 ]; then
101      PROCESS=$1
102      LEVEL=$2
103      DATAFILE=$3
104 else
105      echo "$USAGE" 1>&2
106      exit 1
107 fi
108
109 if [ "$LEVEL" = 0 ]; then
110      #
111      # Determine which options to use with the ps command.
112      #
113      case $SYSTEM in
114          SUNBSD | ULTRIX )   PS_OPTS="-auxw"      ;;
115          * )                 PS_OPTS="-ef"        ;;
116      esac
117
118      #
119      # Build the data file.
120      #
121      rm -f $DATAFILE $PSFILE
122      ps -ef | sed '1d' | sort >$PSFILE
123
```

```
124        exec <$PSFILE
125        IFS=
126        while read LINE
127        do
128              IFS=$OLD_IFS
129
130              set $LINE
131              OWNER=$1
132              PID=$2
133              PPID=$3
134
135              #
136              # Determine column where the process name begins.
137              #
138              case $SYSTEM in
139                    AIX | HP | SGI | SOLARIS )    COL=48 ;;
140                    SUNBSD | DECOSF)             COL=57 ;;
141                    ULTRIX )                     COL=51 ;;
142                    * )  echo "Unexpected system type." 1>&2
143                         exit 1
144                         ;;
145              esac
146
147              LINE=`echo "$LINE" | cut -c$COL-`
148              set dummy $LINE
149              shift
150              NAME=$1
151
152              echo $PID $PPID $OWNER $NAME >>$DATAFILE
153              IFS=
154        done
155        IFS=$OLD_IFS
156 fi
157
158 #
159 # Print the current process.
160 #
161 INDENT=`expr $LEVEL \* 2`
162 OUTLINE=`FillLine "" $INDENT`
163
164 LINE=`grep "^$PROCESS " $DATAFILE`
165 set $LINE
166 OUTLINE=$OUTLINE   $1"
167 OUTLINE=`FillLine "$OUTLINE" 30`
168 OUTLINE="$OUTLINE   $3    $4"
169 echo "$OUTLINE"
170
171 if [ "$RECURSIVE" = "TRUE" ]; then
```

```
172          LEVEL=`expr $LEVEL + 1`
173          while read LINE
174          do
175              set $LINE
176              #
177              # For every process that is a child of the
178              # current process, invoke this command ($0)
179              # recursively.
180              #
181              if [ "$2" = "$PROCESS" ]; then
182                  $0 $1 $LEVEL $DATAFILE
183              fi
184          done  <$DATAFILE
185    fi
186
187    rm -f /tmp/*.$$
188    exit 0
```

This command prints the process tree for a process. If no process is identified on the command line, process 1 is assumed, which will cause the entire process tree to be printed. The information for each process is listed on a separate line. This information includes the process ID, the owner, and the name of the process. If a process has child processes, they are listed following the parent, and the information for the child process is indented two spaces further than the information for the parent process.

Line 27 adds the directory where this shell script is stored to the PATH variable. This is a technique that was discussed in "Reusing Functions" in Chapter 3. It is used in this shell script to allow it to include the file SystemType.sh on line 29.

Line 29 uses the dot command to include the declaration for the SystemType function. This function is described in Chapter 9.

Lines 31–51 assign initial values to the significant variables used in this shell script and provide a brief comment describing the purpose of each variable.

Lines 31 and 32 define the usage message for this command. Line 31 gets the name of this command from the command line. This is used to keep the usage message accurate even if this command is renamed.

On line 37, PSFILE is assigned the name of a temporary file that will be used to hold the output from the ps command. The $$ suffix on the file name will be substituted with the process ID of this command when it is executed. This creates a unique temporary file name so that two simultaneous executions of this command will not use the same temporary file.

On line 40, SYSTEM is assigned the string returned by the function SystemType. This function was defined on line 29 by executing the file SystemType.sh.

Shell scripts that use resources that need to be released when the shell script exits must ensure that the resources are released even when the shell script exits unexpectedly. Line 53 uses the trap command to specify the commands that are to be executed if signal 1, 2, 3, or 15 is received. This command will ensure that any files in the /tmp directory that end with the process ID of the current process are removed before the process exits.

Lines 55–70 define the shell function `FillLine`. This function is used when displaying the output to fill a line with spaces to the indicated column. Notice that the names of the variables used in this function begin with an underscore. This is a technique discussed in Chapter 3; it is used to avoid name collisions with variables used outside the function. (Remember, all variables are global.)

Lines 72–87 process the command line options. This parsing technique was described in "When getopts Is not Available" in Chapter 6. This method is more portable than using `getopts`, but it has the disadvantage that you cannot specify more than one option behind a single hyphen. Since there is only one option to this command, that does not matter in this case.

Once the command line option has been removed from the command line, lines 92–107 ensure that the correct number of parameters are passed to the command and assign appropriate values to any parameters that are omitted. Lines 95 and 99 use the same technique as line 37 for creating a unique file name and storing it in a variable. Notice that the only time there are three parameters is when this shell script is executed recursively.

Lines 109–156 are only executed when this shell script is executed by the user, not when it is executed recursively. The purpose of this section of code is to process the information from the `ps` command and store it into a data file. The data file contains only the fields that are used by this command, and the name of the data file is passed to any recursive executions of this shell script.

Lines 113–116 determine which options should be used with the `ps` command. If the system is a BSD system (`SUNBSD` or `ULTRIX`), the `-auwx` options are used with the `ps` command, otherwise the `-ef` options are used. These options are saved in the variable `PS_OPTS`.

Line 121 removes the temporary files that are used by this command. These files should never exist at this point, but this command makes that point clear to someone who is reading the code.

Line 122 executes the `ps` command, removes the header information, which is in the first line, and then writes the sorted output into the file named by the variable `PSFILE`. Sorting this information causes each level of the process tree to be displayed in process order.

Line 124 causes the standard input of the shell script to be redirected to the file just created.

Line 125 sets the `IFS` variable to be empty. This forces the `read` command to read the standard input without removing any whitespace from the line. This is necessary in order to be able to locate the process name. The number of fields before the process name is not always the same, but the process name always starts in a particular column.

Line 126 begins a `while` loop that reads the standard input one line at a time.

Line 128 restores the original value of the `IFS` variable so that other commands inside the `while` loop will not be adversely affected. On line 153, the `IFS` variable will be set to empty again, just before the next line is read.

Line 130 uses the `set` command to parse the line that was just read and loads the fields into the positional parameters. The only fields that are needed are the process ID, the parent process ID, and the owner. The process name cannot be extracted using a field position because the process name is not always in the same field position. This happens because the fields in the output of the `ps` command sometimes run together without leaving interleaving whitespace.

Lines 131–133 get the owner, process ID, and parent process ID. These values are always in the first three fields in the output from the `ps` command.

Lines 138–145 determine where the name of the process begins in the output from the `ps` command. The `case` statement is used because, depending upon the type of the system, the process name begins in a different column.

Line 147 removes the front of the line so that the process name is moved to the front.

Line 148 uses the `set` command to parse the rest of the line. Since the fields in the line are separated by whitespace, each field will be loaded into the corresponding positional parameter. The "dummy" parameter is used here in case the name of the process begins with a hyphen. This technique is discussed in "The `set` Command" in Chapter 12; it is a portable method to prevent the `set` command from interpreting a value beginning with a hyphen as an option. The `shift` command following the `set` command removes the dummy parameter.

Line 150 copies the process name to the variable `NAME`.

Line 152 appends a new line to the data file. This line contains the process ID, the parent process ID, the owner, and the name of the process.

Line 153 sets the `IFS` variable to be empty again. This is necessary since the `read` command is about to be executed to read the next line from the file.

Line 161 determines the number of spaces to indent the next line of output. The indentation level indicates the number of parents processes of the process to be displayed.

Line 162 uses the `FillLine` function to prefix the output line with the proper number of spaces to represent the process's ancestry.

Line 164 locates the line in the data file that contains the information on the next process to be displayed.

Line 165 uses the `set` command to parse the line that was found in the data file. The positional parameters will be loaded with the process ID, parent process ID, owner, and process name, in that order.

Lines 166–169 format the output line and write it to the standard output. The `FillLine` function is used again on line 167 so that the owner and process name always begin at the same column regardless of the ancestry of the process.

Lines 171–185 are normally executed, but will be skipped if the `-n` option was used. These are the lines that execute the command recursively for every child of the process currently being displayed.

Line 172 increments the indentation level.

Lines 173–184 are a `while` loop that reads the data file one line at a time looking for lines that have the parent process ID set to the process currently being displayed. The standard input of the `while` loop is redirected to the data file on line 184.

On line 181, the parent process ID is compared with the process ID of the process currently being displayed to see if it is a child of this process. If it is, the shell script will be executed recursively to print the process tree for that process.

Line 182 executes the current command recursively. The variable $0 is the name of the current process and, thus, is being used as the name of the command to execute. The variable $1 is the process ID of the child process. The LEVEL variable passes along the cumulative indentation level so that recursive execution has progressively deeper indentation.

Line 187 removes the temporary files created by this process.

# 11

# *Debugging*

## DEBUGGING OPTIONS

Shell scripts are normally executed by entering their name followed by the parameters to the shell script. For example:

$ *scriptfile parm1 parm2* . . .

This same shell script can also be run by passing the command line to the shell, as shown here.

$ sh *scriptfile parm1 parm2* . . .

The advantage of executing a shell script this way is that you can set shell options without modifying the shell script. For example, to turn on the -v option while a shell script is executed, you could enter the command in the next example. The -v option causes the shell to print the lines in the shell script as they are read. Notice that this is not quite the same thing as printing the lines as they are executed because lines that are not executed will be displayed, and lines in loops will not be displayed, each time the loop is executed.

$ sh -v *scriptfile parm1 parm2* . . .

Another way to set the shell options is to execute the `set` command inside the shell script. Using the `set` command, any option can be turned on or off anywhere in the shell script. This allows an option to be turned on for a particular section of the shell script, rather than the whole shell script.

To turn an option on using the `set` command, precede the option letter with a hyphen (`-`). For example:

```
set -v
```

To reset, or turn off an option, use the `set` command and precede the option letter with a plus sign (+). For example:

```
set +v
```

The following example shows how the `set` command can be inserted in a shell script in order to print all of the lines in the shell script as they are read. This is similar to enabling the `-v` option from the command line of the shell.

```
#!/bin/sh
set -v
     .
     .
     .
exit 0
```

The shell provides several options that are useful for debugging shell scripts. Some of these options will be discussed in more detail in the following sections. In addition, there are other shell options not related to debugging shell scripts that are not listed here.

| | |
|---|---|
| e | Exit the shell script if a command exits with a nonzero exit status |
| n | Read the lines in the shell script, but do not execute them |
| u | Treat unset variables as errors if their value is retrieved |
| v | Print the lines in the shell script as they are read |
| x | Print commands and their arguments as they are executed |

## CHECKING SYNTAX

The `-n` option provides a way to check the structure of the shell script without executing the statements in the shell script. If the shell detects an error, it will print a message and quit. This option is usually used together with the `-v` option. For example:

```
$ sh -nv scriptfile parm1 parm2 ...
```

In the following shell script, there is an `else` statement without an `if` statement. Since this is not allowed, this file will result in an error if you attempt to execute it.

```
#!/bin/sh
else
    echo "This is an else clause."
fi
```

If this shell script is executed using the -n and the -v options, the shell will display the following information. The output may be slightly different on some systems, but this gives you an idea of what to expect.

```
$ sh -nv sample
#!/bin/sh
else
sample: syntax error at line 3: `else' unexpected
$
```

As you can see, the lines are listed up to the point where the error is detected. Then an error message is printed and the shell process quits. Notice that the line number in the error message is not exactly correct; this is the line where the shell was processing when it detected the error, but it may not be the line that actually contains the error.

## TRACING EXECUTION

The -x option causes the shell to print each statement as it is executed. The statements are printed after the shell has evaluated them so that you can see the results from variable substitution, wildcard character expansion, and so forth.

The following example shows a simple shell script containing a variable assignment and an if statement.

```
#!/bin/sh
VAR="abc"
if [ "$VAR" = "abc" ]; then
    echo "The if statement is true."
else
    echo "The if statement is false."
fi
exit 0
```

If this shell script is executed with the -x option, the shell will display the following information.

```
$ sh -x sample
VAR=abc
+ [ abc = abc ]
+ echo The if statement is true.
```

```
The if statement is true.
+ exit 0
$
```

Frequently you will see a shell script that leaves a command to enable execution tracing near the front of the file, but preceded by a comment character. Thus, to turn on execution tracing, all you have to do is edit the file and remove the comment character. This technique, while very common, seems to be of dubious value since you must edit the shell script to uncomment the command; you could just as easily edit the file to add the command.

```
#!/bin/sh
# set -x
...
```

## CONDITIONAL OUTPUT

Another common way to debug a shell script is to print key information at various points in the shell script using the `echo` command. Oftentimes these `echo` commands will be temporary statements that are removed after the shell script is debugged. However, sometimes this information will be a permanent part of the shell script. In these cases, the information is printed conditionally, depending upon a command line option.

Many commands use `-v` as the verbose option. This option is usually used for information about the execution of the command that the user of the command will find helpful.

Command line options to enable debugging information are usually undocumented because they are not intended for normal use. There is no consistent standard for naming debugging options, but `-d` and `-x` are common choices.

The shell function `Question`, presented in Chapter 9, allows the user to enter `-x` or `+x` in response to any question asked during the execution of the shell script. These responses, in turn, are passed on to the `set` command to enable and disable the shell execution tracing facility.

## COMMON CODING PROBLEMS

This section discusses a variety of coding problems that frequently occur when developing shell scripts. By being aware of these problems, you may be able to avoid them in the future.

### Variable Assignment

You cannot put whitespace on either side of the equal sign when assigning a value to a variable, and if the value contains whitespace, it needs to be enclosed in quotes.

```
VAR="this is the value"
```

## Braces

When you use braces to group commands and put a closing brace on the same line as the last command, remember that you must put a semicolon and a space between the last command and the closing brace. For example:

```
{ command1; command2; ...; }
```

This also applies to braces when they are used to bracket a function declaration.

## The `case` Statement

The ; ; symbol in the `case` statement is used to terminate each individual case. Be sure to precede it with whitespace or put it on a line by itself. Also, do not put a space between the two semicolons.

## Line Continuation

The backslash must be the last character on a line if it is to be interpreted as a line continuation character. If you are not getting the behavior you expect when ending the line with a backslash, look for anything following the backslash character, such as a space. Also, you cannot put a comment on a line that is continued, either before the backslash or after it.

```
echo "This will not work."      \<space>
echo "This will not work."      \   # Comment
echo "This will not work."          # Comment \
```

## Wildcard Characters

When using the [ ! ... ] wildcard notation, ! must be the first character following the left bracket or it will be treated as one of the characters to match.

Also, if you want to include the hyphen as one of the characters to match, rather than to specify a range, it must be the first character following the left bracket.

## The `test` Command

The `test` command evaluates an expression that is passed to it on the command line. It evaluates the expression and returns a successful status if the expression is true and an unsuccessful status if the expression is false.

When composing the expression, each option, value, and symbol used in the expression must be passed as a separate parameter to the `test` command, and, therefore, they must be separated by whitespace. In the following example, you can see that the equal sign is separated from the two strings that it is comparing so that each string and the equal sign will be passed to the `test` command as separate parameters.

```
if test "$NAME" = ""; then
    echo "NAME is empty."
fi
```

This is also true of the brackets that are usually used to represent the `test` command; they must be separated from the parameters by whitespace.

```
if [ "$NAME" = "" ]; then
    echo "NAME is empty."
fi
```

When constructing complex expressions with the `test` command, remember that the expression is part of a command line; do not try to break the expression into multiple lines without using line continuation.

If you are using parentheses in an expression, be sure to quote them to prevent them from being interpreted by the shell. Parentheses are usually quoted by preceding each parenthesis with a backslash character.

```
if [ \( "$NAME" = "" \) ]; then
    echo "NAME is empty."
fi
```

When creating an expression for the `test` command that tests for equality, be sure to notice that there are two equality operators—one to test whether or not two strings are equal (=), and one to test whether or not two numbers are equal (`-eq`). The difference between these two operators is shown here:

```
0  =  00  is false
0 -eq 00  is true
```

## The `expr` Command

The `expr` command also evaluates expressions, and its values and operators also need to be separated by whitespace so that they can be passed as individual parameters. For example:

```
expr 4 + 17
```

Parentheses are used with the `expr` command only when the colon operator (`:`) is used. (See "Extracting Substrings Using `expr`" in Chapter 8).[1] When parentheses are used with this operator, they must be preceded with a backslash, even though they are inside a quoted string.

```
expr "string" : "pattern\(.*\)"
```

---

[1] Some versions of the `expr` command also allow parentheses to be used to group expressions.

Also, when using the asterisk operator for multiplication, it must be quoted to prevent the shell from interpreting it as a wildcard character. This is usually done by preceding the asterisk with a backslash, as shown in the next example.

```
expr 2 \* 3
```

Be sure not to quote the entire expression because each value and operator must be passed to the `expr` command as a separate parameter. For example, in the following example, the entire expression is passed to the `expr` command as a single parameter, which is not what you want.

```
expr '2 * 3'     # Wrong
```

The `expr` command is frequently used to determine if a string is numeric by using the string in an arithmetic expression and then testing the result to see if there is an error. However, this is usually done incorrectly, as shown in the following example:

```
if expr "$NUMBER" + 1 >/dev/null 2>&1     # Probably wrong
then
    echo "Numeric"
else
    echo "Not numeric"
fi
```

The problem with this example is that the `expr` command does not follow the normal conventions for setting its exit status to zero for success and not zero for failure. The `expr` command returns both zero and one when the command is successful. It returns a value of two or greater to indicate an error. As you can see, the problem occurs when the value of one is returned, which is any time the expression evaluates to zero. For this to occur in this example, the number would have to be -1, but since you suspect that the number might not even be numeric, why couldn't it be -1?

The correct way to detect an error from `expr` is to test the return value for a value of two or more. Most systems will return a value of two if there is an error, however, some systems use additional values to give a more precise indication of the error.

```
expr "$NUMBER" + 1 >/dev/null 2>&1
if [ $? -lt 2 ]; then
    echo "Numeric"
else
    echo "Not numeric"
fi
```

## Input-Output Redirection

When more than one redirection syntax is used on a command line, remember that they are evaluated from left to right. For example, the following statement discards the standard output and the standard error.

```
command >/dev/null 2>&1
```

But the following command does not do the same thing. (See "Redirection Syntax" in Chapter 4 for more information.)

```
command 2>&1 >/dev/null        # Probably wrong
```

It is common to redirect the standard error to the same file as the standard output, but the reverse is not as common. One common exception is when using the echo command to write error messages. Since the normal output is written to the standard output, it must be redirected to write it to the standard error.

```
echo "Error message." 1>&2
```

Be careful not to inadvertently reverse the redirection. Since this code is executed only when an error occurs, it is possible that this problem will go undetected for a long time.

```
echo "Error message." 2>&1    # Probably wrong
```

When using file redirection with the read command, you need to be sure to use the correct syntax.[2] For example, at first glance the following code might appear to read three lines from the file. However, this will actually read the first line from the file three times.

```
read LINE1 <file        # Probably wrong
read LINE2 <file        # Probably wrong
read LINE3 <file        # Probably wrong
```

This code was probably intended to open the file and redirect the read command to read from the descriptor assigned to the newly opened file. The following examples show how this should have been done:

```
exec 3<file
read LINE1 <&3
read LINE2 <&3
read LINE3 <&3
```

---

[2] Very old versions of the shell do not allow file redirection on built-in commands.

In many versions of the shell, using file redirection with a shell statement, such as a `while` statement, will cause that statement to be executed in a subshell. Since a subshell is a separate process, it cannot make changes that affect the current process. Thus, any changes made to variables within the loop will be lost when the loop exits. Some solutions to this problem are discussed in "Reading Files" in Chapter 4.

```
while read LINE
do
      ...
done <file
```

## Unusual File Names

Remember that file names in UNIX can contain any combination of ASCII characters except the slash character (/) and the NULL (ASCII value of zero). In particular, watch out for file names that contain newlines, `IFS` characters, or wildcard characters. For example, the following names are all valid file names:

```
file
fi'le
fi"le
fi le
fi`le
fi*le
```

File names that begin with a hyphen are particularly troublesome because they frequently cause problems for the code that parses command line options; that code might not be able to distinguish an option from a file name that begins with a hyphen.

## Missing Quotes

Probably one of the most common mistakes in shell scripts is not using quotes when they are needed. A statement that is missing quotes may work fine in most situations, but it may fail when an unusual situation is encountered.

Notice in the following example the usage message is not printed correctly.

```
$ touch b
$ USAGE="Usage: command [abc]"
$ echo $USAGE
Usage: command b
$
```

In this example, the variable `USAGE` is not enclosed in double quotes when it is passed as a parameter to the `echo` command. When `USAGE` is replaced with its value, the characters `[abc]` are treated as wildcard characters. If `[abc]` matches one or more file names, these characters will be replaced in the command line with the names of the files that they match. In this example, they are replaced with the name of file b. Since the shell does not replace the wildcard characters in the command line unless they match a file name, this code will work fine until it is executed in a directory that has a file named a, b, or c.

To prevent the shell from evaluating [abc] as wildcard characters, you need to quote the variable when it is passed to the echo command.

```
echo "$USAGE"
```

The following example shows the DownShift function (discussed in Chapter 9, "Examples of Shell Functions") the way I originally wrote it.

```
DownShift() {
    echo $@ | tr '[A-Z]' '[a-z]'          # Missing quotes
}
```

This function was being used to downshift the input entered by the user so that the text could be evaluated in a case insensitive way. However, one of the responses typically entered by the user was a question mark (?). When the question mark in the variable $@ is echo'ed to the tr command, it is treated as a wildcard character. Thus, whenever the current directory contained a file with a one-character file name, the question mark would be replaced with the name of the file. To correct the problem, the variable $@ must be quoted, as shown here:

```
DownShift() {
    echo "$@" | tr '[A-Z]' '[a-z]'
}
```

## Empty Variables

An empty variable, when passed as a parameter to a command, will be treated in one of two ways, depending upon whether or not it is quoted. If an empty variable is not quoted when it is passed as a parameter to a command, it will simply disappear. After the variable has been substituted into the command line, there is nothing to indicate that it was ever there. This technique (having an empty variable disappear from the command line) can be useful when it is intentional.

The following lines are taken from the findstr command presented in Chapter 10. In this example, the variables I and L will either be empty or they will contain an option that is to be passed to the grep command. Since they are not quoted, these variables will disappear from the command line when they are empty, and they will pass an option to the grep command when they are not. This technique prevents having to build a complex if statement to construct the proper command line.

```
find . \( -type f -o -type l \) -name "$FILENAME" -print |
    xargs -e grep $I $L -- "$STRING" /dev/null
```

While it can be useful for an empty variable to disappear, it is more common that you want the value of a variable to be passed to a command even if it is empty; that is, you want to pass an empty parameter to a command. In the following example, the values between the square brackets are passed as parameters to the `test` command. Since the parameters to the `test` command are used to specify an expression, each parameter must be in its proper place when it gets to the `test` command or the `test` command will print an error indicating that the expression is not constructed correctly.

```
$ NAME=
$ if [ $NAME = "" ]; then
>    echo "Name is empty."
> fi
test: argument expected
$
```

In the example above, the variable `NAME` is empty and it is not quoted; therefore, after variable substitution, it disappears and will not get passed to the `test` command. Since the `test` command requires a value on both sides of the equal sign, it prints an error. To correct the problem, the variable `NAME` must be quoted, as shown here:

```
$ NAME=
$ if [ "$NAME" = "" ]; then
>    echo "Name is empty."
> fi
Name is empty.
$
```

Another common situation in which an empty variable causes problems occurs when the `set` command is used to parse the value of a variable (see "Parsing Data" in Chapter 8). In the following example, the variable `VAR` is empty; thus, it will disappear after it is substituted into the command line. However, when the `set` command is used without any parameters, it prints a list of the current variables.

```
VAR=
set $VAR        # Does not work.
```

To make matters worse, you cannot quote the variable because then the `set` command will not parse the value of the variable. In this case, you need to use the `- -` option of the `set` command, which will allow the parameter list of the `set` command to be empty. Some old versions of the shell do not support the `- -` option. ("The `set` Command" in Chapter 13 discusses some alternatives for situations in which the `set` command does not support the `- -` option.

```
VAR=
set -- $VAR
```

## STYLE

Discussions on coding style are usually controversial, and the characteristics of good coding style can be debated endlessly. However, while not endorsing any particular style, the following guidelines usually contribute to good style:

- Stay away from complex code sequences. Even though you understand what your code does, very few of us write code for ourselves. Most of us write code for a company that wants to ensure that the code we write will be easy for someone else to maintain in our absence.

- Software always lasts longer than you expect. This is especially true of shell scripts, since people frequently save old shell scripts so that they can be used as a template for another shell script.

- Conform to the style of the surrounding code when making changes. Even though you do not like the style, it is usually easier to understand code that is all written in the same style.

- Whitespace is not wasted space. When it comes to improving the readability of code, there is no substitute for liberal use of whitespace. This includes blank lines, as well as consistent indentation.

- Shorter is not necessarily faster. For some reason, small shell scripts give us a false sense that the shell script is fast or efficient.

Good programming style is as important when writing shell scripts as it is when writing any other type of code. Pick a style that you like and use it consistently. The days of programmers writing quick and dirty programs that no one else can understand are coming to an end. In the interest of saving time and money, companies expect their engineers to write programs that can be used, updated, and maintained by others. When a shell script grows to be more than a few lines, clear, well-commented code will be the single biggest asset when debugging, especially if you are not the author.

The remainder of this section shows examples of techniques that are used less frequently or that may be difficult to understand the first time they are seen. These examples are not necessarily good or bad; they are explained here so that if you see one of them, you will understand what the person who developed the code is trying to accomplish.

### Different Ways to Format Statements

There are many ways to format the control flow statements, and the format you choose will be the most distinguishing feature of your coding style. The examples in Chapter 1 presented each of the control flow constructs in what is probably the most common format. This section will show a variety of styles for an `if` statement so that you can see some other possibilities. Each of these examples does the same thing; it performs a test to determine if the directory `tmp` exists, and if not, it will create it. When reading these examples, remember that brackets (`[...]`) can be used interchangeably with the `test` command.

```
test -d tmp && mkdir tmp

[ -d tmp ] && mkdir tmp

if test -d tmp
then
    mkdir tmp
fi

if test -d tmp; then
    mkdir tmp
fi

if [ -d tmp ]
then
    mkdir tmp
fi

if [ -d tmp ]; then
    mkdir tmp
fi
```

## Another `if` Statement

The following example shows how you can use the standard shell syntax to create another type of conditional execution that is similar to an `if` statement.

[ *expression* ] && { *command-list1* } || { *command-list2* }

This syntax is intended to be equivalent to:

```
if [ expression ]
then
    command-list1
else
    command-list2
fi
```

However, this convention should be used carefully, since it does not provide any benefit over the standard `if` statement, and, more importantly, it does not always work as you might expect. If the last command in *command-list1* does not execute successfully, both *command-list1* and *command-list2* will be executed. Since there are many commands that use the exit status to return information from a normal execution (for example, `expr` and `diff`), this convention is prone to errors.

## Another Method of Quoting

In the following example, the letter x is appended to the front of the value of $1. This value is then compared with the letter x. If the two strings are equal, then $1 must be empty. This technique ensures that if the value of $1 is empty, it will not disappear when it is substituted into the command line.

```
if [ x = x$1 ]
then
    echo '$1 is empty.'
fi
```

In this example, it would probably be clearer to use quotes to prevent an empty variable from disappearing. The next example shows the same code, using quotes instead of the x's.

```
if [ "" = "$1" ]
then
    echo '$1 is empty.'
fi
```

This technique is more useful when the value of a string might be confused with an option to the command. For example, if you want to compare the value in $1 with the string -f, you must do something to prevent the test command from interpreting either string as an option. The following code will not work because the test command will interpret the string -f as the option to determine if a file exists:

```
if [ -f = $1 ]; then        # Wrong
    ...
fi
```

To avoid this problem, you can append the letter x to the front of both strings to ensure that they do not begin with a hyphen character and, thus, will not be misinterpreted as an option to the test command.

```
if [ x-f = x$1 ]; then
    ...
fi
```

## Using Variables

Do not forget that braces may be used around variable names even when they are not necessary. Since they are usually not needed, most people do not use them. Then, if you are not accustomed to seeing variables in braces, you may not recognize their purpose when you do see them.

```
echo $VAR
echo ${VAR}
```

An even more unusual place to see braces when they are not necessary is with the variables that are built into the shell. For example, in the following list, the variables in the first column are equivalent to the variables in the second column. The second column shows the more common way that the variable is written. The braces shown in the first column are not necessary, but they are allowed.

```
${1}                        $1
${*}                        $*
"${@}"                      "$@"
${FOO:=${BAR}}              ${FOO:=$BAR}
```

To carry the last example a little further, the following example shows that you can nest the variable initialization syntax to arbitrary levels:

```
$ UGH=ugh
$ echo ${FOO:=${BAR:=${BAZ:=${UGH}}}}
ugh
$
```

Do not forget that a variable can be assigned a value at the front of a command line in order for that assignment to be placed in the environment of the command without affecting the environment of the current process. For example, to display a clock on an X Window with the time from another time zone, you can set the TZ variable in the process environment of the xclock command without changing that variable in the current environment.[3]

```
TZ=EST5EDT xclock -title "East Coast"
```

Another style that is not used very often is to place more than one variable assignment on the same line. This only contributes to the compactness of the code, and, thus, it is not used very often.

```
VAR1=abc VAR2=def
```

## The : (null) Command

Whenever you see the null command used, you may wonder why it is being used, since the null command does not do anything. The section describing the null command in

---

[3] Look in the file /usr/lib/tztab for other time zones.

Chapter 3 shows examples of several common uses for the null command. In particular, remember that the null command can be used to invoke the behavior of the variable initialization syntax, while discarding the variable returned by that syntax.

```
: ${VAR="VAR is not set."}
```

Another common example is to use the null command with one of the file redirection syntaxes to truncate a file, as shown below.

```
: >file
```

In the next example, the null command is used as a comment character. Since the values passed on the command line of the null command are ignored, the null command can be used as a comment. However, there is no advantage to using this technique, and it can cause undesirable side effects if the comment contains shell metacharacters, such as a greater than sign ($>$); therefore, it is more of a novelty than a practical technique.

```
: This is a comment.
```

## Here Documents

Remember that the string used to mark the end of a here document can be any sequence of nonblank characters. The following example shows the exclamation mark used to mark the end of the here document:

```
cat <<!
This is a here document.
!
```

It is more common, and better practice, to use short words or mnemonics such as END, End, EOF, or EOD.

```
cat <<EOF
This is a here document.
EOF
```

## Input-Output Redirection

The shell allows the output redirection operator ($>$) to be used on a line without the command. This is useful if you want to delete the contents of a file or to create an empty file. For example:

```
>file
```

This is equivalent to using this operator with the null command.

```
: >file
```

The shell also allows the input-output redirection syntax to be placed anywhere on the command line. The following examples are all equivalent; they write the parameters of the echo command into the file tmp.

```
echo a b c >tmp
>tmp echo a b c
echo >tmp a b c
echo a >tmp b c
```

In practice, the input-output redirection syntax is almost always put at the end of the command line. Placing it at any other location does not improve the command in any way and is bound to cause confusion.

### Passing the Command Line

The following sequence is very cryptic if you have not seen it before. However, it is also very common. This syntax is usually used when it is necessary to pass the entire command line without introducing any changes. (For more information on this technique, see the "Positional Parameters" in Chapter 2.)

```
command ${@+"$@"}
```

This statement is equivalent to the following sequence:

```
if [ $# -eq 0 ]; then
    command
else
    command "$@"
fi
```

### Unusual Braces

Some versions of the shell allow braces to be used in place of the do and done keywords in the for statement and the in and esac keywords in the case statement. While this may arguably improve the readability of the code, it is an undocumented feature and, thus, it may not be portable.

```
case value {
    * ) echo "This is a test." ;;
}

for f in a b c {
    echo $f
}
```

## Unusual Semicolon

It is not uncommon to see a line in a shell script terminated by a semicolon. This is probably because it is common in C and other languages to terminate a line with a semicolon, and it was accidentally entered that way in the shell script. Since a semicolon is a statement separator in the shell, a semicolon can be at the end of most commands without causing any problem and, thus, go unnoticed. For example:

```
$ date;
Tue Jan  1 00:00:01 PDT 1991
$
```

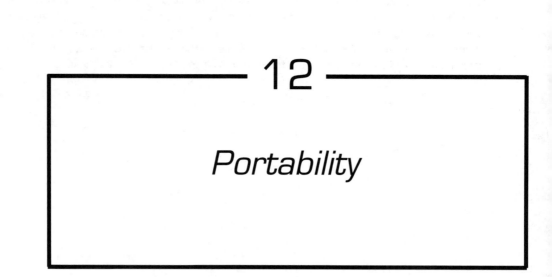

# *Portability*

One of the advantages of using a shell script rather than an executable program is that a shell script is portable from one system to the next without need of modification or compilation. The only catch is that to be portable, the shell script can only use those commands and features that are available on each system where it will be used. This chapter discusses some problems that you are likely to encounter when writing portable shell scripts, and it describes some of the techniques that you can use to make shell scripts more portable.

## DISTINGUISHING VERSIONS OF UNIX

This section discusses a variety of ways that you can distinguish one UNIX system from another.

### System V or BSD

There are two main types of UNIX systems: System V and BSD. System V is the version of UNIX that was developed at Bell Laboratories. BSD, which stands for Berkeley Software Distribution, was developed at the Computer System Research Group at the University of California at Berkeley.

In practice, the distinction between System V and BSD is not very useful because most systems include a combination of features from both types of system. Thus, knowing that the system is based on one of these types of UNIX does not ensure that a particular feature will behave as it normally does on that type of system. There are usually more reliable ways to determine how a feature works or if a feature is available on any particular system.

However, if you still want to determine whether the system is based on System V or BSD, you may be able to determine its type by looking at the name of the kernel. On System V systems, the kernel is usually in a file named /unix. On BSD systems, the kernel is usually in a file named /vmunix. This test may not always work, since some manufacturers use a completely different name for their kernel. For example, on HP-UX 9.0 the kernel is in the file /hp-ux. And on systems that conform to the System V Release 4 file layout, the kernel is in a file in the directory /stand rather than the root directory (/).

## By Manufacturer

There are a variety of commands on UNIX systems that differ, depending upon which company manufactured the system. These commands are usually associated with system administration, but they also include such everyday commands as df and du.

The uname command is usually used to get information that identifies the current system. The -s option is used to get the name of the operating system, the -r option is used to get the revision number of the operating system, and the -m option is used to get the model name of the computer hardware. The following table shows typical output from the uname command for a variety of systems.

| System | uname -s | uname -r | uname -m |
|---|---|---|---|
| DEC ULTRIX | ULTRIX | 4.3 | RISC |
| DEC OSF/1 | OSF1 | V3.0 | alpha |
| HP 9000 | HP-UX | A.09.05 | 9000/750 |
| IBM RS/6000 | AIX | 2 | |
| NEC | UNIX_System_V | | |
| SCO | *hostname* | 3.2 | i386 |
| SGI | IRIX | 5.2 | IP17 |
| Sun BSD | SunOS | 4.1 | |
| Sun Solaris | SunOS | 5.4 | sun4d |

To identify the company that manufactured the system you can usually use the uname -s command. Most manufacturers use this option to return the proprietary name of their operating system. On Digital Equipment's OSF systems, they return the more general name OSF1. Also, a few systems use the -s option of the uname command to return the name of the current system rather than the name of the operating system. (See "The uname Command" later in this chapter.)

The function SystemType in Chapter 9 encapsulates the interpretation of the information returned from the uname command and returns a string that uniquely identifies the current system. This function also provides examples of how to identify systems that return the name of the system rather than the name of the operating system for the `-s` option of the `uname` command.

## By Implementation

While `uname -s` can be used to identify the manufacturer of a system, it usually will not distinguish different implementations of UNIX that are produced by the same manufacturer. For example, even though SunOS changed significantly (from BSD to System V) when Solaris was released, `uname -s` still returns `SunOS`. Thus, to distinguish Sun's older BSD-based system from their newer System V system, you need to examine the version number of the operating system using `uname -r`.

When you examine the version number of the operating system, you need to be familiar with the numbering scheme used by the manufacturer. For example, when Sun released Solaris, they changed the version number of the operating system from 4 to 5. However, the number returned by `uname -r` will contain more than a single digit; for example, it might return 4.1 or 5.1. The function `SystemType` in Chapter 9 shows an example of how to distinguish Sun's older BSD-based system from their newer Solaris system by examining only the first digit of the version number.

Some manufacturers provide commands that return information about the model of the computer on which you are executing. This information is not usually used in shell scripts because there are usually more reliable ways to identify a system than by model of the computer. In addition, these commands are not standardized and, therefore, may not be available on all systems. The following commands, if they are available, are examples of commands that return success or failure to identify the current computer model. These commands may have been intended for use in make files and such, but they are not very useful in shell scripts.

```
hp-pa       i386        m68k        m68000      mips
pdp11       sparc       sun         u3b         u3b2
u3b5        vax
```

The `uname -r` command returns a string that identifies the model of the computer hardware, but on some systems this option does not return anything at all.

On Sun systems, the `arch` command can be used to distinguish computer models based on different architectures. For example, the `arch` command can be used on a Sun system to determine if the computer hardware is an Intel architecture or a SPARC architecture.

## By Version Number

As discussed in the previous section, the version number of the operating system can be used to identify different implementations of the same operating system. By checking the entire version number (rather than just the most significant digits of the version number), you may be able to identify minor update and fix levels of the operating.

It is usually not necessary to identify small revisions of the operating system, such as updates and fix level, because manufacturers try to maintain compatibility from one release to the next. However, testing for a specific version of the operating system may be necessary, for example, if a shell script takes advantage of a new feature that is not available on previous versions of the system. In that case, you may want to identify a particular revision so that you can print an appropriate error message or take some other action when the feature is used on the wrong version of the system.

## By Functionality

The most reliable method for determining whether or not you can use a feature is to devise a test that tests for that specific feature. There are several examples in this book that use this type of test. The following three examples give you an idea of how these tests can be used.

On systems that support the `getopts` command, the shell has been changed to initially set the variable OPTIND to 1 as an indicator that the `getopts` command is available. Since this will never happen on a system that does not have the `getopts` command, this is a reliable method for determining whether or not the `getopts` command can be used to parse the command line options. If `getopts` is not available, the shell script usually contains a less robust parser than it uses. An example of this technique is discussed later in this chapter (see "The `getopts` Command"), and it is used in the `findstr` command in Chapter 10.

When testing to see if a feature is available, it is unusual to have a variable that indicates whether or not it is available, as in the previous example. The `Clear` function in Chapter 9 takes a different approach; it simply executes a command that may or may not exist and then tests to see if it was successful. If the command fails, it tries another command. If that command also fails, the function executes a command that always works, although not quite as well.

Another common example of testing to determine if a feature is available is to execute the `echo` command with the `-n` option to determine if it is the System V version or the BSD version of the `echo` command. If it is the System V version, the `-n` will be displayed in the output, since it will be treated as a parameter instead of an option. If it is the BSD version, there will be no output, since `-n` is the option to suppress the newline at the end of the line. This was discussed in "Printing a Prompt" in Chapter 8.

## PORTABILITY TECHNIQUES

### Common Subset of Commands

The first thing that must be done in order to write a portable shell script is to identify a common subset of commands and features that are available on each system where your shell script will be used. Even though UNIX has a rich set of commands and features, many of them are not standard or not implemented the same on all systems.

The subset of commands and features that are available on every UNIX system is probably too small to be of any practical value. Fortunately, most people do not write shell scripts that will be used on every UNIX system. In practice, a shell script only needs to be portable to a small subset of the UNIX systems. It will be up to you as the developer of the shell script to identify where the shell script will be used and, further, to identify the set of commands and features that are needed by the shell script that are common to each of these systems.

Try to stick with standard UNIX commands. For example, the examples in this book use many different commands, but whenever there is a choice, they generally use very standard commands, such as the commands listed here:

| awk | cat | cmp | cp | echo |
|-----|-----|-----|-----|------|
| expr | grep | ln | mkdir | mv |
| pwd | sed | test | touch | tr |

You will certainly need other commands as well, but the fewer of those commands that you use, the less you will have to change when your shell script is used on a new system and one of them is not available. This will make your shell script easier to port to other systems later on.

The following commands are also likely to be available on most UNIX systems. However, even though these commands are likely to be available, some of them may work differently depending upon the type of the system (System V or BSD).

| ar | at | awk | basename | bc |
|------|-------|-------|----------|--------|
| cat | cd | chmod | chown | cmp |
| col | comm | cp | cut | date |
| dc | dd | df | diff | dirname |
| du | echo | ed | expr | false |
| file | find | grep | kill | ln |
| ls | mail | make | mkdir | mv |
| nohup | nice | od | pr | ps |
| pwd | rm | rmdir | sed | sh |
| size | sleep | sort | stty | su |
| tabs | tail | tar | tee | test |
| touch | tr | true | tty | uniq |
| what | who | write | wc | |

There are several other commands that are commonly used or needed, but these commands tend to be more closely associated with either System V or BSD UNIX.

System V Commands:

| cpio | env | id | line | logname |
|------|--------|-------|------|---------|
| lp | lpstat | mailx | tput | xargs |

BSD Commands:

```
compress    finger      head        hostname    last
lpq         lpr         lprm        more        printenv
ranlib      strings     which       whoami
```

Even when using relatively common commands, you will have to stick with the established features and options in these commands. You must take the least common denominator approach to selecting commands and features. That is, if a command or feature is not available on every system, then it may as well not be on any system. Since you have to find an alternative on one system, you may as well use the alternative that works on all systems.

Your best reference for information on the portability of commands and options will be the manual pages on the systems where the command will be used. Whenever you are attempting something that is out of the ordinary, be sure to read the manual page. If the manual page does not explicitly allow an action, it is not portable. Even if it works today, if the feature is not there intentionally, it may work differently or it may not work at all in a future release.

Another good reference to use when trying to identify portable commands and their options is the *X/Open Portability Guide.* While not strictly adhered to by the manufacturers, it is pretty reliable in defining a common subset of commands and their options that are available on most platforms. More often than not, the manufacturers will provide everything in this guide and a lot more. You may find a few instances where a manufacturer does not conform to the guide, and you will frequently need commands or options that are not listed in the guide, but it is a good starting point.

## Conditional Execution

The section "Distinguishing Versions of UNIX" earlier in this chapter discussed information that can be used as a basis for conditional execution. The function `IsSystemType` in Chapter 9 provides an abstraction for this information that lets you write statements such as shown below.

```
if IsSystemType "HP-UX"
then
      ...
fi
```

The `IsSystemType` function will return true (success) if the string that is passed to it matches one of the strings that is returned by the `uname` command. This abstraction lets you bracket nonportable code using a method that is similar to the `ifdef` facility of the C preprocessor.

The function `SystemType`, also presented in Chapter 9, provides a different abstraction for determining the type of the current system. It not only hides the method of comparing the strings returned by the `uname` command, but it hides the strings that are returned by `uname` as well. In their place is a set of strings that are defined and controlled by the implementation of the `SystemType` function. When a new system is added or the manufacturer changes the value of a string, there is only one place in the code that must be changed.

The following example show how this function can be used. In this example, the string returned by the `SystemType` function is saved in a variable so that it can be reused, which is more efficient than calling the function again.

```
SYSTEM=`SystemType`
if [ "$SYSTEM" = "SUNBSD" ]
then
      . . .
fi
```

Here is another example; this time the value returned from `SystemType` is used in a `case` statement.

```
SYSTEM=`SystemType`
case "$SYSTEM" in
    SCO )    ... ;;
    SGI )    ... ;;
    * )      echo "Unexpected system type." 1>&2 ;;
esac
```

## Abstraction

A common technique for writing portable code is to use shell functions to provide an abstraction for a task that is not portable from one system to the next. The idea is that you can implement a complicated task in a function and from then on, the function is used in its place. This prevents a shell script from becoming unnecessarily complicated with the code that is needed to perform the task on a variety of systems. The shell script can stay focused on the problem at hand.

As an example, the function `SpaceAvail` in "Determine Space Availability" in Chapter 8 provides an abstraction for determining how much space is available in a directory. This function first determines the type of system that it is executing on, and then it executes one of several code sequences depending upon the type of system.

A beneficial side effect of abstraction is that it causes you to encapsulate tasks in functions, which, in turn, improves the modularity and maintainability of the shell script.

## Providing a Standard Environment

Another common technique used in portable shell scripts is to provide a standard environment for such things as command names, command options, file names, and so forth.

This technique uses variables to store nonportable information. Then whenever the information is needed, the variable is used in its place. The task of determining the correct information for the current system is encapsulated in a startup file.

An example of a file that can be used to initialize a standard environment is shown below. To use this file, a shell script executes the following statement (assuming the file is named `environ.sh`):

```
. environ.sh
```

This causes the statements in `environ.sh` to be executed in the current shell script without creating a new process. You may need to ensure that the directory that contains this file is listed in the PATH variable, since the shell uses the PATH variable to locate files using the dot command.

```
#
# File: environ.sh
#
# This file initializes the variables used to setup a
# standard environment.  These variables contain values that
# are typically not the same from one system to the next.
# By storing these nonportable pieces of information in
# variables, the information can be determined once when the
# shell script is initialized, and the value in the variable
# can be used from then on.
#
# To use this file, execute the following statement near the
# beginning of your shell script:
#
#     . environ.sh
#
# The following variables are defined in the standard
# environment initialized by this file.
#
SYSTEM=`SystemType`     # String identifying the system
C=                      # Suppress newline of echo (Sys V)
N=                      # Suppress newline of echo (BSD)
L=                      # Symbolic link option for test cmd
RSH=                    # Name of remote shell command

#
# Initialize the variables.
#
case $SYSTEM in
     HP)  C='\c'
          N=
          L=h
          RSH=remsh
          ;;
```

```
    SCO)  C=
          N='-n'
          L=h
          RSH=rcmd
          ;;

    SGI)  C='\c'
          N=
          L=l
          RSH=/usr/bsd/rsh
          ;;



          .
          .
          .



    *)    echo "environ.sh: Unexpected type of system." 1>&2
          exit 1
          ;;
  esac
```

After this file is executed, the variables SYSTEM, C, N, L, and RSH will be initialized with values specific to the current system. The next few examples show how these
variables can be used in shell statement.

The variables C and N are used to hold options that suppress the newline at the end
of the output from the echo command. (This technique was discussed in "Printing a
Prompt" in Chapter 8.) The following example shows how these variables can be used
with the echo command:

```
echo $N "Would you like to ... [y/n]? $C"
```

The variable L holds the option that is used with the test command to test for
symbolic links. This option is either an h or an l, depending upon the type of system.
The initialization file determines the appropriate option for the current system and stores
it into the variable L. The following example shows how you can use the variable L with
the test command:

```
if [ -$L file ]; then
    echo "file is a symbolic link."
fi
```

The variable RSH holds the name of the remote shell command. This is necessary, since
the name of this command and its location are not standard from one system to the next

(see "Remote Command Execution" in Chapter 5). The following example shows how to use this variable in a remote command:

```
$RSH host echo foo
```

## LOCATING COMMANDS AND FILES

### File System Layout

The location of files on UNIX systems is not standard, but, with a few exceptions, most of the common commands and files are located in the same directory on most UNIX systems. However, on systems based on SVR4, the location of files is completely different. Here are some key directories and where they were moved to:

| | |
|---|---|
| /bin | /usr/bin |
| /lib | /usr/lib |
| /usr/adm | /var/adm |
| /usr/lib/cron | /etc/cron.d |
| /usr/mail | /var/mail |
| /usr/man | /usr/share/man |
| /usr/spool | /var/spool |
| /usr/tmp | /var/tmp |

Also, all executable files have been moved out of /etc and put in either /sbin or /usr/sbin.

On systems that use the new SVR4 file layout, there are usually symbolic links that allow files to be referred to by their old names. However, as time progresses, more and more of these systems will exist, and the need for them to have symbolic links to provide compatibility with older systems will fade. Thus, you cannot count on the links to be there if you are writing portable software.

### BSD Commands

Many of the commands from BSD UNIX are included on System V systems as standard commands. On some systems, there are additional BSD commands, but they are located in a special directory, since they are not part of the standard system. When such a directory exists, it is frequently named /usr/ucb, except on SGI systems, where it is named /usr/bsd.

Sometimes the same command is in both the /bin and /usr/ucb directories. When this happens, the command in /usr/ucb is usually a symbolic link to the corresponding command in /bin, but not always. If it is not a symbolic link, be careful because the two commands may not be the same. This may occur if the BSD version of the command and the System V version of the command are not the same.

The following list shows some of the commands you may find in /usr/ucb:

```
clear      compress     finger      ftp          head
hostid     hostname     lpq         lpr          lprm
mail       more         quota       printenv     rcp
renice     rlogin       rsh         ruptime      rwho
talk       uptime       users       whatis       whereis
which      whoami
```

### Which Files Are Portable?

The file /dev/null is available on all systems. Writing to /dev/null is always successful, and any data written to /dev/null is discarded. If /dev/null is read, the file will always appear to be empty.

The file /dev/tty is a synonym for the controlling terminal of a process. This device can be used to read and write messages to the terminal, even when the standard input or standard output has been redirected to another file. (There is an example of this technique in the Kill command in Chapter 10.)

The following file descriptor numbers are always used for the standard files:

```
0          standard input
1          standard output
2          standard error
```

## SHELL FEATURES

Even though the shell is available on all UNIX systems, the features of the shell are not the same on all systems. This section discusses some of those differences.

### Executing the Shell

When a command is executed on a UNIX system, the system must determine whether the command is an executable program or a shell script. If it determines that the command is a shell script, it must then determine which shell should be used to execute the shell script (see "Identifying Shell Scripts" in Chapter 5). So far in this book, I have indicated that you should start every shell script with the following line:

```
#!/bin/sh
```

This is probably the most accepted method for ensuring that a shell script will be executed by the Bourne shell, but there are times when this will not work:

- Some systems do not support the feature that allows this to work. For example, on SCO systems, a special option in the kernel (Hash Pling) must be enabled before this feature will work.

- Some systems, such as ULTRIX, provide a very limited shell as /bin/sh. In the case of ULTRIX, a more modern version of the shell is provided in the file /bin/sh5; however, if you change the first line of a shell script to use /bin/sh5, your shell script will not be portable to other systems.

- On some systems, the directory /bin no longer exists. The SVR4 file system layout does not provide a /bin directory. Instead, most commands are located in /usr/bin. Thus, if the first line of a shell script indicates that it should be executed by the program /bin/sh, that file may not exist. On these systems, the administrator will usually put a symbolic link between /bin and /usr/bin so that commands can be accessed by their old names; however, as time progresses, more and more of these systems will exist, and the need for them to have symbolic links to provide compatibility with older systems will fade. Thus, you cannot count on the links to be there if you are writing portable software.

## Variable Initialization

In Chapter 2, the following syntaxes were discussed as a means to initialize variables:

$\{ variable : -value \}$
$\{ variable : =value \}$
$\{ variable : ?message \}$
$\{ variable : +value \}$

As discussed in Chapter 2, these four types of initialization can be used with or without the colon. The colon tells the shell whether or not to treat an empty variable (one that has been assigned an empty string) the same as an uninitialized variable (one that has never been assigned a value). If the colon is present, uninitialized variables and empty variables will be treated the same. If the colon is omitted, empty variables are not treated as uninitialized variables.

Some older versions of the shell, such as /bin/sh on ULTRIX, do not support the colon in these syntaxes.

## File Redirection with Shell Built-ins

Some older versions of the shell, such as /bin/sh on ULTRIX, do not allow input-output redirection to be used with commands that are built into the shell, such as the read command. For example, the following statement may not be allowed:

```
read line 0<&3
```

In the case of the read command shown here, you may be able to use the line command instead. The line command does not provide the parsing capabilities of the read command, but because it is not a built-in command of the shell, its input can be redirected. Alternatively, you could put the `read` command in a subshell to perform the read and redirect the input of the subshell (see "Reading Files" in Chapter 4).

## Shell Functions

Some older versions of the shell, such as `/bin/sh` on ULTRIX, do not support shell functions. Since shell functions are so useful, you may consider one of the following alternatives if you must use a shell that does not provide them.

You can store commands in a variable and then execute the contents of the variable with the `eval` command. This works well with simple functions, but when the task gets more complicated, you probably are not contributing to the overall maintainability of the shell script. The following example shows a reasonably complicated function implemented this way. This function can be used to get a y or n answer from the user.

```
getyesno='(while read _ANSWER
        do
              case "$_ANSWER" in
                   [yY] )   exit 0  ;;
                   [nN] )   exit 1  ;;
                   * )       echo Please enter y or n." ;;
              esac
        done)'
```

To use this function, you would display the question and get the answer, as shown here:

```
echo "Would you like to ... [y/n]? \c"
if eval "$getyesno"; then
    echo "Yes"
else
    echo "No"
fi
```

Since executing a function uses the same command line format as executing a command, you can also simulate functions by using temporary shell scripts. To do this, each function is stored in your shell script as a here document. The here document is then copied to a temporary file when the shell script is executed.

```
cat <<\EOD >FunctionName
#!/bin/sh
    .

    .

    .
exit 0
```

```
EOD
chmod +x FunctionName
        .
        .
        .
```

*FunctionName parm1 parm2 . . .*

For example, the function `DownShift` from Chapter 9 can be implemented using this technique, as shown in the next example. Notice that to change a function into a shell script, all you need to do is remove the function name, the parentheses, and the opening brace at the front of the function, and the closing brace at the end of the function. You also have to be sure that the function does not rely on any side effects such as using variables that are global to the shell script and the function.

```
cat <<\EOD <DownShift
#!/bin/sh
#
# NAME
#     DownShift - downshift the alphabetic characters in a
#     string
# SYNOPSIS
#     DownShift string
#
# DESCRIPTION
#     This function will downshift the alphabetic characters
#     in the string.  Nonalphabetic characters will not be
#     effected.  The downshifted string will be written to the
#     standard output.

echo "$@" | tr '[A-Z]' '[a-z]'

exit 0
EOD

chmod +x DownShift
        .
        .
        .
```

If you use this technique, you may want to do some additional tasks, such as removing the temporary shell script when you are done, or creating it only if it does not already exist.

There is also a difference in the way functions are implemented in the shell on various systems. Some shells have only one set of positional parameters for the shell script and the functions within the shell script. This causes any function call to overwrite the positional parameters of the shell script. Newer versions of the shell save and restore the positional parameters around function calls. Therefore, if you are writing a portable shell script, be sure to save any of the command line parameters that are still needed before using a shell function. This is true for shells based on the original shell function implementation in SVR2, which includes HP-UX and ULTRIX `/bin/sh5`. The shell was modified in SVR3 to save and restore the positional parameters, but not all systems picked up that change.

### Using Another Shell

Sometimes when the shell on a system is very old or it is missing a feature that you need, you can use another shell on the system that is compatible with the Bourne shell. For example, on ULTRIX, you may be able to use `/bin/sh5` in place of `/bin/sh`.

Another possibility is to use the POSIX shell or the Korn shell, since they provide nearly all of the functionality of the Bourne shell, and these shells contain all of the Bourne shell's syntactic constructs. These shells primarily differ from the Bourne shell in that they have many additional capabilities beyond what is available in the Bourne shell. The following list discusses some differences that might cause a Bourne shell script to behave differently if it is executed by the Korn shell or the POSIX shell.

- Both the Korn shell and the POSIX shell support shell functions. Positional parameters are saved during a function call. When the function returns, the positional parameters are restored. Some versions of the Bourne shell do not save the positional parameters when a shell function is executed.

- Positional parameters are not limited to nine addressable parameters ($1 through $9) in the POSIX shell.

- The `for` and `while` loops are executed in the current process even when there is input or output redirection. Thus, assignments to variables inside these loops always remain after the loop completes.

- The `set` command uses `- -` to delimit the parameter list, not a single hyphen.

- The colon is supported in the variable initialization syntax.

- Korn shell sets $0 to the function name while the function is executing; the Bourne shell and the POSIX shell do not change the value of $0 when a function is executed.

- The x and v shell options must be set in each function where they are needed. In the Bourne shell, these options are global to the entire shell script including shell functions.

## ISSUES WITH SPECIFIC COMMANDS

This section discusses some of the portability issues that arise with specific UNIX command. This is an incomplete list, but it includes some of the most common problems that you are likely to encounter.

## The `cp` Command

On Sun BSD systems, you should not use the `cp` command to copy library files (library files usually end with the `.a` suffix). If you do use the `cp` command to copy a library file, the creation date of the file will not match the date stored in the symbol table of the library file, and the next time you use the library, you will get a message indicating that the symbol table is destroyed or out of date. It is easy enough to correct the problem; you simply use the `ranlib` command on the library, and it will repair the symbol table.

To avoid this problem, you can use the `cpio` command to copy the library, or you can put the library in a `tar` file while it is being copied and extract the library from the `tar` file at its new location.

## The `df` Command

The `df` command is a common source of information on the space allocation in a file system. However, the information is formatted differently by each manufacturer. In addition, some manufacturers report the information in units of 512 byte blocks, and others report the information in units of 1024 byte blocks.

These differences make it difficult to use a common method to extract information from the output of the `df` command. The section "Determining Space Availability" in Chapter 8 discusses how to parse the output of the `df` command on a variety of systems, and it shows a shell function that encapsulates the complexity of finding the amount of available space on those systems.

## The `du` Command

The `du` command reports the amount of space used in a directory; however, on some systems, the amount of space used is reported in units of 512 byte blocks, and on others it is reported in units of 1024 byte blocks. (The section "Determining Space Usage" in Chapter 8 shows an example of a shell function that will determine the amount of space used on a variety of system types.)

## The `echo` Command

There have been several places in this book where it was mentioned that there are two implementations of the `echo` command—the System V version and the BSD version. (The section "Printing a Prompt" in Chapter 8 explains how you can determine which version of the `echo` command you are using.)

The two versions of the `echo` command differ in the way they allow you to specify special characters. The System V version of the `echo` command allows you to specify special characters using the following conventions:

| | |
|---|---|
| `\b` | Backspace |
| `\c` | Print the line without a newline |

| | |
|---|---|
| \f | Form feed |
| \n | Newline |
| \r | Carriage return |
| \t | Horizontal tab |
| \v | Vertical tab |
| \\ | Backslash |
| \0*n* | Where *n* is an octal number representing an ASCII character |

The BSD version of the echo command supports one option, -n, to allow you to print the line without a newline at the end of the line. Any other special characters that you want in the output must be entered using the standard control sequences for the ASCII characters. These control sequences will also work with the System V echo command, but they are not frequently used because they represent nonprinting characters. Here are some common examples; however, these control sequences may be slightly different in some environments.

| | |
|---|---|
| ^H | Backspace |
| ^L | Form feed |
| ^J | Newline |
| ^M | Carriage return |
| ^I | Horizontal tab |
| ^K | Vertical tab |
| ^G | Bell (control-G) |

Be careful when you are testing the echo command, since the version of the echo command may be different in different shells on the same system. Thus, the version of the echo command that you are using in your interactive shell may not be the same as the echo command that is used by the Bourne shell. This is frequently a problem for C shell users who write Bourne shell scripts.

## The env **and** printenv **Command**

The env command and the printenv command will print out a complete list of the environment variables and their values. The env command is System V version of this command, and printenv is the BSD version. System V systems frequently support both of these commands.

The set command, when used without any parameters, also prints a list of variables and their values. But this list is a list of shell variables. It may look similar to the list of environment variables because the environment variables are copied to shell variables whenever a shell script is executed. (See "Environment Variables" in Chapter 5 for more information.)

## The getopts **Command**

The getopts command is not available on many systems; however, its use is encouraged whenever it is available. Therefore, on systems that do support the getopts command, the shell has been modified to assign an initial value of 1 to the variable OPTIND. Since this will never happen on a system that does not support the getopts command, this is a reliable method for determining whether or not the getopts command can be used to parse the command line options.

Since this assumes that a shell script will do something useful if it determines that the getopts command is not available, these shell scripts usually include additional code that will parse the command line when the getopts command is not available.

The following example shows how to test whether or not the getopts command is available. (The two parsing techniques that are used in this example are both explained in Chapter 6.) This example shows how to combine the two methods so that the getopts parsing technique will be used if it is available, and the other technique will be used if it is not.

```
FLAG=FALSE
VALUE=
OPT=
if [ "$OPTIND" = 1 ]; then
    while getopts fv: OPT
    do
        case $OPT in
            f)  FLAG=TRUE
                ;;
            v)  VALUE=$OPTARG
                ;;
            \?) echo "Usage: ..." 1>&2
                exit 1
                ;;
        esac
    done
    shift `expr $OPTIND - 1`
else
    while [ $# -gt 0 ]
    do
        case $1 in
            -f) FLAG=TRUE
                shift
                ;;
            -v) VALUE=$2
                shift 2
                ;;
            -v*)VALUE=`echo "$1" | sed 's/^..//'`
                shift
                ;;
            --) shift
                break
                ;;
            -*) echo "Usage: ..." 1>&2
```

```
                                    exit 1
                                    ;;
                           *)    break
                                    ;;
                    esac
              done
       fi
```

## The `hostname` **Command**

The `hostname` command returns the name of the current system. Usually the name of the system returned by this command is the simple name of the system, but on some systems, this name will include the domain name of the system. (The section "Getting the Name of the System" in Chapter 5 shows how to remove the domain name from the name of the system.)

Also, the `hostname` command is usually located in the directory `/bin`, except on SGI systems, where it is in the directory `/usr/bsd`.

## The `ls` **Command**

The output of the `ls -l` command is slightly different on System V systems and BSD systems. In the System V version of the `ls -l` command, the file information includes the group ownership of the file in the fourth field. On BSD systems, the group ownership of the file is not printed unless the `-g` option is used.

These two different formats of the `ls -l` command will cause problem for any shell script that parses the output of the command to get the size of the file. On System V systems, the file size is in the fifth field of the output, and on BSD systems, the file size is in the fourth field.

## The `mkdir` **Command**

The `-p` option of the `mkdir` command causes it to create any missing components in the directory path leading up to the directory in addition to creating the directory itself. Some versions of the `mkdir` command do not support this option, and on some systems, it will not work if the directory being created is on an NFS mounted file system.

The `MkDir` Command (discussed in Chapter 10) is a shell script that provides the same functionality as the `mkdir` command with the `-p` option.

## The `ps` **Command**

The `ps` command is frequently used to get general information about the processes that are executing on a system. However, there are two versions of this command—the System V version and the BSD version. These versions differ both in the options that are provided and in the format of the output:

The following two commands show the options that are typically used with the two versions of the `ps` command to print a full display of process information:

```
ps -ef      # System V systems

ps -aux     # BSD systems
```

With the BSD style `ps` command, you can use the `w` option (wide) to prevent the process name from being truncated if the output from the `ps` command extends beyond 80 characters.

If you parse the output from the `ps` command, there are some things you need to watch for. The fields are usually separated by whitespace, except that some fields with large values may run together with the previous field, in which case, there will be no whitespace separating those fields. Also, some fields contain a time value that may be in the format *hh:mm:ss* or *Month Day* depending upon the value. Notice that the former value does not contain whitespace, but the later one does.

The `Kill` command in Chapter 10 is an example of a command that parses the output of the `ps` command. In that example the process ID, the owner, and the name of the process are extracted from the output of the `ps` command.

## The `pwd` Command

Through the use of symbolic links, a directory may have more than one valid path name. For example:

```
mkdir /abc
mkdir /def
ln -s /def /abc/xxx
```

The names `/def` and `/abc/xxx` both refer to the same directory. If you change directories to `/abc/xxx`, what would you expect the `pwd` command to print? Either `/abc/xxx` or `/def` would be correct. The answer is that it depends on which version of `pwd` you use. The `pwd` command is built into the Bourne shell, but it is also a command in `/bin`. The following example shows the output from these two versions of `pwd` when they are executed on a SunOS 4.1 system:

```
$ cd /abc/xxx
$ /bin/pwd
/def
$ sh -c "pwd"
/abc/xxx
$
```

## The Remote Shell Command

There are several different names for the remote shell command:

```
rsh         rcmd        remsh
```

These versions of the remote shell command are interchangeable other than their names, although some versions of the remote shell command require the host name to the first parameter, while others allow options to precede the host name.

You also need to be careful on systems in which the remote shell command is named `rsh` because that may also be the name of the restricted shell. For example, on SGI systems, `/bin/rsh` is the restricted shell, and `/usr/bsd/rsh` is the remote shell.

## The `set` Command

Many commands allow the `- -` option to indicate that there are no more options, and the remaining values on the command line are parameters. (This was discussed in "Command Line Conventions" in Chapter 6.) The `- -` option is frequently used with the `set` command to load the positional parameters. It prevents the parameter list from appearing to be empty when the value to be loaded into the positional parameters is empty, and it prevents the value to be loaded into the positional parameters from being interpreted as an option if it happens to begin with a hyphen.

However, the `set` command in very old versions of the shell (for example, ULTRIX) uses a single hyphen for this purpose rather than a double hyphen. While some systems will allow either the single hyphen or the double hyphen, not all systems that use the double hyphen also allow the single hyphen (for example, HP-UX).

A common technique for terminating options to the `set` command is to pass a dummy parameter in place of the double hyphen. Since the first parameter that does not begin with a hyphen terminates the list of options, and it is easy to remove the first parameter with the shift command, passing a dummy parameter works just as well as the double hyphen. This technique works with all versions of the shell.

```
set dummy $VAR
shift
```

## The `shift` Command

It is common to see multiple shifts written as multiple executions of the `shift` command rather than specifying the shift count as a parameter to the `shift` command. This is a more portable technique, since some very old shells do not support a shift count as a parameter on the `shift` command.

```
shift; shift
```

Or:

```
shift 2
```

## The `test` Command

The section on the `test` command in Chapter 3 listed the options that are available with the `test` command on most systems. The `test` command usually supports many other options as well, but they are not very standard and, thus, not very portable. Two of these options are used frequently enough that they deserve special attention—the option to test whether or not a file is a symbolic link, and the option to test whether or not a file has execute access.

Many systems support an option to determine whether or not a file is a symbolic link; however, the name of the option is not consistent across all systems. For example, SGI systems use the `-l` option to test for a symbolic link. Most other systems use the `-h` option. While the `-h` option is less of a mnemonic, it is consistent with the corresponding option of the `tar` command.

The `-x` option is an option in the `test` command on most systems to determine whether or not a file has execute access. However, this option is not provided in the `test` command in the shell on ULTRIX systems.

## The `touch` Command

The date specification of the `touch` command is evolving to a new format. In most older versions of the `touch` command, you specify the date as follows:

```
touch [mmddhhmm[yy]] file ...
```

In newer versions of the `touch` command, required for X/Open compliance, you specify the date as follows:

```
touch [-t [[CC]YY]MMDDhhmm[.SS] file ...
```

Fortunately, most systems that support the newer format of the date specification also support the older format of the date specification for backwards compatibility.

## The `tr` Command

Some versions of the `tr` command require you to enclose ranges of characters in brackets, while others do not.

```
tr '[a-z]' '[A-Z]'        # System V system
```

Or:

```
tr 'a-z' 'A-Z'            # BSD systems
```

If the brackets are used with a version of the `tr` command that does not require them, they will be translated, `[` to `[` and `]` to `]`, which is harmless, except in a situation in which you actually want the bracket characters to be translated to some other character.

## The `uname` Command

The `uname` command allows the manufacturer to return information that identifies various aspects of the system. As discussed earlier in this chapter, this information is very useful for writing conditional statements to make shell scripts portable. However, there are two common problems with this command:

1. The `-m` option of the `uname` command is used to return the model name of the computer system; however, on some systems this option does not return anything at all. This makes the use of this option unreliable.

2. Most manufacturers use the `-s` option of the `uname` command to return the proprietary name of their operating system. On Digital Equipment's OSF systems, they return the more general name `OSF1`. Also, a few systems use the `-s` option to return the name of the current system rather than the name of the operating system. The `-s` option is defined to be the "system name," which is somewhat ambiguous. Most manufacturers interpret the system name to be the name of the operating system and the "node name" to be the name of the system as defined by the user. I have seen two systems that return the name of the system as defined by the user for the command `uname -s`:

   1. SGI's IRIX version 3.3 and before; newer versions of IRIX return the string `IRIX` for the command `uname -s`.

   2. As of version 3.2 of SCO's operating system, it still returned the name of the system as defined by the user for `uname -s`.

## The `unset` Command

Some older shells do not support the `unset` command to remove variables from the shell environment. This is not usually a problem, since the `unset` command is rarely used in shell scripts.

## The `until` Command

Some versions of the shell support an `until` control flow statement. Since it is not available in many versions of the shell, and it is easily replaced with a `while` statement, this control flow statement has not been mentioned elsewhere in this book.

## OTHER PORTABILITY PROBLEMS

### Short File Names

There are still some systems that only allow fourteen character file names. Also, this restriction may be an attribute of individual file systems rather than the whole system. Therefore, some directories on a system may have the restriction, while others do not.

If you use a file name that is more than fourteen characters, these systems will silently truncate the name to fourteen characters. This may cause unexpected file name collisions if the file names used by a shell script are not unique within the first fourteen characters. This may also cause interoperability problems if the file names are passed between systems that have different restrictions on the length of a file name.

To determine if a system restricts file names to fourteen characters, you can create a file with a file name that is greater than fourteen characters and use the `ls` command to see whether or not the system truncated the file name.

### Explicit Path Names

Using explicit path names for commands is likely to cause a problem since the commands may be in different directories on different systems (see "Locating Commands and Files" earlier in this chapter). Unless there is a reason not to, it is usually better to name a command without its path and make sure all of the possible paths for the command are in the PATH variable (see "The PATH Variable" in Chapter 5).

# 13

## Common Questions and Problems

**I COPIED ONE OF THE EXAMPLES FROM THIS BOOK**
**BUT IT DOES NOT WORK. WHAT IS WRONG?**

The syntax of the shell and the syntax of UNIX commands can be very picky at times. Pay particular attention to the following pitfalls:

- Be sure that you have transcribed the example exactly as it is printed.
- Occasionally, tab characters will be required and must not be confused with spaces. When this is necessary, the accompanying text will make this clear; otherwise, spaces and tabs can be used interchangeably.
- Be sure to include spaces where they are shown and not to add spaces where they are not shown.
- Be sure to distinguish between characters that look the same. Even though they look the same, they will have very different meanings:

  The single quote ( ' ) and the back quote ( ` ).
  The backslash character ( \ ) and the forward slash character ( / ).
  The letter ell ( l ) and the number one ( 1 ).
  The capital letter oh ( O ) and the number zero ( 0 ).

232

## WHY DO I ALWAYS SEE THE FOLLOWING LINE AT THE FRONT OF SHELL SCRIPTS?

```
#!/bin/sh
```

This is a directive to the UNIX kernel. Whenever a file is passed to the `exec` system call, the system reads the first two characters to get the magic number. The character sequence `#!` identifies this file as an interpreted file. The system then reads the rest of the line to get the name of the interpreter. In this case, the name of the interpreter is `/bin/sh`, which is the file name of the Bourne shell. (This is discussed in more detail in "Identifying Shell Scripts" in Chapter 5.)

## WHAT DOES THE FOLLOWING LINE MEAN IN A SHELL SCRIPT?

```
# @(#) Some descriptive comment.
```

Since the line begins with a `#`, the line is interpreted by the shell as a comment; however, the character sequence `@(#)` is a special pattern that is used by the `what` command to locate comments in files. It is a common practice to put a line, such as the one shown, in a shell script to give a brief description of what the file does. For example, if you have a file named `MyCommand` that contains the following lines:

```
#!/bin/sh
#
# @(#) This is my command.
#
```

Then, the `what` command will extract the comment as shown here:

```
$ what MyCommand
MyCommand:
    This is my command.
$
```

## HOW DO YOU DO A GOTO IN THE SHELL?

There is no goto in the shell, but you can use the control flow statement described in Chapter 1 to add structure to your code, which may eliminate the need for a goto statement.

## HOW DO YOU INCLUDE A FILE IN A SHELL SCRIPT?

The dot command, shown below, is a shell command that instructs the shell to execute the contents of another file. It behaves the same as if the contents of the file are included in the shell script in place of the statement.

```
. file
```

## WHY AM I HAVING TROUBLE CONTINUING A COMMAND
## ON THE NEXT LINE?

A backslash character immediately followed by a newline causes the newline to be ignored by the shell. If you are having trouble with this, it is probably caused by inadvertently entering a space or tab character after the backslash. You should also make sure you have not put a comment after the backslash and that you are not trying to continue a line that ends in a comment.

```
echo "This will not work."      \<space>
echo "This will not work."      \    # Comment
echo "This will not work."           # Comment      \
```

## HOW CAN I USE PARENTHESES IN AN EXPRESSION
## WITH THE test COMMAND?

If you enter something such as the following, you will surely get a syntax error.

```
$ if [ ( 2 -eq 2 ) -a ( 5 -eq 5 ) ]; then
syntax error: '[' unexpected
$
```

The problem is that the shell is trying to evaluate the parentheses when you intended them to be passed through to the test command. (Remember, the square brackets are actually an alias for the test command.) To get this to work, all you need to do is quote the parentheses so that they will be ignored by the shell.

```
$ if [ \( 2 -eq 2 \) -a \( 5 -eq 5 \) ]; then
>     echo "Now it works."
> fi
Now it works.
$
```

## WHY DO CHANGES TO THE VALUE OF A VARIABLE DISAPPEAR?

This occurs when the shell decides to execute a portion of the shell script in a subshell. When this happens, the value of any variable will revert to its value before the subshell was created. This frequently happens when the standard input or standard output of a `while` loop is redirected. For example:

```
$ I=before
$ while :
> do
>     I=after
>     break
> done < file
$ echo $I
before
$
```

The section "Reading Files" in Chapter 4 shows how you can use the `exec` command to prevent this `while` loop from executing in a subshell.

## WHY DO THE COMMAND LINE PARAMETERS DISAPPEAR OR CHANGE?

If the command line parameters change after the shell script begins to execute, it is probably the side effect of one of the commands in the shell script. In particular, the `shift` command or the `set` command has been executed in the shell script.

The `shift` command shifts the positional parameters one position to the left. It is unlikely that this command will be used accidentally. However, the `set` command is commonly used to parse information. When the `set` command is used this way, it assigns the parsed information to the positional parameters. Thus, using the `set` command will destroy the original command line parameters.

Also, on some systems, there is only one set of positional parameters for both the parameters of the shell script and the parameters of functions that are executed by the shell script. If this is the case, you will need to save the command line parameters before the first function is called.

## WHY DOES MY SHELL SCRIPT PRINT A LIST OF VARIABLES?

When the `set` command is used to parse its parameters and store them into the positional parameters, it is easy to inadvertently pass an empty parameter to the `set` command. However, the function of the `set` command, when it does not receive any parameters, is to print a list of the current variables.

In the following example, if the variable VAR is empty, it will disappear after it is substituted into the command line.

```
VAR=
set $VAR      # Does not work.
```

If you see this behavior, you can correct it by preceding the variable with `- -`, as shown in the next example.[1]

```
VAR=
set -- $VAR
```

Notice that you cannot enclose the variable in quotes because that would prevent the shell from parsing the contents of the variable, which is probably not what you want. (See "Parsing Data" in Chapter 8 for more information on parsing data with the `set` command.)

```
VAR=
set "$VAR"    # Does not work.
```

## HOW CAN I PASS A VARIABLE TO sed?

Many of the examples in this book use shell variables to pass information into `sed` scripts. The important thing to remember is that the shell will perform variable substitution inside double quotes but not inside single quotes. Then, all you have to do is put the variable where you want the shell to substitute its value. In the following example, the value of the variables `OLD_TEXT` and `NEW_TEXT` will be substituted into the `sed` script before it is executed.

```
sed "s/$OLD_TEXT/$NEW_TEXT/g" file >newfile
```

The next question shows a technique that is more commonly used with `awk`, but it works equally well with `sed`.

## HOW CAN I PASS A VARIABLE TO awk?

Since `awk` scripts tend to be longer than `sed` scripts and they often contain dollar signs, they are usually quoted with single quotes. To pass a variable to an `awk` program, you simply end the quote just before the variable and start the quote immediately after the variable. It is usually a good idea to enclose the variable in double quotes to prevent any problems that could occur if the variable contains whitespace. For example:

```
who | awk '/^'"$LOGNAME"'/ { print $2 }'
```

When reading this example, remember that the first instance of a quote character begins the quote. The next instance of the quote characters ends the quote. This pattern is repeated across the command line as many times as necessary.

---

[1] On some systems, the `- -` option is not supported with the `set` command. On these systems, you can use a single hyphen for the same purpose.

## HOW CAN I SUBSTITUTE A PATTERN THAT CONTAINS
## A / USING sed?

The use of the slash character as a delimiter in sed scripts is a frequently followed convention, but any character that is not in the text can be used. For example, you will often see the % character used as the delimiter in sed scripts that process file names. Even though the % character can be used in a file name, it is much less likely to be used than the / character. For example, the following two sed commands are the same, except for the choice of the delimiters.

```
sed -e "s/OldText/NewText/g" file >newfile

sed -e "s%OldText%NewText%g" file >newfile
```

You can also use backslashes to escape the slashes that are part of the pattern. For example:

```
sed "s/old\/pattern/new\/pattern/g" file >newfile
```

## HOW CAN I WRITE MESSAGES TO THE STANDARD ERROR FILE?

The echo command is typically used to display messages from shell scripts. Since the output of the echo command is normally written to the standard output, you will need to redirect its output to the standard error, as shown here:

```
echo "Message" 1>&2
```

## HOW DO I READ FROM THE TERMINAL?

This is probably easier than you think; you simply use the read command. This command is built into the shell; therefore, it does not have its own manual page. The read command reads one line at a time, and it will block until the user enters a response followed by the return key. For example:

```
read ANSWER
echo "The user entered $ANSWER"
...
```

## WHY DOES MY FILE APPEAR EMPTY AFTER READING ONLY ONE LINE?

This problem is encountered quite frequently, and it is certainly not obvious the first time you see it. It is caused by one of the commands inside the loop reading the remainder of the standard input. The most common way for this to occur is to execute a remote shell command inside the loop. When a remote shell command is executed, the shell sends the standard input to the remote command. Since the shell has no way of knowing how much, if any, of the standard input is needed by the remote command, it sends it all. Thus, when the remote shell returns, the standard input is empty. For example:

```
while read LINE
do
        rsh host command
done <file
```

This problem can be corrected by redirecting the standard input of the remote shell to /dev/null. Some versions of the remote shell provide a -n option to do this for you.

```
rsh host command </dev/null
```

## HOW CAN I READ A FILE ONE LINE AT A TIME?

You can use a while loop and the read command to read a file one line at a time. In the following example, each line of the file is read into the variable LINE, one line for each execution of the loop. When the end of the file is reached, the status from the read command will cause the loop to complete.

```
while read LINE
do
        . . .
done <file
```

When the standard input or standard output of a while loop is redirected, as in the example above, the loop will be executed in a subshell. This in turn causes modifications to variables made inside the loop to be lost when the loop completes. (The section "Reading Files" in Chapter 4 discusses ways to avoid this problem.)

## WHY DOES A FOR LOOP READ A FILE ONE WORD AT A TIME?

The for loop normally separates its input into words delimited by the characters in the IFS variable. Since the IFS variable usually contains a space, tab, and newline, the for loop processes its input one word at a time. If you set the IFS variable to contain only the newline character, the for loop will read its input one line at a time.

```
IFS='
'
for line in `cat file`
do
      . . .
done
```

Since the `IFS` variable is used for purposes other than parsing the word list of the `for` loop, its original value should be restored as soon as the temporary value is no longer needed to prevent undesirable side effects.

Using a `for` loop to read a file has the advantage over the `while` loop from the previous example because it is not executed in a subshell. Therefore, any modifications to variables made inside the loop will not be lost when the loop completes.

## HOW CAN I READ A FILE ONE WORD AT A TIME?

The problem from the previous question is now the behavior that we would like to achieve. Therefore, we could use a `for` loop, as in the previous question. Inside the loop, the `echo` command is used to write each word to the standard output, one word per line.

```
for WORD in `cat file`
do
      echo $WORD
done
```

If you want to change a file so that every word is on a line by itself, you can use the following command to change spaces to newlines. If the original file contains more than one space between words, this command will change the extra spaces to blank lines.

```
tr ' ' '\012' <infile >outfile
```

## HOW CAN I STRIP THE CARRIAGE RETURNS (^M)
## FROM A DOS FILE?

This is a common problem when moving text files from DOS to UNIX. Each line in a DOS text file usually ends with a carriage return and a newline. In UNIX, each line in a text file ends with a newline. When DOS text files are viewed on UNIX, the carriage return appears as a ^M at the end of each line.

The following command deletes all carriage return characters from the file. Be sure you only execute this command on text files; it would most likely destroy a binary file.

```
tr -d '\015' <infile >outfile
```

## HOW CAN I COPY A DIRECTORY?

The simplest way to copy a directory is to use the `cp` command with the `-r` option, as shown below:

```
cd  directory1
cp  -r  .  directory2
```

This command, however, does not preserve some of the file attributes, such as file access permissions and file modification times. The `cpio` command allows more control over how the files are copied. The following command will probably be sufficient for most situations:

```
cd  directory1
find  .  -depth  -print  |  cpio  -pdmu  directory2
```

This topic is covered in more detail in "Copying Directories" in Chapter 8, and the `dircopy` command in Chapter 10 is an example of a shell script that can be used to copy a directory.

## HOW CAN I SEARCH A DIRECTORY FOR A FILE?

With heavily populated hierarchical directories, it is often difficult to locate files, even when you know the name of the file. The following command will search the current directory for a file and print the path name of the file if it is found.

```
find  .  -name  file  -print
```

If you do not know the exact name of the file, you can use wildcard characters as long as they are quoted. For example:

```
find  .  -name  "*pattern*"  -print
```

(See "Searching Directories" in Chapter 8 and the `findfile` command in Chapter 10.)

## HOW CAN I SEARCH A DIRECTORY FOR A FILE
## THAT CONTAINS A STRING?

This has to be one of the most requested and duplicated functions of all time. Everyone seems to have a copy of a command that does something like this (except the vendors, of course).

The `find` command is indispensable for traversing through directories and processing the elements in a variety of ways. In this example, we use the `find` command to locate every regular file and pass its name on to the `grep` command.

```
find . -type f -exec grep "string" /dev/null {} \;
```

The `xargs` command is not available on all systems, but when it is, it can provide a considerable performance boost to commands such as this. In the example above, the `grep` command is executed on every file. Using the `xargs` command, the file names are collected into groups, and then a group of file names is passed to the `grep` command. The following example shows the equivalent command written using `xargs`.

```
find . -type f -print | xargs -e grep "string" /dev/null
```

(See "Searching Directories" in Chapter 8 and the `findstr` command in Chapter 10.)

## HOW CAN I DOWNSHIFT ALL THE FILE NAMES IN A DIRECTORY?

This may be necessary, for example, when moving files between incompatible file systems, such as DOS and UNIX. The following command takes each file in the current directory and renames it to its downshifted namesake. Note that this command does not prevent you from renaming a file to an existing file, thereby deleting that file. For example, if you had two files, ABC and Abc, when this command is completed, there will only be one file named abc.

```
for f in *
do
    mv $f `echo $f | tr '[A-Z]' '[a-z]'`
done
```

## HOW CAN I RENAME ALL OF THE FILES NAMED xxx* TO yyy*?

The `mv` command is used to rename files in UNIX, but it does not allow more than one file to be renamed at the same time. The following example shows how to use a `for` loop to rename each file in a current directory that begin with the prefix xxx to the corresponding file name that begins with yyy.

```
OLD=xxx
NEW=yyy
for f in $OLD*
do
    SUFFIX=`expr $f : '$OLD\(.*\)'`
    mv $OLD$SUFFIX $NEW$SUFFIX
done
```

The `for` statement is used to process each file that begins with the original prefix. Inside the `for` loop, the `expr` command is used to remove the prefix so that only the suffix remains. Then, the new and old file names are constructed and used as parameters to the `mv` command.

## HOW CAN YOU TELL IF ONE FILE IS NEWER THAN ANOTHER?

The following code sequence provides a simple comparison of the modification dates of two files.

```
if [ -n "`find file1 -newer file2 -print`" ]
then
    echo "Yes; file1 is newer than file2."
else
    echo "No; file1 is not newer than file2."
fi
```

(This topic is covered in more detail in "Comparing File Dates" in Chapter 8 and the `IsNewer` function in Chapter 9.)

## HOW CAN I SET AN ENVIRONMENT VARIABLE IN A SHELL SCRIPT AND HAVE THAT CHANGE AFFECT MY CURRENT ENVIRONMENT?

The simple answer is that you can't. However, there are clumsy ways to accomplish this. The problem is that when a shell script is executed, a new process is created to execute the shell script, and UNIX is designed so that a process cannot make changes to the environment of the process that created it.

However, if all you need to do is define some common shell commands in a separate file, you can use the dot command.

```
. file
```

This command instructs the shell to execute the commands inside the file without creating a new process. Thus, any variables defined or changed inside the file will affect the current environment. (For more information on this topic, see the sections "Changing the Child Environment" and "Changing the Parent Environment" in Chapter 5.)

## HOW CAN I PASS THE ENTIRE COMMAND LINE TO ANOTHER COMMAND?

The special variable `$@` refers to all of the positional parameters. When it is enclosed in quotes, it will reliably reproduce the parameter list. (Without the quotes, parameters that contain whitespace will be split into separate parameters.)

```
#!/bin/sh
command "$@"
```

However, if there are no parameters, the shell on some systems interprets "$@" to mean one empty parameter. But one empty parameter is not the same as no parameters at all. The following command corrects this problem by using one of the variable initialization syntaxes:

```
#!/bin/sh
command ${@+"$@"}
```

This is equivalent to the following command:

```
#!/bin/sh
if [ $# -eq 0 ]; then
    command
else
    command "$@"
fi
```

## WHEN EXECUTING A COMMAND I GET THE MESSAGE
*command*: `arg list too long`. WHAT SHOULD I DO?

There is a limit to the maximum length of a command line. This limit is usually very large[2]; however, some commands allow an unlimited number of parameters to be passed on the command line. When the parameter list is a list of file names, it is common to use wildcard characters or other commands such as the `find` command to create a list of file names to be passed to the command on the command line. Thus, it is easy to inadvertently exceed the maximum command line length, which will result in this message being printed.

On System V systems, and some BSD systems, the `xargs` command can provide a solution to this problem. The `xargs` command is used to gather a large number of parameters and package them into smaller groups that are then passed on to another command. The `xargs` command receives the parameters from its standard input rather than on the command line so that it can avoid the limit on the command line length.

In the following command, the `grep` command will be passed the names of every file in the current directory:

```
grep "pattern" *
```

If there are so many files in the current directory that this command exceeds the maximum command line length, it could be rewritten using `xargs`, as follows:

```
echo * | xargs grep "pattern"
```

---

[2] The command line length is limited by the number of characters, not the number of parameters. The limit can usually be found in `/usr/include/limits.h` as a define called `ARG_MAX` or in `/usr/include/sys/param.h` as a define called `NCARGS`.

# Appendix A

## Comparison of UNIX Shells

### OVERVIEW

As you know, the shell is the interface between the user and the UNIX system. Its purpose is to execute the commands entered by the user. The shell can be used to execute commands in one of two ways—it can execute commands that are entered interactively, or it can execute commands that are read from files or shell scripts. This book is concerned with using the shell to execute shell scripts; however, when comparing the various shells that are available on UNIX systems, you need to consider the capabilities of the shell as an interactive command interpreter, as well as its ability to execute shell scripts.

The features of a shell that make it useful for interactive work do not necessarily make it good for executing shell scripts and vice versa. The features of a shell that make it useful for interactive work are those that help the user enter and execute commands more efficiently, such as:

- Aliases to allow abbreviations of commonly used commands. This cuts down on the amount of typing the user must do.
- File name completion to assist the user to enter file names. Once the user has entered enough of the file name to make it unique, the shell will fill in the remainder of a file name. Some shells also provide this capability for other information, such as user names.

244

- Command history substitution to allow previously executed commands to be repeated or edited and then executed again.

The features of a shell that make it useful for executing shell scripts are the features that make the shell a good programming language. As you can see from the examples in this book, shell scripts can be much more than a simple list of commands that are executed one after another. Entering fewer keystrokes is not an asset in shell scripts, so features like aliases, command completion, and command history substitution are of little or no value in shell scripts. The features that make a shell useful for executing shell scripts are features such as:

- Control flow constructs, such as conditional execution and loop control statements
- Flexible control of input and output operations
- Signal processing
- Functions

And of course, there are many features that are useful in both interactive shells and shell scripts.

There are many shells available to chose from, and choosing the right shell is important in order to work efficiently on UNIX systems; however, this does not mean that the same shell is right for every user. You may also find that the best shell for interactive work is not the best shell for executing shell scripts.

The remainder of this appendix gives a brief description of the most common shells available on UNIX systems. The relative strengths and weaknesses of these shells are compared. This information is intended to help you decide which shell is best for you. While this appendix may not contain all of the information you need to make this decision, it should help you to understand the issues that you need to think about when you select a shell.

## THE BOURNE SHELL

The Bourne shell (sh) is the original UNIX shell. It was written by Stephen R. Bourne at Bell Laboratories. As you have seen from the examples in this book, the Bourne shell is an excellent shell for shell scripts. It contains a full set of control flow constructs, expression matching capability, and a very powerful syntax for controlling input and output.

The Bourne shell is available on every UNIX system; therefore, this shell is often the standard to which other shells are compared. If a shell is not better than the Bourne shell in some way, then why bother with that shell?

The main strengths of the Bourne shell are that it is an excellent script writing language and that it is available on every UNIX system. This makes the Bourne shell the most commonly used shell for shell scripts. If you need to write a shell script that will be used by others and you do not know what shells they have available on their system, you will almost certainly have to use the Bourne shell. This makes the Bourne shell useful for scripts such as the ones that are used to install new products.

The weakness of the Bourne shell is that it does not have any of the features needed to make it an efficient interactive shell. For this reason, the Bourne shell is almost never used as an interactive shell. This combination of being a good shell for shell scripts but a poor shell for interactive work creates the situation in which engineers frequently use a different shell for these two purposes.

## THE C SHELL

The C shell (csh) was developed by Bill Joy at the University of California at Berkeley. It remedied the Bourne shell's lack of support for interactive users, and it also changed the fundamental syntax of the shell so that it resembled the C programming language, for which this shell is named. This new syntax was considered an improvement because the shell was intended to be used in the C language development environment at Berkeley. However, the C shell turned out to have problems of its own. The control operators for redirecting input and output are not as powerful as those of the Bourne shell, and the C shell is reputed to contain numerous defects. Nevertheless, the C shell is a vast improvement over the Bourne shell for interactive work, but its defects have prevented it from being widely used for writing shell scripts.

Some of the features in the C shell that were added to make it more useful for interactive users are:

- The C shell maintains a history of commands and allows the user to substitute information from the command history stack into new commands. This allows a rudimentary form of command line editing, and it facilitates the repetition of commands.

- The C shell allows aliases for common commands. This lets the user create short or mnemonic names for common command sequences.

- File name completion causes the shell to finish entering a file name after the user has entered the first few characters of the file name.

- Job control allows the user to control the execution of multiple processes so that long running processes, or jobs, can be executed in the background while the user continues to enter commands from the terminal (foreground).

- The C shell syntax resembles the C programming language, which is more familiar to many users than the syntax of the Bourne shell.

For many years, the Bourne shell and the C shell were the only shells to choose from. This allowed these two shells to become the standard shells included on every UNIX system, and this practice continues today. The C shell is still one of the most commonly used shells for interactive use.

Since the C shell is better than the Bourne shell for interactive users, it became the common choice for interactive use. And since the Bourne shell was better for writing shell scripts, it was usually used for that purpose. This led to the situation in which users would use one shell for interactive work and another shell for writing shell scripts.

## THE KORN SHELL

The Korn shell (ksh) was written by David Korn at Bell Laboratories. The Korn shell uses the same syntax as the Bourne shell, but it has many additional features that make it very useful for interactive work. Many people feel that the Korn shell has the best features from both the Bourne shell and the C shell. It kept the superior programming capabilities of the Bourne shell, while adding the features that are useful for interactive users from the C shell. Since the Korn shell is a good shell for both interactive users and shell scripts, Korn shell users need to learn only one shell.

The following list shows some of the features that are available in the C shell and are also incorporated into the Korn shell:

- Command history and history substitution
- Command aliases
- File name completion
- Job control
- Arrays of variables
- Integer arithmetic evaluation
- Tilde substitution
- An option to prevent accidentally removing a file (noclobber)

There are also many features in the Korn shell that have been added beyond the capabilities in either the Bourne shell or the C shell:

- The `select` and `function` statements
- New built-in commands: `time`, `whence`, and `getopts`
- New shell variables: `REPLY`, `PPID`, `EDITOR`, `OLDPWD`
- Line editing capabilities based on the `vi` and `emacs` editors
- Extended parameter substitution capabilities

This shell is rapidly gaining in popularity. It is included as one of the standard shells on System V systems, and it is also the basis of the POSIX shell, which will probably replace the Bourne shell in the next few years. While the Korn shell is readily available, it is not standard on many UNIX systems, and since it is relatively new, it will not be found on many older systems. This may cause problems for users that need to write portable shell scripts.

## OTHER SHELLS

There are several other shells besides the Bourne shell, the C shell, and the Korn shell, but these three shells are the most commonly used shells. This section briefly describes several other shells. While the shells mentioned here are all good shells, they have the disadvantage of not being widely available. If you want to use one of these shells, you may have to locate and install it yourself.

The POSIX shell is an implementation of the shell defined by the IEEE POSIX Shell and Tools Specification (IEEE Working Group 10003.2), and it is a replacement for the Bourne shell on systems that comply with the POSIX standard. The Korn shell was used as a starting point for the definition of the POSIX shell, and, therefore, these two shells are very similar. If the POSIX shell is available, it is a very good choice for both interactive use and for writing shell scripts.

The Bash shell, which stands for the "Bourne Again SHell," is a shell that was developed by the Free Software Foundation. This shell is a POSIX-compatible shell with some additional features added in. Two significant considerations of this shell are that it is POSIX compatible and that, like all products from Free Software Foundation, it is free.

The tcsh shell is an improved version of the C shell. It fixes many of the defects in the C shell, and it also has some additional features from the Korn shell, such as improved command line editing. Some of the inherent problems of the C shell still remain in this shell. Since the system vendors continued to ship the C shell rather than replace it with the improved tcsh shell, the use of this shell is not very widespread.

Perl is not a shell, but it is worth mentioning here because it can be used in place of a shell for writing scripts. It has all the capabilities of `sh`, `sed`, and `awk`, and scripts written in Perl are very efficient. Its only drawbacks are that it causes you to use one shell for interactive work and another tool for scripts, and that it is not as pervasive as the Bourne shell for portable scripts.

## SELECTING A SHELL

When you are trying to decide which shell you want to use, there are many things to consider. The following table lists the major UNIX shells and shows how they compare in some key area:

| Shell | Suitable for Interactive | Suitable for Scripts | Syntax Style | Availability |
|---|---|---|---|---|
| Bourne | No | Yes | Bourne | Excellent |
| Korn | Yes | Yes | Bourne | Good |
| POSIX | Yes | Yes | Bourne | Rare |
| Bash | Yes | Yes | Bourne | Rare |
| C Shell | Yes | No | C Shell | Excellent |
| tcsh | Yes | No | C Shell | Rare |
| Perl | No | Yes | | Good |

## Interactive Capabilities

The first thing to consider when selecting a shell is whether you will use the shell for interactive work or for writing shell scripts. The following guidelines may help you select an interactive shell:

- The Bourne shell is not suitable for interactive work. On systems that only have the Bourne shell and the C shell installed, you will have to use the C shell as your interactive shell.
- The tcsh shell is a reasonable upgrade for users who are currently using the C shell.
- If possible, pick a shell that can be used for both your interactive shell and for writing shell scripts, that is, the Korn shell, POSIX shell, or the Bash shell.

The C shell is a very popular shell, but its popularity stems from the fact that for a long time, it was the only suitable shell for interactive work. Since there is no compelling reason for C shell users to change to a new shell, there continues to be many C shell users. However, new users would be better off selecting the Korn shell, POSIX shell, or the Bash shell.

## Shell Script Capabilities

The following guidelines may help you select a shell for writing shell scripts:

- The C shell and the tcsh shell are generally not used for nontrivial shell scripts due to the inherent problems of the shell's syntax.
- The Bourne shell is the shell of choice when maximum portability is important, but otherwise one of the other Bourne shell derivatives is also suitable for writing shell scripts.
- You may also want to consider using Perl as an alternative to using one of the shells for writing scripts.

## Syntax Style

Most shells use an input language, or syntax, that is derived from either the Bourne shell or the C shell. This is true for all of the shells discussed in this appendix (except Perl, which is not a shell). The tcsh shell uses the same syntax as the C shell, and the other shells use the same syntax as the Bourne shell.

The syntax of the C shell is generally considered inferior to the syntax of the Bourne shell for writing shell scripts. The Bourne shell provides more flexibility for controlling the input and output of commands, and there are some aspects of the C shell's syntax that do not work correctly. Naturally, for small tasks, whichever shell gets the job done is the right choice, but as the task gets more complex, you should use one of the shells that use the Bourne shell syntax.

For interactive use, the shell syntax is not too significant. Most of the time, you will simply enter commands one after another. The most involvement that you will have with the syntax of the shell is to redirect the input or output of a command, use quotes around a parameter, or use wildcard characters to refer to a group of files. For these everyday tasks, the syntax of the Bourne shell and the C shell are nearly identical. For example, the following items are the same in both the Bourne shell and the C shell:

- Executing commands
- Redirecting standard input ($<$)
- Redirecting ($>$) and appending ($>>$) standard output
- Pipelines ($|$)
- Background execution ($\&$)
- Single and double quotes
- Grave quotes for command substitution ($`$)
- Wildcard characters ($*$, ?, [ . . . ])
- Using (but not setting) variables

## Availability

The availability of a shell in the context of this discussion refers to the likelihood that a particular shell is already installed on a system. For a variety of reasons, most users are not willing to locate and install a particular shell on their system, but, instead, they will limit their selection to one of the shells that is already there. This is probably the most significant factor in limiting the choice of which shell to use. As an example, even though the Bash shell is easily obtainable and it is free, it is not as pervasive as the Korn shell, which is standard on system V systems.

Availability is also important when considering the portability of a shell script. If the shell is not available to execute the shell script, the shell script is not portable. This is a common problem for product installation scripts. If the installation script is written for a shell that the customer does not have on his or her system, the customer will not be able to install the product. In this regard, the Bourne shell is the most widely available shell.

## SUMMARY

The Bourne shell is the only shell that is available on every UNIX system, and, therefore, it is the only shell that can be used when a shell script must be portable to a wide variety of systems. However, the Bourne shell is not suitable for interactive work.

The Korn shell is arguably the best all around shell. It is good for both interactive work and shell scripts; thus, you only need to learn one shell. Since the Bourne shell and the Korn shell share the same syntax, it is not difficult to switch from one shell to the other if you occasionally need to write a Bourne shell script. Since the Korn shell is standard on System V systems, it is available on most new systems.

The C shell is still more common as an interactive shell than the Korn shell, primarily because it has been around longer and it is available on more systems, but it requires the user to use a different shell for interactive work and shell scripts.

The remaining shells are suitable for persons with a special interest in one of these shells, but most users will not want to bother with locating and installing one of these shells.

# Appendix B

## *Syntax Summary*

## VARIABLES

| | |
|---|---|
| $\$\#$ | Number of positional parameters |
| $\$-$ | Current flags set in shell |
| $\$?$ | Exit status of last command executed |
| $\$\$$ | Process number of the current process |
| $\$!$ | Process number of the last background command executed |
| $\$*$ | The complete parameter list, $\$1$ though $\$n$ |
| $\$@$ | Same as $\$*$, but parameters are quoted if $\$@$ is quoted (e.g. "$\$@$") |
| $\$0$ | Positional parameter 0; always contains the command name |
| $\$1-\$9$ | Positional parameters 1 through 9 |
| | |
| $\$variable$ | Return the value of the variable |
| $\${variable}$ | Return the value of the variable |
| $\${variable:-value}$ | If not empty return variable, otherwise value; variable unchanged |
| $\${variable-value}$ | If defined return variable, otherwise return value; variable unchanged |
| $\${variable:=value}$ | If not empty return variable, otherwise set to value and then return |
| $\${variable=value}$ | If defined return variable, otherwise set to value and then return |

| | |
|---|---|
| $\${ variable:?message }$ | If not empty return variable, otherwise print message and exit |
| $\${ variable?message }$ | If defined return variable, otherwise print message and exit |
| $\${ variable:+value }$ | If not empty return value, otherwise return empty string |
| $\${ variable+value }$ | If defined return value, otherwise return empty string |

## PATTERNS

| | |
|---|---|
| * | Matches any (zero or more) characters |
| ? | Matches any single character |
| [ . . . ] | Matches any single character in the enclosed set |
| [ ! . . . ] | Matches any single character that is not in the enclosed set |

## QUOTES

| | |
|---|---|
| \ | Quote the next character |
| ' . . . ' | Quote the enclosed characters except for ' |
| " . . . " | Quote the enclosed characters except for $ ` \ " |

## INPUT-OUTPUT

| | |
|---|---|
| *p1* \| *p2* | Connect standard output of process *p1* with standard input of process *p2* |
| >*file* | Write standard output to *file* |
| >>*file* | Append standard output to *file* |
| >&*m* | Write standard output to file descriptor |
| >& - | Close standard output |
| *n*>*file* | Write output from file descriptor *n* to *file* |
| *n*>>*file* | Append output from file descriptor *n* to *file* |
| *n*>&*m* | Write output for file descriptor *n* to file descriptor *m* |
| *n*>& - | Close file descriptor *n* |
| <*file* | Read standard input from *file* |
| <&*m* | Read standard input from file descriptor *m* |
| *n*<&*m* | Read input for file descriptor *n* from file descriptor *m* |
| <& - | Close standard input |
| *n*<& - | Close file descriptor *n* |
| << [ - ] *word* | Here document with substitution |
| << [ - ] \ *word* | Here document without substitution |
| << [ - ] '*word*' | Here document without substitution |

## OTHER SPECIAL CHARACTERS

| | |
|---|---|
| # | Comment |
| & | Execute command in the background |
| ; | Command separator |
| && | Conditional AND |
| \|\| | Conditional OR |
| ;; | Case delimiter |
| () | Command group executed in a subshell |
| { ...; } | Command group with combined input and output |
| `command` | Substitute the output of the command |
| *name*() {...} | Define the function *name* |

## BUILT-IN COMMANDS

| | |
|---|---|
| : [*parm* ...] | This command does nothing; returns exit code zero |
| . *file* | Execute *file* without creating another process |
| break [*n*] | Exit enclosing loop |
| cd [*directory*] | Change current directory |
| continue [*n*] | Resume at the next iteration of the enclosing loop |
| echo [*parm* ...] | Writes parameters, separated by blanks, to standard output |
| eval [*parm* ...] | Evaluate parameters and execute result |
| exec [*parm* ...] | Execute parameters in place of this shell without creating a new process |
| exit [*n*] | Terminate this shell with status *n* |
| export [*name* ...] | Export name to environment for use by subprocesses |
| pwd | Print the current working directory |
| read [*name* ...] | Read one line from the standard input and store it in *name* |
| readonly [*name* ...] | Prevent assignment to *name* |
| return [*n*] | Return from function with status *n* |
| set [-ekntuvx] [*parm* ...] | Change setting of shell options and positional parameters |
| shift [*n*] | Shift the positional parameters *n* positions left |
| test [*expr*] | Evaluate conditional expressions |
| times | Print accumulated user and system execution time |
| trap [*command-list*] [*n* ...] | Read and execute *command-list* if signal *n* is received |
| type [*name* ...] | Indicate how *name* would be used if executed as a command |
| umask [*nnn*] | Set the default file creation mask to octal *nnn* |
| unset [*name* ...] | Remove the variable or function corresponding to *name* |
| wait [*n*] | Wait for process *n* to terminate |

## CONTROL FLOW

```
if command-list
then
      command-list
```

```
[elif command-list
then
     command-list]
[else
     command-list]
fi

for variable [in word-list]
do
     command-list
done

while command-list
do
     command-list
done

case string in
     [ pattern [ | pattern ] ... ) command-list ;; ]
     ...
esac
```

# Index

# LICENSE AGREEMENT AND LIMITED WARRANTY

READ THE FOLLOWING TERMS AND CONDITIONS CAREFULLY BEFORE OPENING THIS DISK PACKAGE. THIS LEGAL DOCUMENT IS AN AGREEMENT BETWEEN YOU AND PRENTICE-HALL, INC. (THE "COMPANY"). BY OPENING THIS SEALED DISK PACKAGE, YOU ARE AGREEING TO BE BOUND BY THESE TERMS AND CONDITIONS. IF YOU DO NOT AGREE WITH THESE TERMS AND CONDITIONS, DO NOT OPEN THE DISK PACKAGE. PROMPTLY RETURN THE UNOPENED DISK PACKAGE AND ALL ACCOMPANYING ITEMS TO THE PLACE YOU OBTAINED THEM FOR A FULL REFUND OF ANY SUMS YOU HAVE PAID.

1. **GRANT OF LICENSE:** In consideration of your payment of the license fee, which is part of the price you paid for this product, and your agreement to abide by the terms and conditions of this Agreement, the Company grants to you a nonexclusive right to use and display the copy of the enclosed software program (hereinafter the "SOFTWARE") on a single computer (i.e., with a single CPU) at a single location so long as you comply with the terms of this Agreement. The Company reserves all rights not expressly granted to you under this Agreement.

2. **OWNERSHIP OF SOFTWARE:** You own only the magnetic or physical media (the enclosed disks) on which the SOFTWARE is recorded or fixed, but the Company retains all the rights, title, and ownership to the SOFTWARE recorded on the original disk copy(ies) and all subsequent copies of the SOFTWARE, regardless of the form or media on which the original or other copies may exist. This license is not a sale of the original SOFTWARE or any copy to you.

3. **COPY RESTRICTIONS:** This SOFTWARE and the accompanying printed materials and user manual (the "Documentation") are the subject of copyright. You may not copy the Documentation or the SOFTWARE, except that you may make a single copy of the SOFTWARE for backup or archival purposes only. You may be held legally responsible for any copying or copyright infringement which is caused or encouraged by your failure to abide by the terms of this restriction.

4. **USE RESTRICTIONS:** You may not network the SOFTWARE or otherwise use it on more than one computer or computer terminal at the same time. You may physically transfer the SOFTWARE from one computer to another provided that the SOFTWARE is used on only one computer at a time. You may not distribute copies of the SOFTWARE or Documentation to others. You may not reverse engineer, disassemble, decompile, modify, adapt, translate, or create derivative works based on the SOFTWARE or the Documentation without the prior written consent of the Company.

5. **TRANSFER RESTRICTIONS:** The enclosed SOFTWARE is licensed only to you and may not be transferred to any one else without the prior written consent of the Company. Any unauthorized transfer of the SOFTWARE shall result in the immediate termination of this Agreement.

6. **TERMINATION:** This license is effective until terminated. This license will terminate automatically without notice from the Company and become null and void if you fail to comply with any provisions or limitations of this license. Upon termination, you shall destroy the Documentation and all copies of the SOFTWARE. All provisions of this Agreement as to warranties, limitation of liability, remedies or damages, and our ownership rights shall survive termination.

7. **MISCELLANEOUS:** This Agreement shall be construed in accordance with the laws of the United States of America and the State of New York and shall benefit the Company, its affiliates, and assignees.

**8. LIMITED WARRANTY AND DISCLAIMER OF WARRANTY:** The Company warrants that the SOFTWARE, when properly used in accordance with the Documentation, will operate in substantial conformity with the description of the SOFTWARE set forth in the Documentation. The Company does not warrant that the SOFTWARE will meet your requirements or that the operation of the SOFTWARE will be uninterrupted or error-free. The Company warrants that the media on which the SOFTWARE is delivered shall be free from defects in materials and workmanship under normal use for a period of thirty (30) days from the date of your purchase. Your only remedy and the Company's only obligation under these limited warranties is, at the Company's option, return of the warranted item for a refund of any amounts paid by you or replacement of the item. Any replacement of SOFTWARE or media under the warranties shall not extend the original warranty period. The limited warranty set forth above shall not apply to any SOFTWARE which the Company determines in good faith has been subject to misuse, neglect, improper installation, repair, alteration, or damage by you. **EXCEPT FOR THE EXPRESSED WARRANTIES SET FORTH ABOVE, THE COMPANY DISCLAIMS ALL WARRANTIES, EXPRESS OR IMPLIED, INCLUDING WITHOUT LIMITATION, THE IMPLIED WARRANTIES OF MERCHANTABILITY AND FITNESS FOR A PARTICULAR PURPOSE. EXCEPT FOR THE EXPRESS WARRANTY SET FORTH ABOVE, THE COMPANY DOES NOT WARRANT, GUARANTEE, OR MAKE ANY REPRESENTATION REGARDING THE USE OR THE RESULTS OF THE USE OF THE SOFTWARE IN TERMS OF ITS CORRECTNESS, ACCURACY, RELIABILITY, CURRENTNESS, OR OTHERWISE.**

**IN NO EVENT, SHALL THE COMPANY OR ITS EMPLOYEES, AGENTS, SUPPLIERS, OR CONTRACTORS BE LIABLE FOR ANY INCIDENTAL, INDIRECT, SPECIAL, OR CONSEQUENTIAL DAMAGES ARISING OUT OF OR IN CONNECTION WITH THE LICENSE GRANTED UNDER THIS AGREEMENT, OR FOR LOSS OF USE, LOSS OF DATA, LOSS OF INCOME OR PROFIT, OR OTHER LOSSES, SUSTAINED AS A RESULT OF INJURY TO ANY PERSON, OR LOSS OF OR DAMAGE TO PROPERTY, OR CLAIMS OF THIRD PARTIES, EVEN IF THE COMPANY OR AN AUTHORIZED REPRESENTATIVE OF THE COMPANY HAS BEEN ADVISED OF THE POSSIBILITY OF SUCH DAMAGES. IN NO EVENT SHALL LIABILITY OF THE COMPANY FOR DAMAGES WITH RESPECT TO THE SOFTWARE EXCEED THE AMOUNTS ACTUALLY PAID BY YOU, IF ANY, FOR THE SOFTWARE.**
**SOME JURISDICTIONS DO NOT ALLOW THE LIMITATION OF IMPLIED WARRANTIES OR LIABILITY FOR INCIDENTAL, INDIRECT, SPECIAL, OR CONSEQUENTIAL DAMAGES, SO THE ABOVE LIMITATIONS MAY NOT ALWAYS APPLY. THE WARRANTIES IN THIS AGREEMENT GIVE YOU SPECIFIC LEGAL RIGHTS AND YOU MAY ALSO HAVE OTHER RIGHTS WHICH VARY IN ACCORDANCE WITH LOCAL LAW.**

## ACKNOWLEDGMENT

**YOU ACKNOWLEDGE THAT YOU HAVE READ THIS AGREEMENT, UNDERSTAND IT, AND AGREE TO BE BOUND BY ITS TERMS AND CONDITIONS. YOU ALSO AGREE THAT THIS AGREEMENT IS THE COMPLETE AND EXCLUSIVE STATEMENT OF THE AGREEMENT BETWEEN YOU AND THE COMPANY AND SUPERSEDES ALL PROPOSALS OR PRIOR AGREEMENTS, ORAL, OR WRITTEN, AND ANY OTHER COMMUNICATIONS BETWEEN YOU AND THE COMPANY OR ANY REPRESENTATIVE OF THE COMPANY RELATING TO THE SUBJECT MATTER OF THIS AGREEMENT.**

Should you have any questions concerning this Agreement or if you wish to contact the Company for any reason, please contact in writing at the address below.

Robin Short
Prentice Hall PTR
One Lake Street
Upper Saddle River, New Jersey 07458